Understanding International Trade

Understanding International Trade

Insights from Trade Theory

RETO FOELLMI AND STEFAN LEGGE

OXFORD
UNIVERSITY PRESS

OXFORD
UNIVERSITY PRESS

Oxford University Press is a department of the University of Oxford.
It furthers the University's objective of excellence in research, scholarship,
and education by publishing worldwide. Oxford is a registered trade mark of
Oxford University Press in the UK and in certain other countries.

Published in the United States of America by Oxford University Press
198 Madison Avenue, New York, NY 10016, United States of America.

Library of Congress Cataloging-in-Publication Data
Names: Foellmi, Reto author | Legge, Stefan author
Title: Understanding international trade : insights from trade theory /
Reto Foellmi and Stefan Legge.
Description: New York, NY : Oxford University Press, [2026] |
Includes bibliographical references and index.
Identifiers: LCCN 2025049466 (print) | LCCN 2025049467 (ebook) |
ISBN 9780197821077 hardback | ISBN 9780197821084 epub
Subjects: LCSH: International trade
Classification: LCC HF1379 .F64 2026 (print) | LCC HF1379 (ebook) |
DDC 382—dcundefined
LC record available at https://lccn.loc.gov/2025049466
LC ebook record available at https://lccn.loc.gov/2025049467

DOI: 10.1093/9780197821107.001.0001

Printed by Marquis Book Printing, Canada

The manufacturer's authorized representative in the EU for product safety is
Oxford University Press España S.A. of Parque Empresarial San Fernando de Henares,
Avenida de Castilla, 2 – 28830 Madrid (www.oup.es/en or product.safety@oup.com).
OUP España S.A. also acts as importer into Spain of products made by the manufacturer.

FSC
www.fsc.org
MIX
Paper | Supporting
responsible forestry
FSC® C103567

Contents

Introduction

For more than 200 years, economists have regarded international trade as a central driver of rising standards of living. Adam Smith saw the division of labor and subsequent exchange of goods in a market as the enabler of productivity gains and thus "the wealth of nations." Collaboration across borders allows for a far greater division of labor, opening the door to higher standards of living.

Not everyone, however, is as convinced of the blessings caused by free trade as the British politician Richard Cobden, who wrote in 1857 that "free trade is God's diplomacy," echoing Montesquieu, who spoke of "*doux commerce*" (sweet commerce) uniting people. Many people strongly oppose free trade: there are many misconceptions about and much criticism of international trade often with simple but ill-conceived arguments. As this book is being printed, the future of the world trade architecture is uncertain. In turbulent times like these, it makes sense to reflect on the basics, what international trade means and what welfare consequences it entails. Generations of economists have developed theories and models to better understand trade's ramifications. And it is the purpose of this book to help readers understand these models and thus international trade.

Aim of the Book

Understanding the determinants and patterns of international trade is important not just for economists but also business leaders, policymakers, and voters. In this book, we provide a thorough yet accessible presentation of key trade theories developed over the past 200 years. The goal of these theories is to shed light on several questions concerning global trade, such as the following:

- Which factors determine the structure, direction, and magnitude of global trade flows?

Understanding International Trade. Reto Foellmi and Stefan Legge, Oxford University Press.
 DOI: 10.1093/9780197821107.003.0001

- How does international trade affect the welfare of countries and individuals?
- Who benefits and who suffers from trade liberalization?
- What is the impact of openness to trade on companies?

There are several rationales for why nations trade with each other. First of all, some goods simply cannot be produced in one country but there is demand for them. This includes, foremost, natural resources such as oil, iron, or gold. To some extent, this group of products can be enlarged to cover agricultural products that require specific climatic conditions and manufacturing goods for which a nation does not have the necessary expertise.[1] However, a nation could—at least in theory and when accepting large costs—produce such products itself. It is possible to grow bananas in the United States, and France could develop its own sophisticated smartphone industry. The large costs involved in such endeavors, however, precisely point out why international trade is beneficial: The costs of production differ across countries. Following the same logic, many of today's highly sophisticated products, like the Apple iPhone, are inconceivable without international trade. In 2021, for instance, Apple reported that it sourced from more than 1,000 suppliers in over 40 countries around the world.

Many of the rationales for international trade can be well understood at the individual level. People in highly developed countries engage in plenty of exchanges every day. Most of the goods and services they want to consume are obtained from others. Put differently, people are highly specialized and trade a lot with others. This is possible because each individual can confidently assume that there is a large number of reliable trading partners. As long as we can find somewhere to provide us with food or someone to cut our hair in exchange for money we earned by "exporting" goods and services we produce, we have little incentive to supply these goods and services ourselves. Instead, we can specialize according to our innate abilities and avoid the costly acquisition of skills necessary to create the goods and services we obtain from others. The same logic applies to firms, regions, and entire countries.

In a market economy, prices are determined by supply and demand. Differences in the costs of production and consumer preferences between countries lead to different prices, but only when those countries do not trade with each other (under autarky, as trade economists usually say). Often, such price differences across nations can be profitably exploited. There is

[1] An early discussion of how the availability of resources and skills determine patterns of trade is provided by Irving B. Kravis (1956).

an arbitrage opportunity as long as trade costs are not too large. In general, it is the interplay of *arbitrage opportunities* and *trade costs* that determines patterns of international trade. The invention of the steamship and other technologies reduced costs of transportation. In addition, policies of trade liberalization lowered political barriers to trade. Together, this reduction of trade costs led to a wave of globalization in the late 19th and early 20th centuries. From the 1980s onward, new information and communications technology allowed Western firms to apply their methods of production in China and Eastern Europe, thereby creating opportunities for arbitrage. This explains the most recent wave of globalization.

Since international trade occurs voluntarily, there must be gains from trade. As theories of international trade illustrate, gains arise for different reasons. Openness to trade allows countries to specialize in the production of a subset of products, which are then traded for others. This can lower overall costs of production while also enlarging the range of products available to consumers. Furthermore, reduced trade barriers can lead to lower prices for consumers if competition between firms increases and markups fall. Finally, openness to trade affects firms differently—with the most productive ones expanding their business. The reallocation of factors of production toward the most productive firms raises overall productivity in a country. In this book, we discuss these mechanisms in detail.

It is also important to point out early what the book does *not* cover. We aim to provide a thorough explanation of the key models of international trade. The book does not, however, discuss trade policy in detail, although occasionally we do use trade policies to explain comparative statics in trade models. Moreover, we focus exclusively on real (≠ monetary) trade. Hence, we do not cover topics such as the balance of payments or exchange rates. And while we describe trade theories using trade in goods, the interpretation carries over to trade in services. Usually, however, the latter faces much higher trade costs. Alongside the cross-border shipment of goods, we briefly examine international factor mobility as well as technology transfers. However, an in-depth analysis of the ramifications of international migration or financial flows is beyond the scope of this book.

Structure of the Book

International trade occurs because of cross-country differences in supply and demand. Theories of international trade usually focus on supply-side explanations, and consumer preferences are assumed to be identical in all countries. Without cross-country differences in demand, all cross-country price differences (which motivate trade) are solely the result of cost differences. This raises the question why costs of production differ across countries. The answer is that nations differ in their technologies and endowments or there are economies of scale in production. This focus on supply-side explanations for international trade does not mean that demand is irrelevant. For instance, in the classical trade models, gains from trade as well as the magnitude of trade flows are determined by goods prices, which in turn are determined by supply *and* demand factors.

More broadly, while taste differences are an obvious reason for trade between consumers, they play a smaller role for trade between regions or countries. Rare examples of nationwide taste differences concern products, especially agricultural ones, that can only be produced jointly but for which the demand varies substantially across countries. Consider poultry meat and chicken feet, the latter of which are typically not eaten in Western Europe but are used in several regional Asian cuisines. Here, the cross-country differences in demand allow for gains from trade. Much more important in quantitative terms are different demand structures of rich and poor countries because of so-called non-homothetic preferences, where the consumption share of different goods depends on income. Non-homothetic preferences generalize *Engel's law*, an economic relationship proposed in 1857 by the German statistician Ernst Engel (1821–1896). The idea is that the share of income that consumers spend on various goods depends on their level of income: Poor individuals spend most of it on food and other necessities, while richer people also buy luxury items.

The figure below illustrates the structure of this book. While we do not explicitly study trade models with demand-side explanations for international trade, we highlight the importance of the demand side throughout the discussion of other models. Chapters 1 to 6 present models based on comparative advantages, competitive markets, and constant returns to scale, focusing on inter-industry trade. This comprises models in which countries differ in their technologies or endowments, which leads to different autarky prices. When trade between these countries is possible, product prices converge, and we can study the impact on production, as well as on wages and capital income.

The models based on competitive markets (shown in the middle of the figure) predict that trade is beneficial if, and only if, countries are different from each other. In fact, the more different they are, the larger *ceteris paribus* the gains from trade. This would suggest that we see large trade

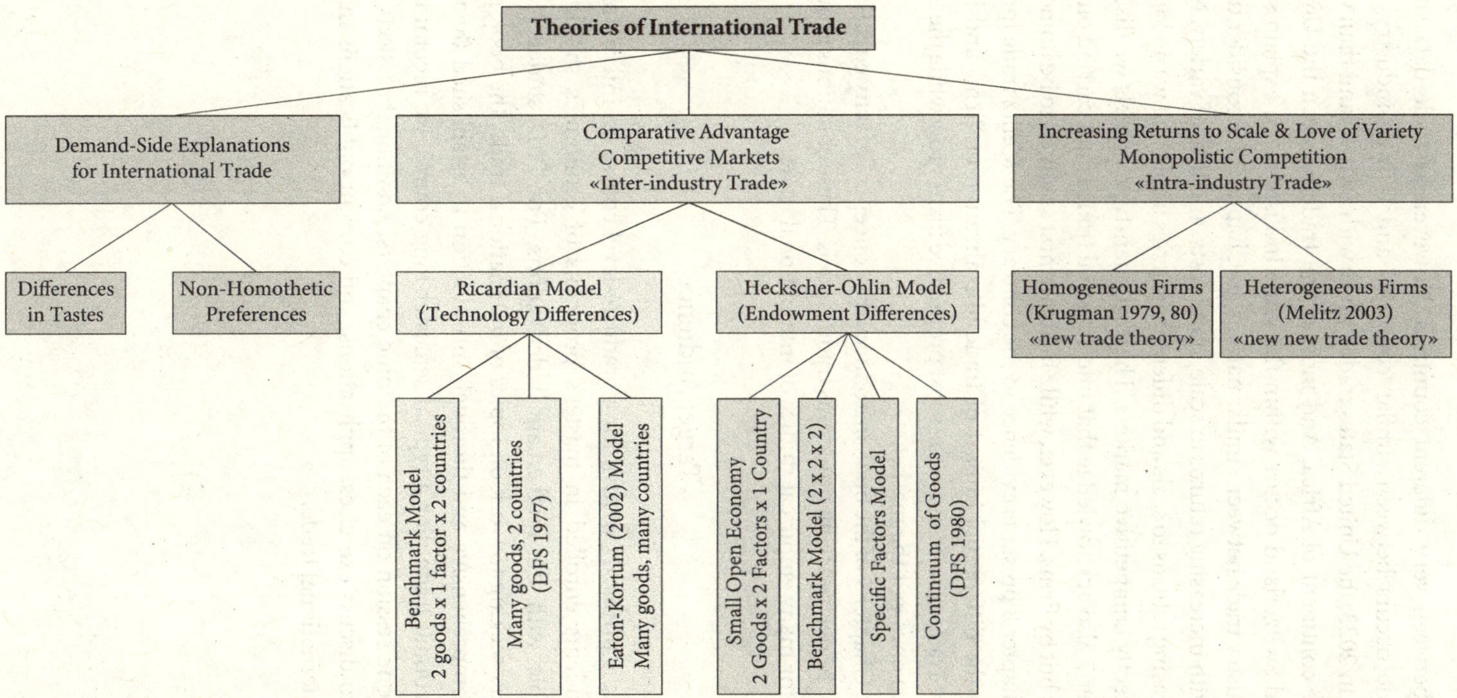

Figure 0.1 Overview of Trade Models

volumes between very different countries. However, as trade data show, most trade occurs between similar countries and is intra-industry. For instance, in 2023, the United States traded more with Switzerland than with the entire continent of Africa. And most of the trade between the United States and Switzerland occurs within the same industries. To explain such intra-industry trade between similar nations, in Chapter 7 we consider trade models with increasing returns to scale, trade costs, and love of variety. Note that increasing returns to scale and different varieties imply that we no longer have perfectly competitive markets. The Krugman-type models we discuss in Chapter 7 also acknowledge that international trade is not carried out by countries but by firms. However, while firms are first assumed to be homogeneous, Chapter 8 presents evidence to the contrary. The Melitz trade model examines the differential impact of trade liberalization on firms and how gains from trade arise because the most productive firms grow while the least productive ones exit the market.

Finally, Chapter 9 of the book introduces the concept of gravity equations, which can be derived from numerous trade models. These equations provide the basis for many empirical studies of international trade.

Target Audience

This book is primarily written for a graduate-level course on international trade. Students enrolled in master's programs of economics should be comfortable with the mathematical derivations. For PhD students and researchers seeking to work on topics of international trade, the book provides a comprehensive and thorough introduction to established theories of international trade. For a typical semester-long course, we recommend focusing one session on each of the nine chapters. Additional sessions can be used to discuss exercises, applications, and current publications in the field of international trade.

1
The Ricardian Trade Model

1.1 Idea and Background

The origins of classical trade theory go back in particular to David Ricardo, who published *On the Principles of Political Economy and Taxation* in 1817. In this seminal work, he laid out the theory of comparative advantage, which argues that all countries can benefit from free trade. This is true even if a nation is less efficient than its trading partners at producing all kinds of goods. In this chapter, we thoroughly analyze the model and the numerous insights it provides.

Before we dive into the details of the model, we should first explain the fundamental ideas in simple terms. Suppose we have two countries, as shown in Table 1.1. Both can produce wine and t-shirts using labor as the sole production input. It is assumed that English workers are more productive in the sense that it takes them fewer hours of labor to produce either good.

If each country wants to have one bottle of wine and one t-shirt, England must put in $2+1 = 3$ hours of work, while the Portuguese must work $3+4 = 7$ hours. In contrast, England could produce two t-shirts in $1 + 1 = 2$ hours, and Portugal two bottles of wine in $3 + 3 = 6$ hours. If they then exchange one t-shirt for one bottle of wine, both have again one t-shirt and one bottle of wine but with less labor input. This is the possible gain from trade.

Table 1.1 Production Time for Goods in England and Portugal

	England	**Portugal**
Bottle of wine	2 hours	3 hours
T-shirt	1 hour	4 hours
Time needed for 1 wine bottle and 1 t-shirt	3 hours alone 2 hours with trade	7 hours alone 6 hours with trade

Assumed trade price: 1 t-shirt = 1 wine bottle

Understanding International Trade. Reto Foellmi and Stefan Legge, Oxford University Press.
 DOI: 10.1093/9780197821107.003.0002

In this simple setup, we already grasp why two countries can benefit from trade. It is because of what is called *opportunity costs*. Spending time on wine production destroys the opportunity to spend that time on t-shirt production. England can spend two hours to directly produce a bottle of wine or instead spend one hour producing a t-shirt that can be traded for a bottle of wine. In some sense, England can produce wine directly or indirectly.

The simple situation of Table 1.1 also highlights that countries must be open to *structural change* in order to realize gains from trade. Effectively, England must send its workers from the wine sector to the textile sector. In reality, of course, such a transition is not as easy as we might assume in a theoretical model.

The simple model also implicitly assumes that England and Portugal can trade frictionless. That is to say, there are no *trade costs*. In reality, there are transportation costs, tariffs, and all sorts of other costs that hamper the exchange of goods and services. Moreover, if the two countries in our setup fully specialize, there is another potential problem: Both are then dependent on the other for the supply of either wine (England) or t-shirts (Portugal). This highlights the importance of *trust* and (trust-building) institutions for international trade.

Finally, we could also tell the story of Table 1.1 in reverse. Suppose England and Portugal are trading as described above. If one nation then prefers, for whatever reason, to stop trading, this will come at a significant cost. Not only are the gains from trade lost but the country would also need to rebuild the sector that it gave up with international trade. Put differently, *deglobalization* is very costly.

1.2 Model Setup

To better understand the mechanisms of the Ricardian trade model, we now describe the setup in more detail.

Home Country

The basic Ricardian trade model can be seen as a 2-goods–1-factor–2-countries model. We assume that there are two goods that are both produced using labor as the only factor of production. To produce one unit of good

$i \in \{1, 2\}$, the fixed amount of a_i units of labor are required. That is to say, there are only variable, no fixed costs of production. With factor markets perfectly competitive, workers are paid the value of their marginal product: $w = p_i * 1/a_i$.

Numerical Example 1.1

Suppose an individual works eight hours a day and it takes $a_1 = 2$ hours of work to produce one unit of good 1. Then the worker produces four units of good 1 per day and is paid the wage w, which is equal to the value of these four units, that is $4 * p_1$. Notice that the wage depends on the worker's *absolute* productivity (a_1). Because there are no other input factors and no profit (due to perfect competition), the worker is paid the entire revenue.

If a country has L units of labor, it can produce a maximum of L/a_i units of output of good i, as shown in Figure 1.1. The limit of production is determined by the country's endowment with labor and its productivity (a_1 and a_2). When using all its labor, the country can at most produce combinations of y_1 and y_2 that are located on the production possibility frontier (PPF). Note that we illustrate the PPF as a linear line. This follows from assuming perfect divisibility.

The PPF, or more precisely the slope of the PPF, tells us how much the country has to give up in terms of y_1 if it wants to have more output of the

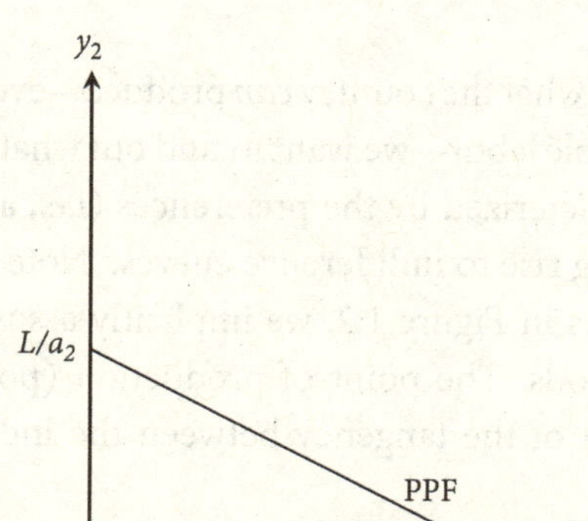

Figure 1.1 Production Possibility Frontier (PPF) in the Ricardian Model

second good. This amount of good 1 that we have to forfeit is called opportunity cost. The slope of the PPF is negative and equal to $-(L/a_2)/(L/a_1)$, or simply $-a_1/a_2$. This is the rate of transformation, and it shows the opportunity cost of producing each product: how much of good 1 (good 2) has to be given up if more of good 2 (good 1) should be produced. If a_1/a_2 is small, the PPF is rather flat, implying that the country is great at producing good 1 and not so great at producing good 2.

We assume that workers are free to offer their labor in either of the two industries $i \in \{1,2\}$. That is, we abstract from any real-world frictions that make it difficult for workers from, say, the textile industry to start working in the car industry. There are also no differences in skill levels, such that workers have identical productive capabilities in both industries. These assumptions imply that the wage in both industries must be identical: $w = p_1 \times 1/a_1 = p_2 \times 1/a_2$. Otherwise, workers would all want to work in the higher-paying sector. If we rewrite this equation, we obtain $p_1/p_2 = a_1/a_2$. This tells us that the relative price of good 1—which we define as $p = p_1/p_2$—is equal to the relative unit labor requirements for good 1. In other words, goods prices are fully determined by the costs of production.

Numerical Example 1.2

Suppose it takes $a_1 = 2$ hours to produce one unit of good 1 and $a_2 = 4$ hours to produce one unit of good 2. In our simple economy, this implies that good 1 will be half as expensive as good 1: $p = p_1/p_2 = a_1/a_2 = 2/4 = 1/2$.

Now that we know what the country *can* produce—every point on the PPF when using all available labor—we want to find out what it *will* produce. The demand side is characterized by the preferences (i.e., a utility function) of the individuals giving rise to indifference curves.[1] Note that by drawing the indifference curves as in Figure 1.2, we implicitly assume the people want to consume both goods. The point of production (point A in the figure) is found at the point of the tangency between the indifference curve and

[1] To obtain country-level preferences, we must assume that all individuals' preferences are identical and that the distribution of income remains constant between different equilibria. This is given in the model because labor is homogeneous and all workers receive the same income share regardless of which equilibrium they are in.

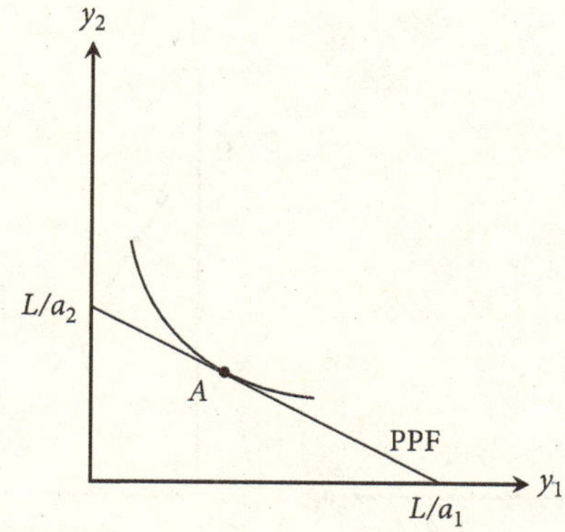

Figure 1.2 Autarky Production in Home Country

the PPF. Point *A* is both the location of production and consumption as long as the country is not open to trade. Depending on the people's preferences, production and consumption could be skewed heavily in favor of one good.

Foreign Country

We consider a situation with two countries, Home Country and Foreign Country, which differ in their relative productivity. Let us assume that $a_1/a_2 < a_1^*/a_2^*$. Note that we indicate variables that refer to the Foreign Country with an asterisk (*). The inequality $a_1/a_2 < a_1^*/a_2^*$ implies that the opportunity costs of producing good 1 are lower in the Home Country. We say that the Home Country has a comparative advantage in the production of good 1.

Numerical Example 1.3

Suppose that $a_1 = 2$, $a_2 = 4$, $a_1^* = 4$, and $a_2^* = 4$. This implies that in the Home Country, the opportunity cost of producing one unit of good 1 is half a unit of good 2. The two hours spent on producing one unit of good 1 is enough to produce half a unit of good 2. In the Foreign Country, the opportunity cost is equal to one unit of good 2. Put differently, when producing good 1, the Home Country has to give up less of good 2. Thus, we say it has a comparative advantage in good 1.

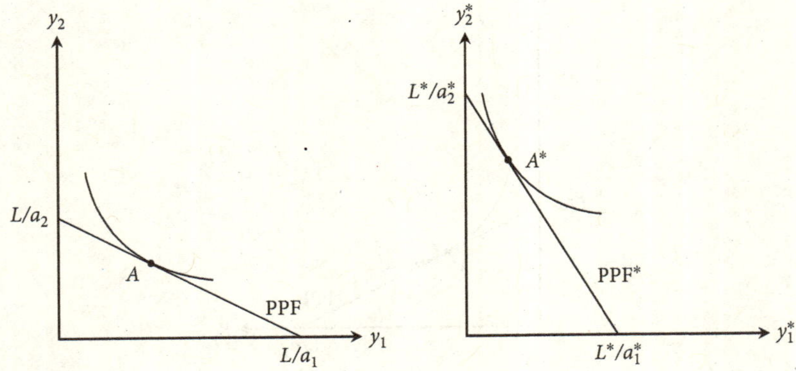

Figure 1.3 Autarky Production in Both Countries

If we plot both the PPF and the optimal point of production and consumption for the Foreign Country, we have the right side of Figure 1.3. Notice that the PPF of the Foreign Country is steeper. The slope is given by $-a_1^*/a_2^*$.

The difference in the two slopes ($-a_1/a_2$ vs. $-a_1^*/a_2^*$) already shows why it is beneficial for the two countries to collaborate (i.e., trade). Suppose the countries want to produce good 1: Which country should produce the first unit? We notice that the amount of good 2 that we have to give up if we use some labor to produce good 1 differs in Home and Foreign. The opportunity costs of producing good 1 are lower in the Home Country. Simply put, the flat PPF of the Home Country (which shows the opportunity costs) is good news for producing good 1: Every unit of labor that is used for the production of good 1 does not cost much in terms of good 2 that is given up. For good 2, with the same logic, we see that it is better to start producing good 2 in the Foreign Country.

One way to illustrate this line of reasoning is shown in Figure 1.4. If we were to merge the two countries' PPFs, we would obtain the combined PPF. Notice that the flatter part of the combined PPF is from the Home Country, while the steep part is from the Foreign Country. When all labor is used for producing good 1, we obtain a total quantity of $L/a_1 + L^*/a_1^*$ and zero output of good 2. If we start from this and want to have at least some positive amount of good 2, it is best to have the Foreign Country start producing good 2.

An alternative interpretation of Figure 1.4 would envision a benevolent dictator who instructs both countries such that total welfare is maximized. As we will see in the next subsection, however, we do not need to merge

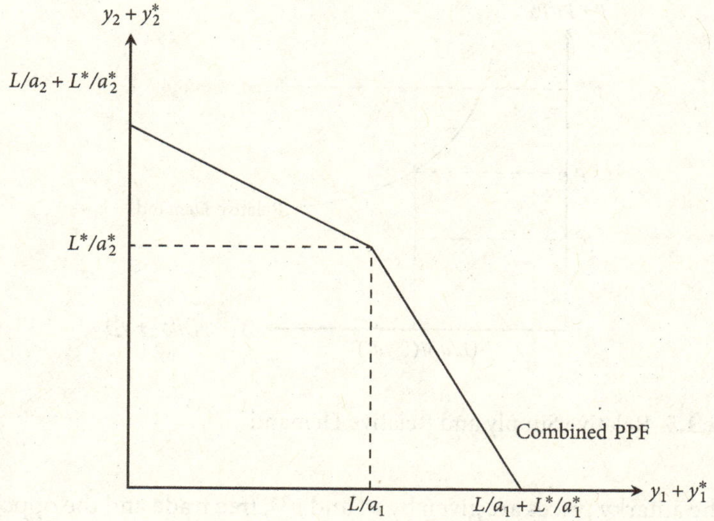

Figure 1.4 Combined Production Possibility Frontier

the countries or have a dictator to achieve an optimal outcome. The price mechanism ensures that both countries behave optimally.

1.3 From Autarky to Trade

As long as the two countries reside in isolation (what we call the *autarky* situation), they will produce and consume at points A and A^*, respectively. Note that this implies different relative autarky prices: $p^a = a_1/a_2$ and $p^{a*} = a_1^*/a_2^*$. These domestic relative prices reflect the marginal rate of substitution in the autarky equilibrium. The fact that autarky prices are different is important as soon as we allow the two countries to trade with each other. Then, one could purchase good 1 at a relatively low price in the Home Country and sell it profitably at a relatively high price in the Foreign Country.

Numerical Example 1.4

Suppose that $a_1 = 2$, $a_2 = 4$, $a_1^* = 4$, and $a_2^* = 4$. Then the relative prices of good 1 are given by $p^a = 2/4 = 1/2$ and $p^{a*} = 4/4 = 1$. In this case, good 1 is relatively cheap in the Home Country.

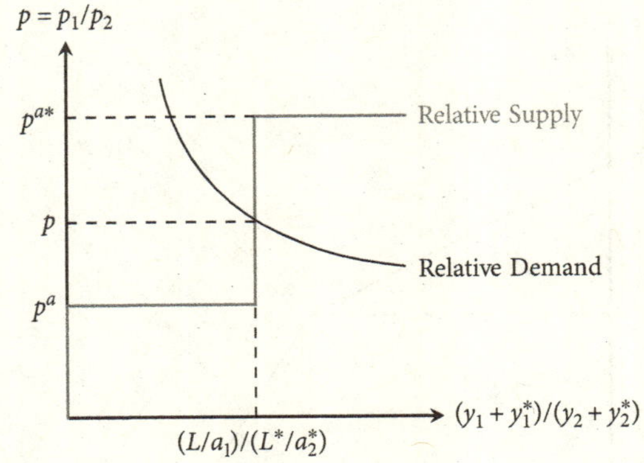

Figure 1.5 Relative Supply and Relative Demand

If the autarky prices are given by p^a and p^{a*}, free trade and the opportunities of arbitrage (i.e., exploiting price differences) will lead to a goods price equalization. Following the law of one price, any arbitrage opportunity will be exploited.[2] This raises the supply of good 1 in the Foreign Country and raises demand for good 1 in the Home Country.[3] As a result, $p^a = p_1/p_2$ will increase, while $p^{a*} = p_1^*/p_2^*$ will decrease.

What will be the equilibrium price? In his original work, Ricardo did not answer this question but stated that the international rate of exchange between two goods will be somewhere between the two countries' autarky rates. It was John Stuart Mill who closed the gap by arguing that the international relative price is determined by world supply and demand. To show this, let us take a look at Figure 1.5.

The step function shows the relative supply curve. It illustrates the *relative* supply of good 1 by the two countries in relation to the prevailing (world market) *relative* price of good 1:

- As long as the relative price p is below p^a, both countries will decide to only produce good 2 (and sell some of the output on the world market at the relative price p to obtain the desired amount of good 1).

[2] This law states that, in the absence of any trade frictions and under conditions of free competition and price flexibility, identical goods sold in different locations must sell for the same price. An early proof of this is provided by William Stanley Jevons in his 1871 book *Theory of Political Economy* and an empirical assessment by Claudia Steinwender (2018).

[3] Those traders who purchase good 1 at a relatively low price in Home and sell it in Foreign exploit arbitrage. However, their actions increase demand for good 1 in Home and raise supply of good 1 in the Foreign Country. This mechanism leads to an equalization of goods prices.

- When $p = p^a$, the Home Country is indifferent between producing good 1 or good 2. It can sell any amount of good 1 (or 2) at the relative price $p = p^a$, which is identical to domestic opportunity costs. If fully specialized in the production of good 1, Home's total supply of good 1 (and also the world's total supply) is (L/a_1).
- If the world market (relative) price is between the two countries' autarky price levels (i.e., $p^a < p < p^{a*}$), both countries will be fully specialized: Home Country only produces good 1, and Foreign Country only produces good 2.
- If the world market price is equal to the autarky (relative) price of the Foreign Country (p^{a*}), it is indifferent between producing good 1 and good 2.
- Finally, if the world market (relative) price exceeded p^{a*}, then both countries will only produce good 1.

To determine which world market price will materialize, we have to consider the demand for good 1 and 2 in the two countries. For simplicity, we make two assumptions: (i) Both countries have the same preferences, and (ii) demand is homothetic. The latter assumption implies that relative demand for good 1 and 2 does not depend on income (i.e., if the someone's income is twice as high, consumption of both good 1 and good 2 simply doubles). These assumptions allow us to draw a simple downward-sloping demand curve as shown in Figure 1.5, regardless of how income differs between the two countries.

The intersection between relative demand and relative supply determines the world market price p. This can (but does not need to) be between the two autarky prices.[4] Notice that if the world market price is between the autarky prices ($p^a < p < p^{a*}$), this implies that the relative price of good 1 increases for the Home Country and decreases for the Foreign Country.

To conclude this analysis, we should reflect upon the fact that we only consider two scenarios here: closed economies and free trade (with zero trade costs). In the real world, there are few examples in recent history for countries under autarky that opened up to international trade. One often-cited example is Japan after the 1858 Treaty of Amity and Commerce with the

[4] If one country is much larger than the other or preferences are extremely skewed, p can be equal to one of the countries' autarky (relative) prices. In this case, the country that does not experience a change in (relative) prices does not benefit from international trade. We discuss this later in the chapter.

United States. However, this treaty was far from creating (equally) free trade between the two countries. Nevertheless, the Ricardian model as a severe simplification of the world economy can be used to establish key principles of international trade.

Pattern of Specialization and Gains from Trade

Opening up to international trade exposes the two countries to a different relative price p, which is larger than the (relative) autarky price in the Home Country and smaller than the (relative) autarky price in the Foreign Country. How will the countries respond to this? For the Home Country, $p > p^a$ implies that good 1 is more valuable (compared to good 2) on the world market than its domestic opportunity cost. Figure 1.6 visualizes this. When only producing good 1, the slope of the black line shows the opportunity costs of producing good 2. Note that the grey line with a slope of $(-p)$ is steeper. Faced with the higher relative price of good 1 on the international market, Home produces only good 1 (output = L/a_1) and consumes at point B. Following a similar logic, the Foreign Country produces only good 2 (output = L^*/a_2^*) and consumes at point B^*. Trade between the two countries is balanced in the sense that the exports of one country are equal to imports of the other country.

Both countries now face the same relative price p, which is equal to the slope of the grey curve. Following our analysis of relative supply and relative demand, we know that the Home Country fully specializes in the production

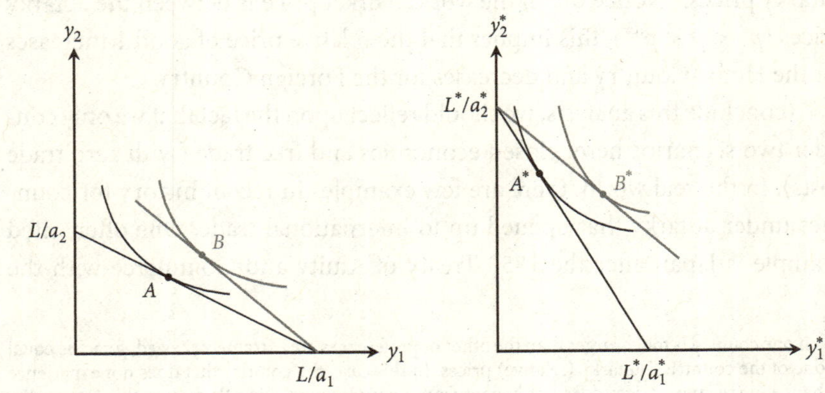

Figure 1.6 Gains from Trade in Both Countries

of good 1 (hence $y_1 = L/a_1$), while the Foreign Country only produces good 2 ($y_2 = L^*/a_2^*$). This provides us with the points of production in both countries. In some sense, the grey lines then represent the budget constraints. The slope ($= p$) shows the terms of trade—the exchange ratio for which they can sell their production.[5] As shown in Figure 1.6, both countries can now reach a higher indifference curve than what was possible under autarky. Thus, we have shown that both countries gain from trade.

Notice that this result emerged without having said anything about the absolute values of a_1, a_2, a_1^*, and a_2^*. The only assumption we made was that $a_1/a_2 < a_1^*/a_2^*$. This, however, specifies only *relative* productivity differences. Even if $a_1 < a_1^*$ and $a_2 < a_2^*$ (i.e., if the Home Country is more productive at producing both goods, or to put it differently, has an absolute advantage in both goods), it will still have a comparative advantage for one of the two goods, while the Foreign Country will have a comparative advantage for the other good. Trade is beneficial for both countries, and the pattern of specialization is derived by comparing costs. The Home Country specializes in the production of good 1 because

$$p_1/p_2 < p_1^*/p_2^* \iff a_1/a_2 < a_1^*/a_2^* \iff a_1/a_1^* < a_2/a_2^* \qquad (1.1)$$

Equation (1.1) provides the key Ricardian logic: With free trade, countries produce those goods for which they have a comparative advantage. We will see this logic again when we extend the Ricardian trade model to many goods in the Dornbusch–Fischer–Samuelson model and to many goods and countries in the Eaton–Kortum model.

We have shown that both countries benefit from trading with each other. The benefit is strictly larger than zero if the world price lies strictly between the autarky prices in equilibrium. Since both countries gain, gross domestic product (GDP) per capita must go up. GDP only consists of wage income, and therefore it suffices to look at wages. While prices equalize, wages do not, as workers are not mobile across countries. Wages are given by the value of the marginal product of labor, equal to $w = p_1/a_1$ and $w^* = p_2/a_2^*$, respectively. If $a_1 < a_1^*$ and $a_2 < a_2^*$ the domestic wage must be higher $w > w^*$. Salaries are determined by absolute advantage, while trade patterns are

[5] Raúl Prebisch (1959) argues that gains from trade are biased against poor countries. This is because their products are sold in competitive markets, whereas the manufactured goods of developed countries are priced in monopolistic markets. The unfavorable terms of trade work like a transfer of income from poor to rich countries. In more recent work, Feenstra, Heston, Timmer, and Deng (2009, p.202) provide empirical support for the idea that countries with higher per capita GDP also have higher terms of trade.

determined by relative advantage. Loosely speaking, the low-productivity country becomes competitive on the world market because wages are lower.

However, we still have to analyze *how much* they benefit and what determines the magnitude of gains from trade. Considering Figure 1.6, we see that each country benefits from being able to trade the good it specializes in at more favorable relative prices. Graphically, the Home Country faces a steeper budget constraint originating from L/a_1, thus allowing higher consumption bundles of both goods (compared to the autarky situation). The same applies, *mutatis mutandis*, to the Foreign Country. Put differently, both countries benefit from the difference in relative goods prices, which are driven by costs in the model.

How much each country benefits depends on the difference between point A and B and between point A^* and B^*. To gain a measure for how much better point B is compared to A, we would need to evaluate a utility function. Hence, consumer preferences play an important role in shaping the gains from trade. The more different consumer preferences are from the sector where the country enjoys its comparative advantage, the larger are the gains from trade. In the extreme case in which the Home Country has a strong preference for good 2 (for which it has a comparative disadvantage vis-à-vis the Foreign Country), the gains from trade will be very large. In contrast, if consumer preferences in the Home Country are skewed toward good 1, gains are smaller. Put simply, gains from within US trade for wine-loving consumers are larger if they live in Wisconsin than in California.

To emphasize that final point, note that the gains from trade are larger the bigger the price changes when moving from autarky to the free trade equilibrium. This price change can be bigger due to larger demand differences, larger productivity differences, or due to large country size differences. That last point illustrates why larger countries see smaller price changes and thus gain less from trade than smaller nations.

1.4 Discussion

The Ricardian model is a starting point for discussing international trade. Despite its many simplifications, it provides us with key insights. Nevertheless, it should also motivate us to think deeper about the ramifications of international trade. This stretches the limitations of the model discussed in this chapter. Nevertheless, we add several remarks at this point to motivate a more detailed study of international trade.

Gains from Trade and Trade Deficits

As the example above illustrates, two countries can gain from the exchange of goods. They are better off when engaging in foreign trade. This refutes a quote that is often (perhaps falsely[6]) attributed to Abraham Lincoln: "When we buy manufactured goods abroad, we get the goods and the foreigner gets the money. When we buy the manufactured goods at home, we get both the goods and the money." While the model discussed in this chapter describes a barter exchange with no money involved, two aspects are worth discussing: the precise cause of gains from trade and the economic interpretation of trade deficits.

Both countries in our example export and import one product, and bilateral trade is balanced. In practice, numerous countries run either large trade surpluses (e.g., Germany, China, and Switzerland) or trade deficits (e.g., United States, India, and France). Sometimes it is argued that a trade surplus (i.e., exports exceeding imports) is a sign of "success," while trade deficits imply a country is losing from trade. To see why such claims are false, reconsider that exports are but a means to an end, with the end being higher consumption. After all, what matters for a country from an economic point of view are higher consumption possibilities, which are achieved through higher production—directly at home or indirectly through export-financed imports.[7]

Gains from trade arise because the terms of trade are more favorable when engaging with foreign countries than the domestic tradeoffs faced under autarky. The confusion about gains from trade, to some extent, might be caused by the perspective of a naive accountant. It is true that companies "gain" revenue from "exporting" their products while they record "imports" as costs. Alas, any intermediate product or service that is not bought from

[6] Frank William Taussig (1914) provides a discussion.

[7] Historically, countries also attempted to achieve higher imports through military force and looting neighboring countries. At best this yields one-time gains compared to sustained gains from (peaceful) international trade.

other companies must be produced in-house. Once we recognize the presence of opportunity costs, we see that it makes no sense to just consider "exports" as favorable. For countries as a whole, a trade deficit does not imply that a country is losing from trading with another country. It obtains goods and services from other nations that it otherwise would have to produce domestically—at higher costs.

The word *deficit* in the term *trade deficit* might also lead to confusion. But as many economists have pointed out, all consumers run a "trade deficit" with grocery stores, barbershops, or gas stations. Yet, in exchange for the money spent, they receive food, haircuts, and gas. Henry George illustrated this in his 1886 book *Protection or Free Trade?* as follows: "To have all the ships that left each country sunk before they could reach any other country would, upon protectionist principles, be the quickest means of enriching the whole world, since all countries could then enjoy the maximum of exports and the minimum of imports."

GDP Growth

While we did not examine imbalanced trade, we did find that each country's GDP went up after trade liberalization: With constant population, the real wage increased. Testing this result empirically is challenging due to reverse causality: Does trade cause GDP growth or vice versa? One well-known attempt to establish causality is the instrumental variables approach chosen by Frankel and Romer (1999). Their results suggest that trade has a quantitatively large and robust, though only moderately statistically significant, positive effect on income. This finding is confirmed in a more recent paper by Dave Donaldson (2018). Analyzing the vast network of railroads built in colonial India, the study shows that railroads decreased trade costs and increased real income levels.

Dependency and Trust

In the example we discussed above, the two countries gained from trade the more they specialized according to their comparative advantage. The maximum benefit is achieved if each country only produces one of the two goods.

It is worth pointing out that such full specialization creates dependencies and requires trust between countries. Suppose the two goods are textiles and food. Not only would it require a substantial amount of trust for one country to fully depend for its food supply on another country, the resilience of the system would also be low: What if, for instance, the food-producing country were hit by a drought? Also, as Albert O. Hirschman (1945) argued in the book *National Power and the Structure of Foreign Trade*, nations can leverage trade dependencies to exert political influence over other countries.

Trade and Competition

A second important aspect to mention is the wider effect of trade liberalization. The Ricardian model like other trade models illustrates why gains from trade are possible, but it also abstracts from other important considerations. Among these is the impact of trade liberalization and specialization on competition in the goods and factor markets. In our simplified example, each country had two industries under autarky but only one after opening up to trade. While we abstract from the implications of this for the labor market, Benmelech, Bergman, and Kim (2022) find that trade openness can lead to more competition in the product market but increased monopsony power in the factor market.

Structural Change

A final important remark concerns the specialization. In the model setup, we assumed workers to be fully mobile. Hence, any worker losing employment in the shrinking sector (after trade liberalization) can easily switch to the growing sector. As numerous examples in the real world illustrate—like Haiti after the trade liberalization in 1994—this assumption must be critically reviewed when deriving policy implications. A frequently cited study by Autor et al. 2013, for example, points out that increased US imports from China led to higher unemployment, lower labor force participation, and reduced wages in local labor markets that house import-competing manufacturing industries. This illustrates that workers often cannot switch sectors as easily as assumed in the simple Ricardian model.

1.5 Comparative Statics

The model framework we developed thus far allows us to understand why trade between two countries can be beneficial. Changing the parameters—technology and labor endowments—provides additional valuable insights. Hence, we discuss technology diffusion and population growth below.

Trade and the Diffusion of Technology

One mechanism through which countries benefit from trade is the diffusion of ideas and technologies. As discussed by Coe and Helpman (1995) and many others, the exchange of goods between two countries often leads to learning from each other. While this should be an important economic argument in favor of trade, some in politics criticize the spread of technology. As an example, we can think of American companies that accuse Chinese rivals of copying intellectual property.

Despite the simplicity of the Ricardian model, it allows us to analyze how changing the technology in one country affects trade and welfare. Suppose in our example from above that the Home Country is the United States and the Foreign Country is China. We had the situation that China exports good 2 while importing good 1 from the United States. Let us assume that good 1 represents a more advanced product, while good 2 describes a less-sophisticated product. What happens if China improves its technology for the advanced product? In the model described above, this translates into a falling a_1^* and a lower relative autarky price for good 1 in China, $p^{a*} = p_1^*/p_2^*$. China's opportunity costs of producing good 2 increase because every unit of labor employed in sector 1 is now more productive. In right-hand plot of Figure 1.3, the Foreign Country's PPF will become less steep.

An improvement in China's productivity for good 2 certainly raises its welfare under autarky. Whether the country also benefits from the reduction of a_1^* under trade is less certain. In Figure 1.6, a small improvement in a_1^* makes China's PPF less steep. As long as it is still steeper than the grey line representing the terms of trade, China will not change its production and continue to sell some of good 2 at the unchanged world market price p. Another way to see this is Figure 1.5: If we lower p^{a*} but keep it above p, nothing changes—the Foreign Country continues to fully specialize in the production of good 2.

If the relative autarky price of good 1 falls sufficiently in the Foreign Country (and the relative demand curve does not change in Figure 1.5), the intersection of relative supply and relative demand would be at $p = p^{a*}$. This is illustrated in Figure 1.7 with the dark grey relative supply curve. With this new setup, China would no longer benefit from international trade because the autarky and world market prices are identical. It would produce according to its domestic PPF and benefit from having better technology for good 1. The "import" of better technology from the United States has benefited the country because it improved China's terms of trade. We come back to this topic in Section 2.7 and call it *import-biased growth* (in contrast to export-biased growth, which worsens a country's terms of trade).

How does the improved technology in China affect the United States? We see from Figure 1.7 that the relative price of good 1 on the world market has fallen. Recall that the terms of trade describe a country's export prices divided by its import prices. Since the United States in our example exports good 1 and imports good 2, the decline in p has worsened America's terms of trade. The impact on its welfare can be described using Figure 1.6: The grey line is now flatter, which implies that the Home Country (still producing only good 1) can no longer reach as high an indifference curve as before. The country is worse off than before the Foreign Country improved its technology, but it still benefits from trade.

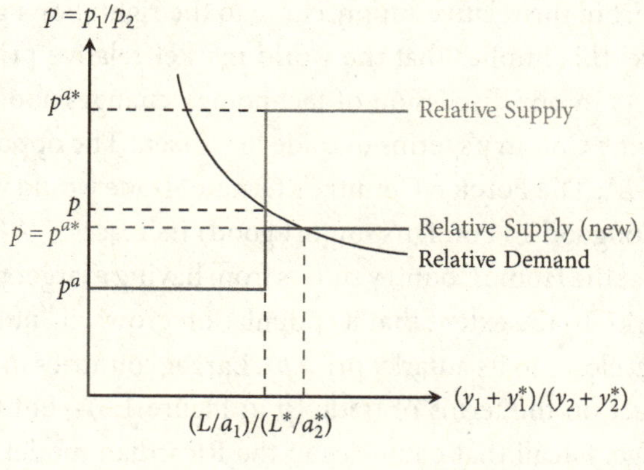

Figure 1.7 Relative Supply and Relative Demand After Technology Improvement

Why is it that the Home Country suffers from a technology improvement in the Foreign Country? The improvement raised Foreign's opportunity costs of producing the product that it exported to Home. Put differently, it is now less bad at producing the good it imports, and is therefore willing to pay less for it. If the change is sufficiently large, this will lead to a change in the terms of trade (i.e., the relative price of good 1). The Foreign Country can use labor in a more favorable way by producing good 1 itself than by importing it from the Home Country. As a result, Home must accept a worsening of its terms of trade and thus sees a reduction in welfare.

It is worth pointing out that the terms of trade also change (in a more straightforward way) if the relative demand curve shifts in Figure 1.5. Suppose the product that the Home Country exports (good 1) becomes more popular. This shifts upward the relative demand curve and improves both Home's terms of trade and welfare. To some extent, this example shows why some nations benefit from having a reputation for quality: Labels like "Made in Germany," originally introduced as a protectionist policy in the United Kingdom in 1887, have been successfully leveraged as a brand synonymous of product quality.

Population Growth

Suppose the Home Country in our example experiences population growth so that L increases to some higher level. How does this affect its trade with the Foreign Country and its own welfare? In Figure 1.5, an increase in L shifts the vertical part of the relative supply curve to the right. For a given relative demand curve, this implies that the world market relative price of good 1 (i.e., p) falls. As in our discussion of technology changes above, a fall in p causes the Home Country's terms of trade to worsen. The opposite happens if we increase L^*: The Foreign Country's terms of trade would worsen as the relative price of good 1 (Foreign's import good) increases.

Why is it that the Home Country suffers from having a larger population in this framework? To the extent that its population grows, it "pulls" the world market price p closer to its autarky price p^a. Larger countries in general have a bigger impact on the terms of trade (p in Figure 1.5)—but this is not to their advantage. Recall that countries in the Ricardian model benefit from trade because they can exchange goods at a relative price that differs from the autarky one.

1.6 Sources of Comparative Advantages

In the model discussed above, we assumed that the two countries differ in their unit labor requirements. This allowed them to benefit from trade by exploiting comparative advantages. But where do these differences in (relative) productivity come from in the real world?

There is a large set of potential explanations for differences in productivity. The most straightforward are climate differences causing heterogeneity in the cost of production. While most vegetables and fruits can be grown anywhere, the costs of doing so differ vastly across countries. For manufactured goods, history and culture can provide an explanation for why unit labor requirements differ. Another cause of cross-country differences in productivity are institutions. As Nunn (2007) explains, countries with good contract enforcement specialize in the production of goods for which relationship-specific investments are most important. This can be extended in the sense that cross-country differences in environmental standards and labor market regulation cause differences in costs of production. Finally, we can mention demographic differences as a cause of comparative advantages. Cai and Stoyanov (2016) find that many skills are age-dependent. As a result, industries relying on skills in which younger workers are relatively more efficient will be more productive in countries with a younger labor force and less productive in countries with an older population.

1.7 Empirical Tests

Before concluding the first chapter, we briefly want to examine whether the basic Ricardian trade model can be brought to the data and explain patterns of trade observed in the real world. Béla Balassa (1963) used data from the early post–World War II period for British exports to the United States. Despite the fact that the United Kingdom had a lower labor productivity in every sector, it was able to export to the United States. Moreover, the empirical results support the Ricardian model's prediction that the United Kingdom should primarily export those goods for which the American productivity advantage was relatively small. Hence, Balassa (1963) provided strong empirical support for the idea that international trade is governed by *comparative*, not *absolute*, advantages.

Later empirical studies had a harder time confirming the Ricardian model with real-world data. This is because, to some extent, increasing levels of specialization imply that we simply do not observe countries' productivity for various goods. Such challenges when confronting the basic model's predictions with the data were pointed out by Deardorff (1984). In some sense, we face a conundrum: Complete specialization is not observed in the data, but when we observe it, we are missing autarky prices and labor costs. Furthermore, it is difficult to compare relative labor costs in international data, partly because relative labor costs are endogenous to trade flows. As Leamer and Levinsohn (1995) concluded, "The one-factor model is a very poor setting in which to study the impacts of technologies on trade flows, because the one-factor model is just too simple."

More recent work by Costinot, Donaldson, and Komunjer (2012) finds that Heckscher–Ohlin models (see Chapter 3) have generated a considerable amount of empirical work. In contrast, much less has been done concerning the Ricardian model. This, the authors write, is "not because of strong beliefs regarding the relative importance of factor endowments and technological considerations." Instead, the "empirical work on Heckscher-Ohlin models shows that technology differences matter."

Revealed Comparative Advantage

When bringing the Ricardian trade model to the data, one question emerges immediately: For which products does a country have a comparative advantage in the real world? To answer this question, Béla Balassa (1965) suggested to use the revealed comparative advantage (RCA). We can define it as

$$RCA_{i,s,t} = \frac{\sum_d X_{i,s,d,t} / \sum_\varsigma \sum_d X_{i,\varsigma,d,t}}{\sum_\iota \sum_d X_{\iota,s,d,t} / \sum_\iota \sum_\varsigma \sum_d X_{\iota,\varsigma,d,t}}$$

where the fraction on the right side is to be read as follows: All exports of country s of product i in year t to all destinations d are given by $\sum_d X_{i,s,d,t}$. Hence, the whole fraction shows a country's share of world exports of a given good divided by the same country's share of total world exports.[8] If $RCA > 1$, we say that the country has a comparative advantage for the good.

[8] Note that we use ζ and ι, respectively, as help variables to summarize over all source countries in the numerator and over all products in the denominator.

Data Example 1.1: Revealed Comparative Advantages in Practice

Data from Base pour l'Analyse du Commerce International (BACI), a collection of bilateral trade flows for about 200 countries and 5,000 products, can be used to estimate revealed comparative advantages in the real world. Switzerland, for example, exported \$33.4 billion worth of watches (Harmonized Section (HS) Section 91) in 2023. In the same year, worldwide exports of watches amounted to \$57.7 billion. Hence, for this product and Switzerland, the numerator is given by 33.4/57.7 = 0.578. Regarding total exports, Switzerland's \$398 billion in 2023 represented just 1.76 percent of global exports worth \$22,604 billion. Using these numbers, we can calculate Switzerland's RCA for watches to be 0.578/0.0176 = 32.8, which is much larger than one. Therefore, we would conclude that Switzerland has a revealed comparative advantage for watches. Similarly, for textiles (HS Sections 61 and 62), Bangladesh has an RCA of about forty, while for cars (HS 8703), we find that in 2023 Slovakia (RCA = 7.1), Japan (3.6), the Czech Republic (3.4), and Germany (2.6) had a revealed comparative advantage.

Comparative advantages are not constant over time. Consider the case of China, a nation that exported \$35 billion worth of textiles (HS Sections 61 and 62) in 1996. This marked about 15 percent of all Chinese exports at the time. In 2023, however, the country exported goods worth \$3.5 trillion, of which only 4 percent were textiles. The RCA fell from about four to two over this time period.

1.8 Conclusion

There is a reason why the Ricardian trade model is usually taught at the beginning of each trade course. Despite its basic setup, the model provides a thoughtful student with several key insights about the origins and impact of international trade. Before we move on to other trade models, we summarize key insights from the basic Ricardian trade model:

- **Prices under autarky differ between countries as a result of different costs of production.** In our example, we had $a_1/a_2 < a_1^*/a_2^*$. There are numerous explanations for such differences in (relative) production costs. These include climate, history, culture, and institutions.

- **International trade occurs because autarky prices differ.** Differences in autarky prices result from different (relative) productivities. They create an incentive to produce (or purchase) a product in one country and sell it profitably at a higher price in another country. Exploiting this arbitrage opportunity raises the demand in the country with the lower price and increases in the supply in the country with the higher price. As a result, we obtain price equalization.
- **Free trade leads to goods price equalization.** As the law of one price states, in the absence of any trade costs the price of a (homogenous) good must be equal in all locations.
- **The effect of opening up to trade, in essence, is exposure to different (relative) prices.** We could just consider the Home Country under autarky and then postulate a world market relative price p. Exposing the Home Country to this different relative price yields the result we discussed. We only include the Foreign Country to see where the world market (relative) price p comes from.
- **Countries are (weakly) better off with trade.** This is illustrated by Figure 1.7. At the core, the gains from trade arise because each country specializes in the production of the good for which it has a comparative advantage. It is access to (relatively) cheap imports that make trade attractive. The Home Country can exchange good 1 for good 2 at a more favorable rate when trading with the Foreign Country than if it lived under autarky ($p > p^a$). Note that we write "weakly better off" because it can be that the free trade relative price is equal to one country's relative autarky price.
- **Gains from international trade are larger the more different the countries.** As Figure 1.7 shows, both countries are better off because after opening up to trade they were able to trade at a relative price that was different from the (relative) autarky price ($p \neq p^a$ and $p \neq p^{a*}$). It follows that gains from trade are larger, the more different the autarky prices are. In the extreme case that $a_1/a_2 = a_1^*/a_2^*$, there are no gains from trade.
- **When countries open up to international trade, they experience structural change.** In our example, the Home Country expands the production of good 1. While we assume workers to be fully mobile (i.e.,

there are no labor market frictions), in reality this points at potential negative effects of international trade.

- **Structural change and bilateral trust are necessary to benefit from international trade.** Gains from trade are limited to the extent that the decline of one sector (for which a country has a comparative disadvantage) is hampered. Similarly, if the transition of factors of production (here: labor) is limited, the benefits of trade are also reduced. Any friction or political intervention that reduces structural change or worker reallocation reduces the gains from trade in the model. Furthermore, both countries' specialization requires mutual trust in the *ex post* exchange of goods.
- **Patterns of trade are determined by comparative advantages.** As we saw in our example above, under free trade each country specializes in the good for which it has lower opportunity costs. A part of the production is then exported.
- **Wages are determined by productivity.** When the two countries trade freely, wages are different across countries. This follows from the fact that free trade leads to goods price equalization, workers are not mobile across countries, and wages are given by the value of the marginal product of labor ($w = p_1/a_1$ and $w^* = p_2/a_2^*$, respectively). Hence, workers in the more productive country earn a higher wage, and we do not have factor price equalization. Empirical evidence clearly supports this result, as wages are correlated positively with labor productivity in a cross-country regression.
- **Trade liberalization (weakly) increases *real* wages.** The workers' well-being is captured by their real wages (w/p), which increase if trade openness reduces goods prices in a country. The higher real wage is matched by a higher average productivity. While the productivity in both sectors remains unaffected—there is no transfer of knowledge and technology—specialization in the relatively more productive sector lifts average productivity.
- **Gains from trade are (weakly) larger for small countries.** When nations open up to international trade, they are exposed to different relative goods prices. Since world market prices are determined by supply and demand in all nations, smaller countries have less influence on them. This implies, *ceteris paribus*, that world market prices are more different from autarky prices in the case of small countries.

- **The Ricardian model also applies to regions.** Adding to the previous point, notice that the Ricardian setup not only applies to nations but also to individuals and regions. The pattern of trade and specialization among regions within a country follows the same logic we see in the Ricardian model. And it is typically the smallest regions that benefit the most from the exchange of goods with other regions.

1.9 Exercises

The following exercises allow students to practice and deepen their understanding of the Ricardian trade model.

Exercise 1 Consider a Ricardian model with two countries and two goods. The countries have the following labor requirements per unit of each good:

	Country A	**Country B**
Bread	5 hours	4 hours
Butter	4 hours	10 hours

(a) Both countries are endowed with 100 hours of labor each. Draw the PPFs for the countries in autarky and when trading.
(b) Which good will each of the two countries specialize in?
(c) What is the range of relative prices for which trade occurs?

Exercise 2 Obtain trade data (either from CEPII's BACI data set or from the United Nations' Comtrade database) and calculate the main revealed comparative advantages (RCA) for a country of your choice. Link your findings to the presence of specific large companies and to the country's economic policies.

Exercise 3 Recall the Ricardian model's setup discuss in this chapter.

(a) Explain why *comparative* advantages, not *absolute* advantages, govern trade flows. Use the term *opportunity cost* in your answer.
(b) Explicitly show the changes in wages that arise when both countries move from autarky to free trade.
(c) Prove that specialization in the relatively more productive sector lifts average productivity.

Exercise 4 Let us think beyond the simple Ricardian model of this chapter.

(a) Instead of free trade, assume that transportation costs exist. Discuss how this might affect trade between the two countries.
(b) Suppose $a_1/a_2 = a_1^*/a_2^*$. What does this imply for trade between the Home Country and the Foreign Country? What if we have $a_1 = a_1^*$ and $a_2 = a_2^*$?

2

The 2x2 Model

2.1 Idea and Background

As much as we can learn from the Ricardian trade model, there are several important aspects of international trade that require a different framework. One fundamental aspect is the distributional impact of trade: If countries as a whole benefit from trade, is that true for all individuals within the countries as well?[1] The 2–goods–2–production–factors (or short, 2x2) model we discuss in this chapter incorporates additional real-world features, like two factors of production (e.g., labor and capital), which enable us to demonstrate a distributional effect of international trade. We will determine factor prices (wages, rental rates) and see how international trade affects those.

Such a model with two factors of production allows us to study another important driver of international trade: cross-country differences in the *relative* endowment with factors of production. Some nations have plenty of capital but little labor, while for others, the situation is reversed. If such countries engage in trade, initially they might possess different technologies but then learn from each other. If eventually two countries employ identical production technology, share identical preferences, and there are no economies of scale, what incentive remains to trade? If cross-country factor mobility is ruled out, nations will continue to differ in their *relative* factor endowment. The scarcity of these factors determines not only factor prices under autarky but also goods prices. Labor-intensive goods will be relatively cheap in countries endowed with plenty of labor. Hence, an incentive for international trade remains.

One important insight from the Ricardian trade model facilitates our analysis in this chapter. We saw that the impact of opening up to trade is equivalent to exposing a country to different (relative) goods prices. Therefore, in

[1] It is possible to show that in a Ricardian model with two countries one nation does *not* benefit in terms of higher per capita income. Galor and Mountford (2008) provide an illustration. This requires, however, that the model is dynamic and features, for instance, human capital and population growth.

Understanding International Trade. Reto Foellmi and Stefan Legge, Oxford University Press.
© Oxford University Press (2026). DOI: 10.1093/9780197821107.003.0003

this chapter, we will only have one country (2-goods–2-factors–1-country model) and study how this country responds to (exogenous) changes in goods prices. In some sense, we "simulate" international trade by altering goods prices and analyze how production and factor prices change.

Before we dive into the details of the model, we explain some key ideas in simple terms. Suppose there are two countries, England and Portugal. While both have five workers, England has five tractors, while Portugal only has one. The two goods they can produce are strawberries and wheat. While tractors are particularly useful for wheat, they are of limited help in harvesting strawberries. In economics parlance, we could say that wheat is a capital-intensive good, while strawberries are a labor-intensive good.

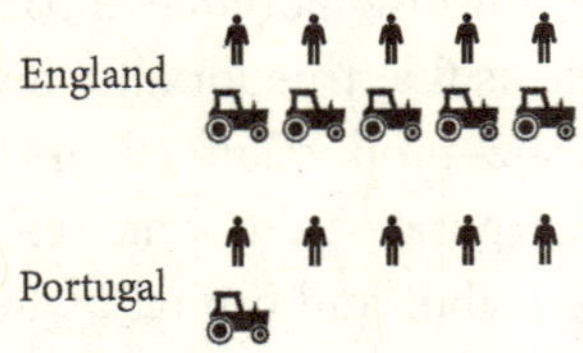

Tractors are much more scarce in Portugal. And because scarcity determines prices in an economy, we would expect tractors to be relative expensive in Portugal compared to England, where there is one tractor per worker. It follows intuitively that wheat will also be relatively expensive in Portugal: Capital is scarce and therefore the capital-intensive good is expensive.

If the two countries open up to economic exchange, there will be a reason to trade because autarky goods prices are different. We would expect England to export wheat and import strawberries. The country has a relatively abundant endowment of tractors, thus a comparative advantage in the capital-intensive good, wheat. Notice that the owners of tractors in England will be happy to learn that wheat is relatively expensive in Portugal and they can now sell into this market. Instead of moving some tractors to Portugal, England can "indirectly export" tractors by selling capital-intensive wheat. Hence, trade in goods is, to some extent, a substitute for trade in production factors. If we were to move some tractors from England to Portugal, we would expect wheat production in Portugal to increase. As the country gets more capital, it will produce more of the capital-intensive good.

Free trade between England and Portugal will lead to an equalization of strawberry and wheat prices in both countries (recall the *law of one price*). This implies that capital-intensive wheat will get relatively more expensive in England, which benefits the owners of tractors, the abundant production factor. As we will see in detail in this chapter, it is generally the abundant factor that benefits from trade liberalization and the scarce factor that suffers. Put simply, the tractor owners in Portugal benefit from the relative scarcity (and thus high factor rewards) under autarky.

2.2 Model Setup

Assumptions

In the economy we now study, two goods $i \in \{1, 2\}$ are produced using labor and capital. Without loss of generality, industry 1 is assumed to be labor-intensive. This implies that at any given factor prices, the production of good 1 always uses more labor relative to capital than the production of good 2. Output is given by $y_i = f_i(L_i, K_i)$, where f is a standard production function (increasing, concave, and homogeneous of degree one in the inputs labor L_i and capital K_i). Notice that this implies constant returns to scale—an assumption that facilitates the analysis but rules out one important reason for trade.[2]

Both factors of production are assumed to be perfectly mobile between industries. This can be seen as a long-run perspective: Over years (or generations), workers or capital can switch from one industry to another. With total factor endowments L and K and full factor employment, it must hold that

$$L_1 + L_2 = L \quad \text{and} \quad K_1 + K_2 = K \tag{2.1}$$

Production

Given the endowments and the production technology, what combinations of the two goods can be produced in the economy? If we maximize the amount of y_2 that can be produced subject to a given amount of y_1, the resource constraints of equation (2.1) give us $y_2 = h(y_1, L, K)$. This function shown in Figure 2.1 represents the production possibility frontier (PPF). The

[2] Increasing returns to scale (IRS) cause average costs of production to fall with increasing output. Thus, IRS are itself an explanation for why there are gains from trade. However, they are incompatible with perfectly competitive markets. We study IRS and trade in Chapter 7.

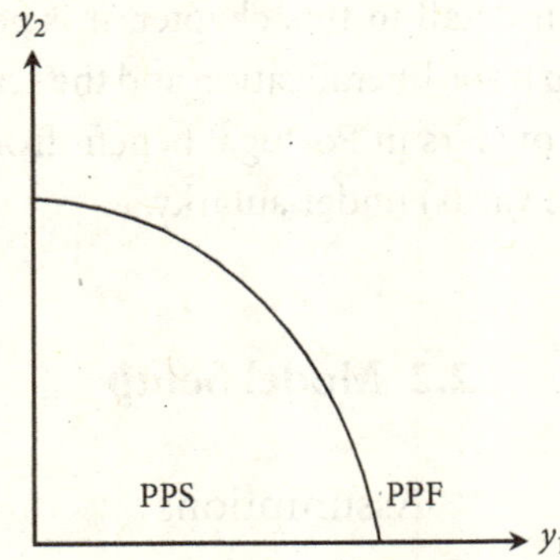

Figure 2.1 Production Possibility Set and Frontier

PPF is concave, unlike the linear PPF we had in the Ricardian trade model of Chapter 1. This follows from the fact that we assumed the production functions $f_i(L_i, K_i)$ to be concave. As a result, the rate of transformation as well as the opportunity costs of producing one good are no longer constant. When we increase the amount of good 1 that we want to produce by fixed amounts, it requires an increasing amount of good 2 that we have to forfeit. The area below the PPF reflects all combinations of y_1 and y_2 that are also possible to be produced, yet without full employment of the factors of production. We call this area (including the PPF) the production possibility set (PPS).

Which of the (y_1, y_2) combinations on the PPF should be produced? To answer this, we could again assume some preferences (i.e., a utility function) and find the highest indifference curve (IC) that intersects with the PPF, as shown in Figure 2.2. However, since we intend to study the effects of international trade—and these can be "simulated" by changing goods prices—we choose a different approach. Suppose that goods prices p_1 and p_2 are exogenously given (e.g., because the country is small in international markets and takes world market prices as given). In this case, we want to maximize the value of our economy's output. Formally, we have

$$\max_{y_1,y_2} p_1 y_1 + p_2 y_2 \quad \text{s.t.} \quad y_2 = h(y_1, L, K) \tag{2.2}$$

To solve this maximization problem, we plug the constraint into the objective function, set the first derivative equal to zero, and solve:

$$\frac{\partial(p_1 y_1 + p_2 h(y_1, L, K))}{\partial y_1} = 0 \quad \Longleftrightarrow \quad p \equiv \frac{p_1}{p_2} = -\frac{\partial h}{\partial y_1} = -\frac{\partial y_2}{\partial y_1} \tag{2.3}$$

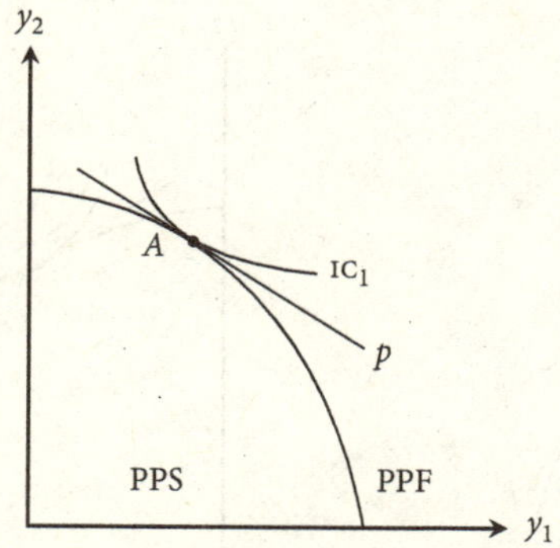

Figure 2.2 Production Under Autarky

Notice that the result says that the optimal point of production is characterized by the equality of the relative price $p = p_1/p_2$ and the (absolute value of the) slope of the PPF ($\partial y_2/\partial y_1$). The latter is the opportunity cost of producing each product (i.e., how much of good 1 (good 2) has to be given up if more of good 2 (good 1) should be produced). We illustrate this optimal point *A* in Figure 2.2.

Note that the straight line with a slope of $-p$ describes the country's budget constraint: $p_1y_1 + p_2y_2 = p_1c_1 + p_2c_2$, where c_i denotes consumption of good $i \in \{1, 2\}$.

Gains from Trade

How will the country adjust to opening up to international trade? Suppose we have a situation in which the country has no impact on the world market price (i.e., it takes world prices as exogenously given) and the relative price of good 1 is lower under autarky than on the world market: $p < p^w$. The economy optimally adjusts to the new situation in which good 1 is more expensive after opening up to trade. Labor and capital will be shifted to the first industry in order to produce more of good 1 and less of good 2. We illustrate this on the left side in Figure 2.3 by changing p to p' and obtain a new optimal point of production A'.

Before changing the relative goods prices—that is, before opening up to trade—the country's point of production *A* was identical to its consumption, allowing the country to reach IC_1, shown in Figure 2.3. Different world market prices of $p' \neq p$ imply different terms of trade at which the

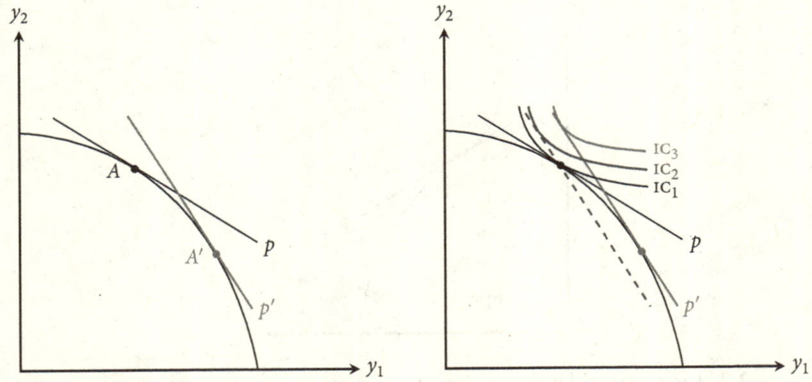

Figure 2.3 Adjustment to Higher Relative Price of Good 1 and Gains from Trade

country can exchange good 1 for good 2 and vice versa. How does this benefit the country? Being exposed to p' but not adjusting its own production, the country can already benefit and reach the superior IC_2. The difference between IC_1 and IC_2 thus illustrates the gains from exchange. Note that the dashed dark grey line goes through point *A* and is parallel to the light grey line. It reflects the country's budget constraint when producing at point *A* and being able to trade internationally. Finally, when the country optimizes its production based on p', it can reach an even higher IC, IC_3. Hence, the difference between IC_2 and IC_3 shows the gains from specialization. Taken together and similar to the Ricardian model, the size of overall trade gains depends on demand and supply forces, captured by the ICs and the PPF.

Both straight lines in Figure 2.3, p and p', describe the country's budget constraint—under autarky and with different relative prices. Note that the country benefits more from having access to world market prices p' the more different those are from autarky prices p.

Equilibrium

We now have determined what amounts of good 1 and 2 should be produced. However, we must still discuss how these amounts are produced. That is, we have to analyze which factor inputs are optimal in each industry. To do this, we define the unit cost functions $c_i(w, r)$, which describe the minimum cost to produce one unit of good i. Given that we assumed constant returns to scale, these unit costs are equal to both marginal costs and average costs. Formally, we have

$$\min_{L_i, K_i \geq 0} \{wL_i + rK_i | f_i(L_i, K_i) \geq 1\} \tag{2.4}$$

The unit-cost functions are nondecreasing and concave in w and r. Note that these do not have a sub-index i because free factor mobility across sectors ensures that factor returns are equal in both industries. We write a_{iL} and a_{iK} for the unit-factor requirements for labor and capital. They are the optimal choice for L_i and K_i in industry i. This gives us the solution to the minimization problem as $c_i(w, r) = wa_{iL} + ra_{iK}$. Because we assume perfect competition in the goods market, there are zero profits and goods prices equal marginal costs:

$$p_1 = c_1(w, r) \quad \text{and} \quad p_2 = c_2(w, r) \tag{2.5}$$

To conclude the description of the equilibrium in the economy, we must state that all available factors of production are fully employed (i.e., factor market clearing):

$$L = a_{1L}(w, r)y_1 + a_{2L}(w, r)y_2 \quad \text{and} \quad K = a_{1K}(w, r)y_1 + a_{2K}(w, r)y_2 \tag{2.6}$$

Thus there are four equilibrium conditions in the 2x2 model: four equations in the four unknowns (w, r, y_1, y_2). Note that the four parameters p_1, p_2, L, and K are exogenously given.

2.3 Factor Price Equalization

We plot the two zero-profit conditions of equation (2.5) in the (w, r) space in Figure 2.4.

Both curves are downward sloping. This follows from the fact that each represents a fixed unit-cost level: If the wage is higher, the rental rate must be lower. Put differently, if w increases, firms will hire less labor (marginal product of labor increases) and more capital (marginal product of capital decreases); thus r decreases. Note that the (absolute value of the) slope of

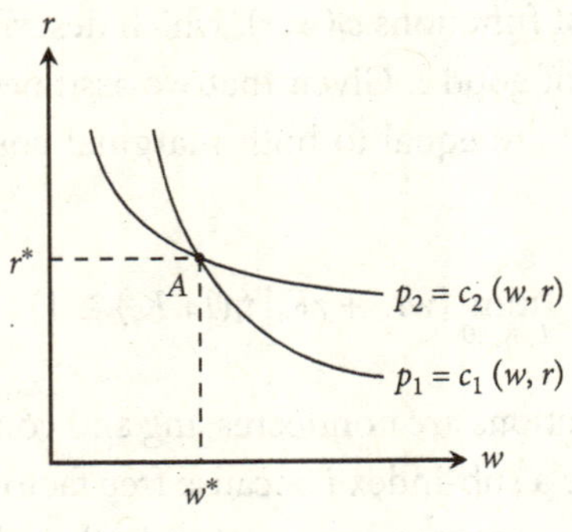

Figure 2.4 Factor Price Equalization

the curves is given by $\partial c_i / \partial w = a_{iL}$. This follows from the envelope theorem.[3] And because industry 1 is assumed to be labor-intensive—that is, at all (w, r) combinations, industry 1 uses relatively more labor—the unit-cost curve c_1 is steeper.

Figure 2.4 provides us with a remarkable result: The two zero-profit conditions pin down unique factor prices w^* and r^*. Factor prices are determined by world market prices and are independent of endowments. If we assume that all countries employ the same production technology, we obtain the factor price equalization (FPE) theorem: *If two countries produce both goods using the same technologies and both goods are freely traded, factor prices are equal across countries.*

Let us provide some intuition for this result. We make three key assumptions: (i) There is perfect competition in all markets, (ii) labor and capital can be used in all countries with the same technology and thus identical productivity, and (iii) trade is free, which leads to an equalization of goods prices across countries. In this situation, there cannot be any cross-country difference in wages or rental rates. Factor rewards equal marginal value products. And both the marginal product and the goods prices are equalized across countries.

Some economists and political commentators see the FPE as a reason for concern. Typically, richer countries are capital abundant and pay higher wages than poor countries. If free trade leads to an equalization of wages,

[3] Formally, we have $\frac{\partial c_i}{\partial w} = a_{iL} + \left(w * \frac{\partial a_{iL}}{\partial w} + r * \frac{\partial a_{iK}}{\partial w} \right)$. Because a_{iL} and a_{iK} are optimal choices of L_i and K_i, the term in parentheses is equal to zero.

then workers in rich countries might want to oppose trade liberalization. Yet, while there is some justification for the concern, it should also be emphasized that FPE only occurs under the many assumptions stated above. Put differently, the FPE theorem also shows why wages (and other factor prices) are *not* equalized in the real world. For one thing, labor productivity is not identical in all countries. And if we recall the Ricardian model of Chapter 1, we analyzed such productivity differences and saw that in this model there is no FPE.

One way to intuitively grasp the FPE theorem is to think about trade in goods as a substitute for trade in production factors.[4] This aspect is nicely illustrated by Wilhelm Röpke (1899–1966), a German economist and one of the spiritual fathers of the social market economy: "If we no longer allow people to export themselves, we must allow them all the more freely to export the products of their labor at the most favorable conditions.... It is bad that under exceptional circumstances you have to take away their permission to migrate. But if you take [away both the free movement of goods and people], you close all valves."

Before we conclude the discussion of the FPE theorem, we should discuss another implicit assumption: We did not allow for factor intensity reversals (FIR). Suppose industry 1 is only labor-intensive (i.e., its slope in Figure 2.4 steeper) for a range of factor prices (w, r) but capital-intensive for others. Then the two curves might intersect twice, and we would not have a unique solution for the factor prices. Such FIRs exist in the real world: Many textiles, for instance, can be produced either in a labor- or capital-intensive way. Robots (i.e., capital) can to some extent replace workers (i.e., labor). However, we rule out FIR in our analysis.

2.4 Stolper–Samuelson Theorem

Step-by-Step Economic Analysis

Since goods prices pin down factor prices in our model, we can ask how factor prices change if we alter goods prices. Graphically, this is a simple

[4] Note that the free movement of goods is *not* a full substitute for the free movement of factors of production. Suppose $K < K^*$ and $L = L^*$, then the two countries' PPF is different, as is the budget constraint (because $rK \neq rK^*$). Welfare in the Foreign Country is higher. Hence, the lack of international factor mobility is not fully "compensated" by free goods trade.

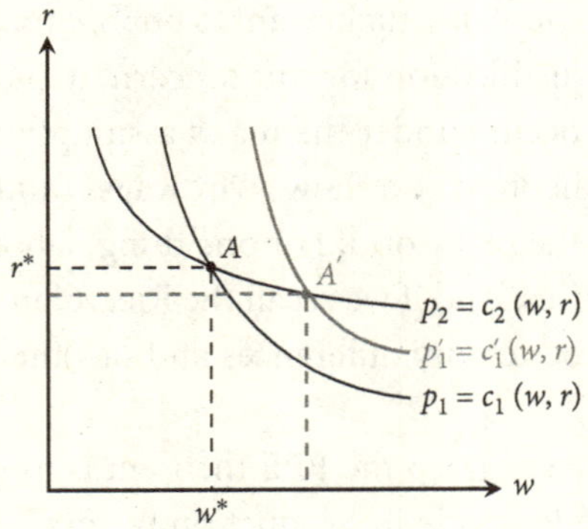

Figure 2.5 Stolper–Samuelson Theorem

exercise. Suppose p_1 increases. This shifts the zero-profit line for good 1 to the right, as shown in Figure 2.5.

In the new equilibrium (A'), the wage w has increased, while the rental rate r decreased. However, these are just the *nominal* factor prices. For statements about welfare—are workers able to purchase more goods when w is up but p_1 is up as well—we have to consider *real* factor prices. For this analysis, it is useful to consider how the economy responds to an increase in p_1 step by step:

1. The price of good 1 increases ($p_1 \uparrow$) while p_2 remains unchanged. This increases the relative price $p = p_1/p_2$.
2. The economy maximizes again the value of its production. Following equation (2.3) and Figure 2.3, an increase in p leads to a higher production of good 1 and a lower production of good 2.
3. To increase y_1, factors of production must be reallocated from industry 2 to industry 1. We denote the amounts of labor and capital that switch sector by $\tilde{L}$ and $\tilde{K}$.
4. If we rule out FIRs, after the reallocation industry 1 must still be labor-intensive: $\frac{K_1+\tilde{K}}{L_1+\tilde{L}} < \frac{K_2-\tilde{K}}{L_2-\tilde{L}}$. But how much capital per worker will be shifted? It must be that $K_1/L_1 < \tilde{K}/\tilde{L} < K_2/L_2$. Proof:
   - We write the two inequalities: (I) $K_1/L_1 < \tilde{K}/\tilde{L}$ and (II) $\tilde{K}/\tilde{L} < K_2/L_2$
   - Rewrite both: (I') $K_1\tilde{L} < L_1\tilde{K}$ and (II') $L_2\tilde{K} < K_2\tilde{L}$
   - Then we divide (I') by (II') but take the smaller numerator divided by the larger denominator on the left side of the inequality: $\frac{K_1\tilde{L}}{K_2\tilde{L}} < \frac{L_1\tilde{K}}{L_2\tilde{K}}$

- This can be solved for $K_1/L_1 < K_2/L_2$, which just states that industry 1 is labor-intensive—something we assumed to be true in the setup.

5. Because the amount of capital $\tilde{K}$ that each worker switching sectors brings to industry 1 is more than the average capital per worker in industry 1, it must be that industry 1 becomes more capital-intensive. At the same time, the amount of capital $\tilde{K}$ that each worker switching sectors takes from industry 2 is less than the average capital per worker in industry 2, it must be that industry 2 becomes more capital-intensive.
6. Both industries end up being more capital-intensive. As a result, the marginal product of labor increases and wages go up. Similarly, the marginal product of capital decreases, and the rental rate goes down.

Numerical Example 2.1

How is it possible that *both* industries end up being more capital-intensive? Let us assume that the economy is endowed with 100 workers ($L = 100$) and 30 machines ($K = 30$). Initially, $L_1 = 70$ workers are employed in industry 1, and they use $K_1 = 10$ machines. That is to say, seven workers share one machine in the labor-intensive industry. The capital-labor ratios for the two industries are then given by $K_1/L_1 = 1/7 \approx 0.14$ and $K_2/L_2 = 2/3 \approx 0.67$.

Suppose after increasing the price of the labor-intensive good ($p_1 \uparrow$) we expand output of industry 1 by shifting $\tilde{L} = 10$ workers and $\tilde{K} = 5$ machines from industry 2 to industry 1. In this case, each worker switching sectors brings with him $\tilde{K}/\tilde{L} = 0.5$ machines. Note that this is less than the 0.67 machines per worker initially in industry 2 but more than the 0.14 machines per worker initially employed in industry 1. As a result, both industries become more capital-intensive (i.e., K_i/L_i increases in both industries): $K_1/L_1 = 15/80 = 0.1875$ and $K_2/L_2 = 15/20 = 0.75$.

This again shows that *nominal* factor prices change. But what about the *real* wage and rental rate? To answer this question, we analyze the costs of production. For industry 1, it must be that $c_1 = wa_{1L} + ra_{1K}$. In other words, costs of production are determined by factor prices (w and r) and by unit inputs (a_{1L} and a_{1K}). Let us divide the expression $c_1 = wa_{1L} + ra_{1K}$ by c_1:

$$1 = \frac{wa_{1L}}{c_1} + \frac{wa_{1K}}{c_1} \tag{2.7}$$

We label the first fraction on the right side as θ_{1L} and call it the share of labor costs in industry 1. Similarly, we obtain θ_{1K} for the cost share of capital.[5] Because we have zero profits, it must hold that changes in costs are equal to changes in prices.[6] Hence, we have

$$\hat{c}_i = \hat{p}_i = \theta_{iL}\hat{w} + \theta_{iK}\hat{r} \tag{2.8}$$

where $\hat{p}_i$ denotes the percent change in the price of good 1. Put simply, equation (2.8) says that the percent change in p_1 must be a weighted average of the percent change in the wage ($\hat{w}$) and the rental rate ($\hat{r}$). We know that $\hat{p}_1 > 0$ (the price of good 1 went up), that the nominal wage increased ($\hat{w} > 0$) and the nominal rental rate decreased ($\hat{r} < 0$). It then follows from equation (2.8) that $\hat{w} > \hat{p}_i$.

> Suppose in industry 1 we have a labor cost share of 80 percent—that is, $\theta_{1L} = 0.8$. Then a price increase of 10 percent ($\hat{p_1} = 0.1$) must be equal to a cost increase of 10 percent because profits are zero. With r falling, this can only occur if nominal wages increase by more than 10 percent. Formally, it must hold that $\hat{w} > \hat{p}_1$. If, for instance, $\hat{r} = 0$, then $\hat{w} = 0.1/0.8 = 0.125$, and if $\hat{r} < 0$, then $\hat{w}$ must be even higher.

From the analysis above, we obtain the *magnification effect*

$$\hat{w} > \hat{p}_1 > \hat{p}_2 = 0 > \hat{r} \tag{2.9}$$

which points out that any change in goods prices has a magnified effect on factor prices. It also states that workers are better off in real terms when we increase the price of the labor-intensive good. Irrespective of how they allocate their income on spending for the two goods, they can afford more after good 1 becomes more expensive. In contrast, capital owners are worse

[5] Following Ronald W. Jones (1968), this is called *Jones algebra* or *hat algebra*, when we look at the notation. We come back to hat algebra in Chapter 6 when discussing the Eaton–Kortum model.

[6] Formally, we totally differentiate the zero-profit condition: $dp_1 = a_{1L}dw + a_{1K}dr$. This we divide by p_1 on the left and by c_1 on the right side, noting that $p_1 = c_1$. Extending the right side by w and r, we obtain $dp_1/p_1 = wa_{1L}/c_1 * dw/w + ra_{1K}/c_1 * dr/r$. With $\hat{w} = dw/w$ and $\hat{r} = dr/r$, we get equation (2.8).

off in real terms. This result was first shown by Wolfgang Stolper and Paul A. Samuelson (1941) and is called Stolper–Samuelson theorem: *An increase in the relative price of a good will increase the real return to the factor used intensively in that good and reduce the real return to the other factor.*

One intuitive way to understand this theorem is to say that the increase in the price of the labor-intensive good 1 leads to structural change: The labor-intensive industry expands, and the capital-intensive industry shrinks. As a result, total demand for labor increases. And because total supply of labor in the economy is unchanged, we now have higher scarcity of labor. A market economy in which prices are determined by scarcity will thus yield a higher (real) wage for workers.

Trade and Income Inequality

The magnification effect shown in equation (2.9) illustrates that there are indeed winners and loser from trade. Even though the country as a whole is better off with trade (see Figure 2.3), some individuals suffer. In theory, this implies that the winners could compensate the losers. However, a large number of studies on the political economy of trade and trade liberalization point out obstacles in this regard. We refer to the collective action problem (Olson, 1965) in addition to research by Fernandez and Rodrik (1991) and Grossman and Helpman (1994). In practice, such obstacles make it difficult to successfully implement programs to support individuals suffering from trade liberalization.[7]

Based on the Stolper–Samuelson theorem, we can think about international trade as one force causing a rise in income inequality observed in numerous rich countries in the past decades. Factors of production—such as labor—are compensated on the basis of scarcity, which is altered by international trade. Does the Stolper–Samuelson theorem and the magnification effect we derived above explain trends in wage inequality of the past decades? An extensive study of this relationship between trade and inequality is provided by Elhanan Helpman in his 2018 book "*Globalization and Inequality*". The central conclusion is that international trade has only modestly contributed to the increase in inequality. The much more important force is

[7] In the United States, John F. Kennedy introduced the Trade Adjustment Assistance (TAA) program on January 25, 1962. Baicker and Rehavi (2004) provide an account of the program's impact.

technological change, altering the rewards for high-skill workers. Nevertheless, the Stolper–Samuelson theorem explains the direction of lobbying or political preferences with regard to trade liberalization. Furthermore, the wage growth observed in the Asian tiger countries Hong Kong, Singapore, South Korea, and Taiwan—countries integrating in the world market—is explained well by the theorem.

2.5 Rybczynski Theorem

Recall that the equilibrium in our economy is guided by four equations in four unknowns (see equations 2.5 and 2.6). What happens to the economy if we alter the endowments *L* or *K*? How will the economy adjust if there is immigration or an inflow of capital? To analyze this, it is useful to employ the Lerner diagram, first introduced by Abba P. Lerner (1952).

Lerner Diagram

Let us assume a production function for apparel like $Q_{Apparel} = AK^{\alpha}L^{1-\alpha}$. Suppose we want to know all possible combinations of K and L that produce one unit of apparel. We rearrange the production function to get $K = L^{(\alpha-1)/\alpha}/(Q_{Apparel})^{-1/\alpha}$. If α is something like two-thirds, the plot would look like Figure 2.6.

The solid curve shows an iso-revenue curve that is equal to an isoquant when prices stay constant. What if we want two units of apparel? The curve must shift out as shown by the dashed iso-revenue curve. It will be

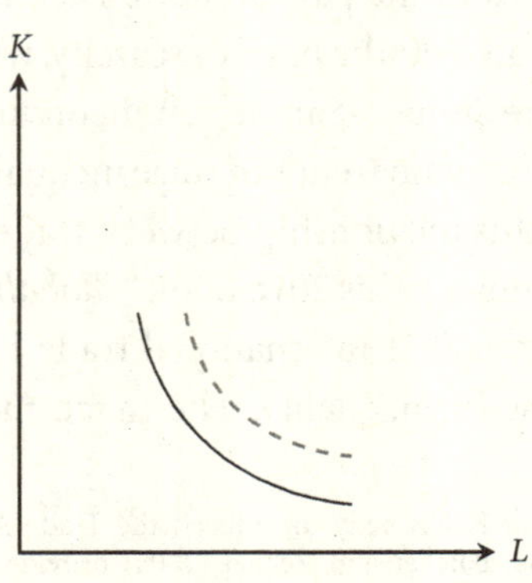

Figure 2.6 Lerner Diagram: Iso-Revenue Curves

convenient to define industry iso-revenue curves in terms of the amount of output that earns \$1. How much apparel earns \$1? To answer that question, we need to know the price of apparel, $P_{Apparel}$. Knowing that, we can compute the quantity of apparel that earns one dollar by diving \$1 by the price:

$$P_{Apparel}Q_{Apparel} = 1 \quad \Longleftrightarrow \quad Q_{Apparel} = 1/P_{Apparel}$$

We plug this into the equation for K above and obtain

$$K = L^{(\alpha-1)/\alpha}/(1/P_{Apparel})^{-1/\alpha}$$

With this equation defining the solid iso-revenue curve in the figure above, it represents all combinations of capital and labor that yield enough apparel output to earn \$1 given the price of apparel, $P_{Apparel}$.

What happens to the curve if the price of apparel falls? If the price of apparel falls, we need a greater quantity of apparel to earn \$1, and this extra quantity requires the use of more capital and labor. Thus, the dollar-value iso-revenue curve shifts out, like it did with the dashed iso-revenue curve. To figure out the combination that is actually used, we need more information. In particular, we need information about how much capital and labor cost. Let us refer to the rental rate of capital as r and the wage as w.

Recall that one of the assumptions of the model is zero economic profit: $wL + rK = 1$. Note that we can rewrite this equation as $K = 1/r - (w/r)L$. The slope and y-intercept of this line are $(-w/r)$ and $(1/r)$, respectively. Furthermore, the horizontal intercept of the dollar-value isocost line is $1/w$. Note that because both the vertical and the horizontal intercept are the reciprocals of r and w, respectively, movements of the intercepts toward the origin represent increases in these factor rewards, while movements away from the origin represent declines. We show the isocost curve as a straight line with slope $(-w/r)$ in Figure 2.7.

The dollar-value isocost line and the iso-revenue curve (i.e., the dollar-value isoquant) are tangent at the point (L_A, K_A). This tangency represents and defines several quantities of interest. First, it represents zero profit: Inputs L_A and K_A cost \$1 to hire, and they can be combined to create \$1 worth of apparel. Second, the tangency point also defines the optimal capital intensity, K_A/L_A, by which apparel will be made. Finally, the slope of the dollar-value isocost line represents the equilibrium relative wage rate, w/r. This follows from the equation $K = 1/r - (w/r)L$ we stated earlier. To gain

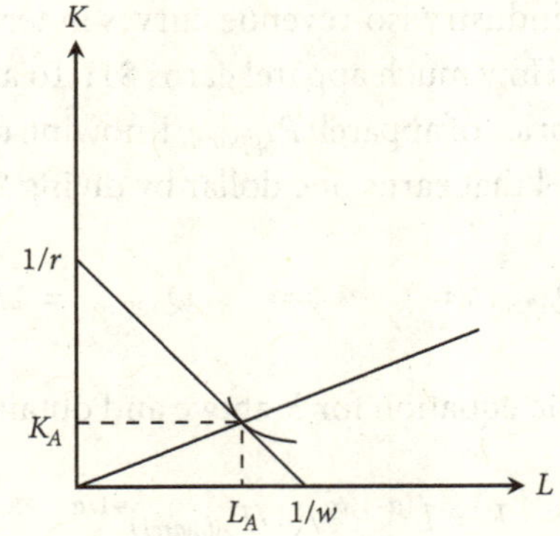

Figure 2.7 Lerner Diagram: Isocost Line and Iso-Revenue Curve

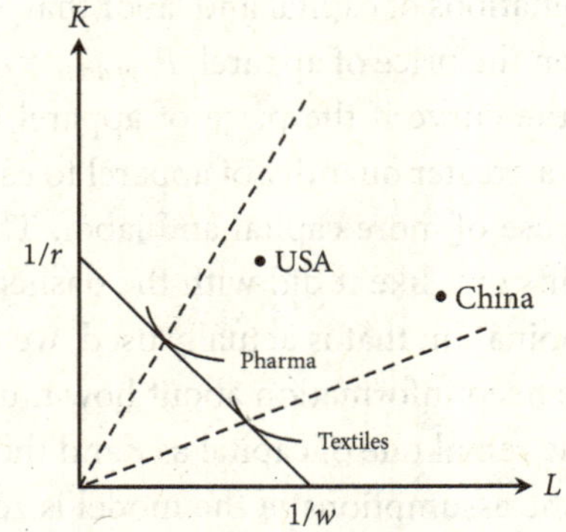

Figure 2.8 Lerner Diagram: Two Industries, Two Countries

some intuition for these quantities, consider what would happen if relative wages were to increase for some reason (i.e., if *w* were to rise, or *r* were to fall, or both). Intuitively, one would expect that an increase in the relative price of labor would lead to an optimal production technique that relies less on labor.

Let us move on by adding another industry, pharmaceuticals, which by assumption is relatively capital-intensive compared to textiles. Figure 2.8 includes a dollar-value pharmaceuticals isoquant as well as a dollar-value textiles isoquant.

Note that we have also placed the pharmaceuticals iso-revenue curve on the same isocost curve as textiles. Why? It reflects our assumption that factors are freely mobile across industries. One way of thinking about this assumption is that it requires the return to capital and the wage rate to be the same across industries within a country. If they were not the same, factors would have an incentive to move to where rewards were higher, and this movement would result in FPE.

We can now complete the Lerner diagram by adding the final ingredient, two countries. Let us assume the United States is capital abundant relative to China—that is, $K_{US}/L_{US} > K_{China}/L_{China}$. Recall that it is assumed that both countries have access to the same technology. It is worth emphasizing that the tangencies between the iso-revenues and the isocost curve in Figure 2.8 do not represent production points. These points only tell us how much capital and labor need to be combined to produce $1 of each good and that these amounts cost $1 to hire.

One of the many useful features of the Lerner diagram is that it is easy to see how much of a country's endowments are devoted to each industry and, therefore, how much each country produces of each good. Start with the full employment assumption we made earlier. This assumption implies that the sum of the amount of each factor devoted to each industry must equal the total endowments of those factors. For the United States, this implies that

$$K_{US,Textiles} + K_{US,Pharma} = K_{US} \quad \text{and} \quad L_{US,Texttiles} + L_{US,Pharma} = L_{US}$$

The dot for each country in Figure 2.8 marks the two countries' total endowments, and the dotted lines emanating from the origin visualize the optimal production techniques. We can see how much of each factor each country devotes to each industry by using vectors with the slopes of these dotted lines to "reach" each country's endowment dot. Figure 2.9 does this for China. Start at the origin and move along the ray for textiles. As you move along this ray, you are increasing the amounts of capital and labor China devotes to textiles. Note that to get to the China endowment point, you eventually have to leave the textiles ray. However, once you leave the textiles ray, you can only travel along a line with the slope of the pharma sector, because that line devotes China's capital and labor in that sector in the optimal proportions necessary to produce it. Getting to the China endowment point, therefore, is just a matter of figuring out how to combine the lines with the two optimal industry factor-intensity slopes to reach China. We can do this for both countries and obtain Figure 2.9.

The factor allocations displayed in the figure highlight the result that the United States devotes more of its endowment to pharmaceuticals than China, while the opposite is true of textiles. A "shortcut" to seeing this is

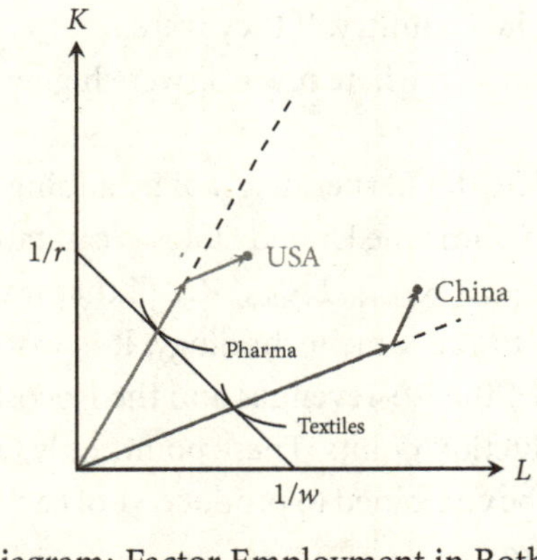

Figure 2.9 Lerner Diagram: Factor Employment in Both Countries

to note that the US endowment point lies closer to the optimal pharmaceuticals capital intensity, while the China endowment point lies closer to the optimal textiles capital intensity. As we will see in the next chapter, the Heckscher–Ohlin theorem states that under the assumptions made above, a capital-abundant country will produce more of, and export, the capital-intensive good.

Note that in Figure 2.9, China and the United States manufacture both goods. This is an outcome of both countries lying inside the same cone of diversification, where the word *cone* refers to the area between the optimal textiles factor intensity and the optimal pharma factor intensity. Suppose that China's endowment point was outside the cone of diversification (lower than shown in Figure 2.9). In that case, there is no way that China would produce pharmaceuticals. If a country lies outside the cone, it specializes completely in the good to which it is closest, and it does so using a capital intensity equal to its capital abundance.

The Impact of Immigration

With the Lerner diagram, we can easily study the impact of migration. Suppose we use (L_1, K_1) to produce y_1. As a vector, this can be illustrated as in Figure 2.10.

Note that the Lerner Diagram is drawn in the factor space (as opposed to the Ricardian model, which we drew in the goods space) with K and L on the axes. If we use the remaining labor and capital in industry 2 to produce y_2, it must be that the total labor and capital used in both sectors adds up to the

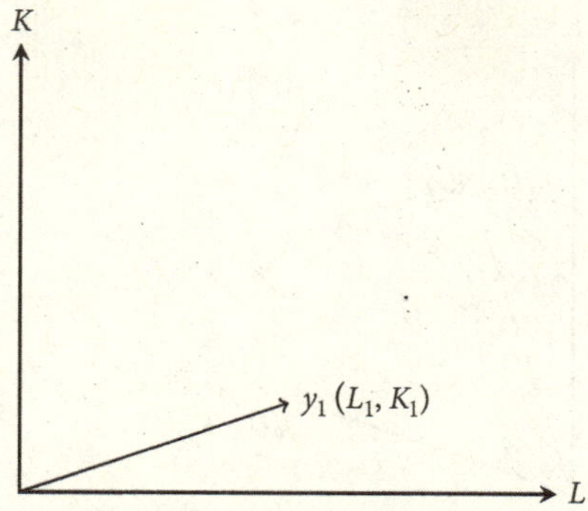

Figure 2.10 Production Vector in the Lerner Diagram

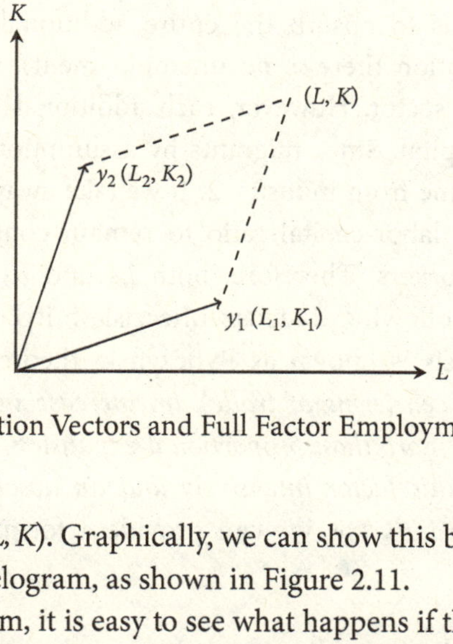

Figure 2.11 Production Vectors and Full Factor Employment

total endowment (L, K). Graphically, we can show this by drawing a second vector and a parallelogram, as shown in Figure 2.11.

Using this diagram, it is easy to see what happens if the economy experiences immigration that raises L to L'. Figure 2.12 illustrates the result.

In grey, we show the new parallelogram—how L' and K are allocated to both industries after immigration. The figure shows that output in industry 1 has expanded, while production in the second industry is reduced. Immigration led to an expansion of the labor-intensive industry and a shrinking of the capital-intensive industry.

Notice that we did not change goods prices (p_1 and p_2 are unchanged). Also, recall that goods prices pin down unique factor price w and r, which then in turn determine a_{1L}, a_{1K}, a_{2L}, and a_{2K}. None of these variables are changed by immigration. Hence, the arrows in the figure above do not change their slope.

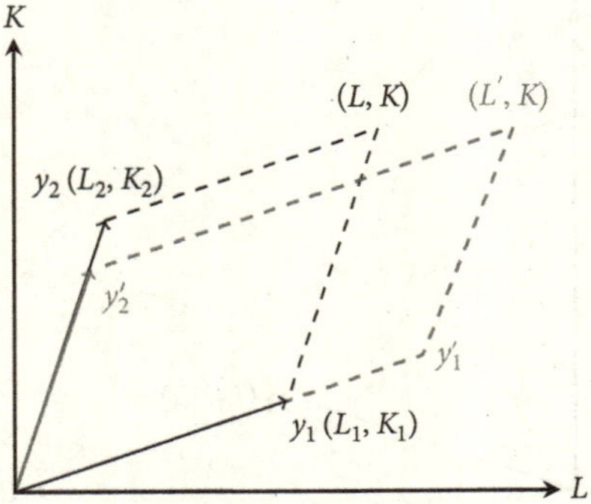

Figure 2.12 Impact of Immigration

If the economy is to absorb the entire additional labor after immigration (by assumption there is no unemployment), we have to expand the labor-intensive sector. However, each additional worker in industry 1 requires some capital. Since migrants by assumption do not bring any, the capital must come from industry 2. If we take away some capital from industry 2, for the labor-capital ratio to remain constant we must also take away some workers. Therefore, both L_2 and K_2 decrease while L_1 and K_1 increase. Following Tadeusz Mieczislaw Rybczynski (1955), the result of our analysis is known as Rybczynski theorem: *At constant relative goods prices (i.e., terms of trade), an increase in one factor endowment will lead to a more than proportional expansion of the output in the industry that uses this factor intensively and an absolute decrease of the output in the other industry.* We can provide a formal proof for this as follows:

- We start with $K = K_1 + K_2$, divide by L, and expand the fractions by L_1/L_1 and L_2/L_2.
- This yields $\frac{K}{L} = \frac{K_1}{L_1}\frac{L_1}{L} + \frac{K_2}{L_2}\frac{L_2}{L}$.
- Note that $L_1/L = (L - L_2)/L = 1 - L_2/L$. Thus, $\frac{K}{L} = \frac{K_1}{L_1}\left(1 - \frac{L_2}{L}\right) + \frac{K_2}{L_2}\frac{L_2}{L}$.
- We multiply with the term in brackets to obtain $\frac{K}{L} = \frac{K_1}{L_1} - \frac{K_1}{L_1}\frac{L_2}{L} + \frac{K_2}{L_2}\frac{L_2}{L}$.
- Note that L_2/L shows up twice on the rightside: $\frac{K}{L} = \frac{K_1}{L_1} + \left(\frac{K_2}{L_2} - \frac{K_1}{L_1}\right)\frac{L_2}{L}$.
- Since the capital-ratio in each sector overall is identical to the ratio for one unit of outcome, we can write $\frac{K}{L} = \frac{a_{1K}}{a_{1L}} + \left(\frac{a_{2K}}{a_{2L}} - \frac{a_{1K}}{a_{1L}}\right)\frac{L_2}{L}$.

- Since we had immigration, the left side (K/L) decreased. On the right side, the first fraction remains unchanged, and the term in parentheses is positive because industry 2 is capital-intensive. It follows that the equation only holds if L_2/L decreased.
- If the share of labor used in industry 2 decreased, it must be that L_1/L increased. Thus, L_1 must increase more than proportionally with L.
- A similar calculation shows that K_1 must expand (and K_2 decrease) after immigration.

Note that both the proof and the illustration of Figure 2.12 only work if there is incomplete specialization (i.e., we remain within the cone of diversification). We discuss this aspect below. While we examined an increase in labor endowment, a similar effect occurs if we change the country's capital endowment. The Rybczynski theorem also informs us about how a country adjusts to cross-country capital movements (e.g., FDI, foreign aid, war reparations, remittances) or capital accumulation. From the late 1970s onwards, China's economic development allowed the country to build up a higher capital stock. In line with the model presented here, Chinese exports shifted away from products that require low-skill labor and little capital. Similarly, Japan was labor-abundant in the aftermath of the Second World War. Reconstruction and high savings rates made it capital-abundant. In the 1960s, Japan was a net exporter of labor-intensive goods such as textiles, while today it mainly exports capital-intensive goods like electronics and sophisticated computer equipment. The example is illustrative but you should always keep in mind that the Rybczynski theorem assumes that technology stays the same. Of course, it is likely that over this long time period, innovations have changed Japan's potential to produce electronics as well.

Another real-world example of the Rybczynski effect is the Dutch disease: After the discovery of the Groningen gas field in the Netherlands in 1959, industries related to natural gas expanded. At the same time, other industries contracted because resources moved to the gas-related industries (and the Dutch currency appreciated).

Cone of Diversification

As we saw in our analysis above, the inflow of additional labor is absorbed in the labor-intensive industry. This raises the question whether any amount of immigration can be absorbed this way. If not, where is the limit?

When L increases, the capital-intensive industry shrinks. And as long as it exists (i.e., as long as we are in the cone of diversification) we can shift K from that industry to the labor-intensive sector. Recall that we abstract from capital inflows such as foreign direct investment (FDI). As long as the increase in L (or K) is such that the endowment vector (L, K) lies between the factor requirement vectors (a_{1L}, a_{1K}) and (a_{2L}, a_{2K}), all labor and capital will be employed in either of the two industries. The space spanned by (a_{1L}, a_{1K}) and (a_{2L}, a_{2K}) is called the cone of diversification.

If the endowment vector lies outside of the factor requirement vectors (e.g., because L increased too much), then it is impossible to add together any positive multiples of the vectors (a_{1L}, a_{1K}), and (a_{2L}, a_{2K}) and arrive at the endowment vector. If this happens because of "too much" labor, then the economy will only produce the labor-intensive good 1—with some labor unemployed. This result is driven by the fact that the economy faces exogenously given product prices as well as fixed technology. In reality, product prices would eventually change, and with them factor prices and the factor requirement vectors. Furthermore, the presence of unemployment might lead to directed technological change (see Acemoglu, 2002).

To bridge the gap between theory and reality at this point, consider the following example. A small open economy always takes goods prices from the world market. When we study the impact of immigration, we can thus hold goods prices constant. But what if the country is "large" and has influence on world market prices? With sufficiently large immigration, even a small country will eventually become "large," and so the assumption of it taking world prices as given becomes invalid. What if we only consider two countries? Suppose that in this setup labor moves from one to the other. As long as both stay within the cone of diversification and there are identical homothetic preferences, world goods prices would not change due to migration.

2.6 Trade Policy

The 2x2 framework also allows us to explore the impact of trade policy. Governments can employ numerous tools to alter international trade flows. These include import duties (tariffs), quotas, export curbs, subsidies, and non-tariff barriers (NTBs). In this book, we focus exclusively on tariffs because the impact of most other measures can be achieved with a tariff of appropriate magnitude.

To understand the impact of trade policy, it is useful to recall why countries benefit from international trade in the two frameworks we discussed thus far: Openness to trade raises a country's welfare because of access to better terms of trade. Hence, one central question is whether a country can use trade policy tools to improve its terms of trade.

Suppose the Home Country introduces a tariff on good 1. To study the welfare effect, we must distinguish between "large" and "small" countries (i.e., countries with and without an impact on the world market price). Furthermore, we have to take account of government revenues arising from the tariff. This implies that we examine the general equilibrium (unlike most undergraduate books, which often focus on the partial equilibrium in one market).

Let us start with the situation illustrated in Figure 2.3. The country produces according to point A', its budget constrain is given by $p' = p_1^w/p_2^w$, and it reaches IC3. It exports good 1 and imports good 2. Note that p_1^w and p_2^w indicate the world market goods prices. When the country introduces an import tariff $t > 0$ on good 2, the economy faces the relative price $p^{\text{tariff}} = p_1^w/(1 + t)p_2^w$. In the case that the country has no influence on world market prices, p_2^w remains unchanged, $p^{\text{tariff}} < p'$, and the budget line is less steep than before. The country will produce more of good 2 and less of good 1.

For the small country that has no influence on world market prices, the introduction of a tariff unambiguously reduces welfare: It can no longer reach as high an IC as before. The situation is different for "large" countries that have an impact on world market goods prices (i.e., they have bargaining power as buyers). Suppose that the United States introduces a tariff on cars from Mexico. Most Mexican car exports go to the United States, where they compete with cars from various other countries (including the United States itself). Hence, Mexican car exporters will not find it optimal to pass on the entire tariff to US customers; instead, they will lower the price to some extent. From the perspective of the United States, this implies an improvement in the terms of trade. In our illustration from above, the country introducing the tariff still faces $p^{\text{tariff}} = p_1^w/(1 + t)p_2^w$, but p_2^w would now fall. If the terms-of-trade gain is sufficiently large—compensating for the distortion of consumption and production—the country might be better off with the tariff than with free trade. For a more in-depth discussion of trade policy, its tools, and its ramifications, refer to the textbook by Krugman, Melitz, and Obstfeld (2024).

2.7 Economic Growth

How does economic growth affect international trade in the 2x2 model? Does economic growth in one country benefit its trading partners as well? To answer these questions, we must first distinguish two possible biases of the economic growth:

- *Import-biased growth* improves a country's terms of trade, generally raising its welfare and decreasing the welfare of foreign countries.
- *Export-biased growth* worsens a country's terms of trade, generally reducing its welfare and increasing the welfare of foreign countries.

In "normal" cases, the net effect of both types of economic growth on domestic welfare is positive. However, it could be negative when growth is export-biased and the world demand is very inelastic. This point was first made by Jagdish Bhagwati (1958), who called this phenomenon "immiserizing growth." We illustrate this special case in Figure 2.13.

The export-biased growth changes the PPF from PPF_1 to PPF_2. As a result, the price of the exported good (relative to the imported good) falls substantially, causing p' to be much flatter than p. This indicates a worsening of the country's terms of trade. The country expands the production of the export good but no longer reaches IC_1 (but some inferior IC). The devaluation of the country's own production causes a welfare loss. Notice that the worsening of the country's terms of trade imply that its trading partners

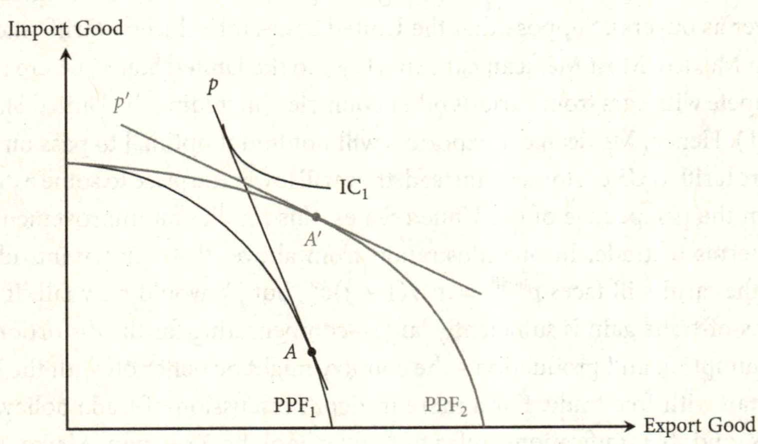

Figure 2.13 Immiserizing Growth

face improved terms of trade. This means that the entire world does *not* suffer from the capacity gains. The question is how these gains are distributed across countries.

The scenario of Figure 2.13 is similar to the case of a monopolist: Increasing the quantity does not necessarily raise revenue if it involves a substantial price cut. Here, the country's export sector cannot take advantage of any monopoly power in the world market. Hence, under rather strong assumptions (heavily export-biased growth and very steep supply and demand curves), economic growth can reduce a nation's welfare.[8] Overall, "immiserizing growth" illustrates an extreme case, but it highlights the problem of a homogeneous export sector. For numerous developing countries focusing exports on primary goods, an excellent harvest does not necessarily increase welfare if world market prices fall strongly. Looked at it from the other perspective, the change in terms of trade that are at the heart of the immiserizing growth can work as a built-in insurance: For a *large* developing country exporting primary commodities the terms of trade improve in bad times and worsen in good times. In contrast, for a *small* exporter of primary commodities, a harvest failure can have devastating effects. Yasuyuki Sawanda (2009), who empirically investigated immiserizing growth, found most cases to occur in Africa and Latin America.

2.8 Conclusion

The analysis of the 2x2 economy provides us with several important insights about the effects of international trade. Recall again that we only considered one economy and how it responds to changes in goods prices. However, trade with a second country would have the same impact for as long as it would entail the same change in goods prices. There are three main takeaways from the 2x2 model:

- **FPE theorem:** Free trade leads to an equalization of goods prices due to the no-arbitrage condition and the law of one price. If two countries use the same technologies, free trade will equalize factor prices (wages, rental rates). In some sense, trade in goods is a substitute for trade in factors of production.

[8] A similar logic applies to the case of import-biased growth: Strong import-biased growth in the Foreign Country can have a detrimental effect on welfare in the Home Country.

- **Stolper–Samuelson theorem:** If opening up to trade increases the relative price of one good, the production factor that is used intensively in this sector will receive a higher reward in real terms. The reward to the other factor is reduced in real terms. This impact of international trade on real factor returns explains political coalitions, as described by Ronald Rogowski (1989).
- **Rybczynski theorem:** At constant relative goods prices, an increase in one factor endowment will lead to a more than proportional expansion in the output of the industry that uses this factor intensively and an absolute decrease in the output of the other industry.

Taken together these results illuminate how international trade can make individuals *within* a country better or worse off than under autarky. In a market economy with perfect competition, individuals who own a given factor of production (e.g., labor or capital) are rewarded according to the scarcity of that factor. The scarcity is determined by supply and demand. With international trade exposing the economy to different goods prices and leading to structural change, the demand for each factor of production changes—and so does the factor reward.

Based on our analysis of international trade so far, we can conclude that the exchange of goods across borders causes countries to be better off. However, within a country, there are winners and losers—which is why trade policies are often controversial.

2.9 Exercises

The following exercises allow students to practice and deepen their understanding of the 2×2 model.

Exercise 1 Consider the introduction of a tariff on imports.

(a) Show that such a tariff unambiguously reduces welfare for a small country that has no influence on world goods prices.
(b) Which assumptions must hold for a tariff to increase welfare in a large country?

Exercise 2 The equilibrium in the 2x2 model is defined by equations (2.5) and (2.6), where $c_j(w, r)$ is the unit-cost function of sector j. $a_{ij}(w, r)$ is the number of factor input $i = L, K$ required in sector j to produce one output unit, and y_j is the total output of sector j. World market prices are exogenously given. Assume further that the cost functions are given by $c_1(w, r) = 4w + r$ and $c_2(w, r) = 2w + 2r$ and that the endowments are given by $L = 500$ and $K = 350$.

(a) Determine the factor input coefficients a_{jL} and a_{jK}, respectively.
(b) Determine the production levels y_1 and y_2 in this economy.

Exercise 3 Consider the 2×2 model with two industries and two input factors (labor L and capital K). We assume that there are no FIRs. The full-employment conditions are given by equation (2.6), where a_{iL} and a_{iK} are the amounts of labor and capital, respectively, required to produce one unit of output in industry $i = 1, 2$. We use y_i for the output produced by industry i.

a) Suppose that $a_{1L} = 3, a_{2L} = 2, a_{1K} = 1, a_{2K} = 3$. Compare the two industries and determine which of the two industries produces with a relatively labor-intensive technology.
b) Suppose that we look at a country that is endowed with $L = 500$ and $K = 400$. Determine y_1 and y_2.
c) Suppose that world consumption equals world production and is given by $D_1 = 12'000$ for good 1 and $D_2 = 8'000$ for good 2. Suppose further that the country we look at accounts for 1 percent

of world consumption and that consumer preferences are identical across countries. Compute the factor content of trade for our country and give a short economic interpretation.

d) The two full-employment conditions can be rearranged to get

$$\lambda_{1L}\hat{y_1} + \lambda_{2L}\hat{y_2} = \hat{L}$$
$$\lambda_{1K}\hat{y_1} + \lambda_{2K}\hat{y_2} = \hat{K}$$

where $\lambda_{iL} = \frac{y_i a_{iL}}{L}$ and $\lambda_{iK} = \frac{y_i a_{iK}}{K}$ and $\hat{z} = dz/z$ for any variable z. Suppose that due to immigration, L increases by 1 percent but K stays constant. Determine $\hat{y_1}$ and $\hat{y_2}$ and provide a short economic interpretation.

Exercise 4 Consider an economy with endowments $L = 100$ and $K = 100$. The capital-intensive industry uses 80 percent of all capital and 20 percent of all labor while the rest is used by the labor-intensive industry. Tragically, half of the capital stock in the economy is lost in a war. Display this in a Lerner diagram and elaborate on the consequence of the war for the two industries.

Exercise 5 Consider the setting illustrated below, where $c_j(w, r)$ denotes the unit-cost function of sector j, and a_{ij} is the unit-factor requirement for the production factor $j \in \{L, K\}$ in sector i.

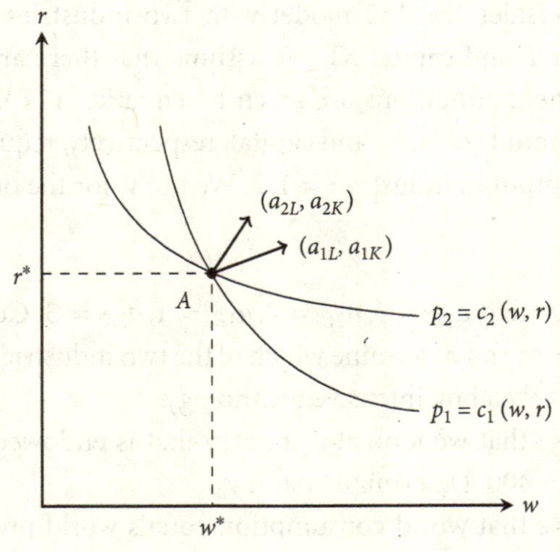

(a) Explain why point A is the equilibrium if p_1 and p_2 are given exogenously.
(b) Considering the figure, which of the two goods is capital-intensive? Explain why.
(c) Assume p_2 increases. Illustrate the outcome and explain whether workers and capital owners are better or worse off.

3

The Heckscher–Ohlin Model

3.1 Idea and Background

Chapter 2 covered the 2x2 model, in which one country produced two goods using two factors of production. To examine the impact of international trade in this setting, we exogenously altered goods prices. This framework can be understood as a simplification of the so-called Heckscher–Ohlin (H–O) model, or 2x2x2 model, in which two countries produce (and trade) two goods using two factors of production.

The origins of this model go back to a book that Bertil Ohlin published in 1933. Therein, he first explained the theory and credited Eli Heckscher as co-developer of the model. The two Swedish economists collaborated at the Stockholm School of Economics in the years before: Many of the ideas of the final model came from Ohlin's 1924 doctoral thesis, which was supervised by Heckscher.

The H–O model seeks to explain patterns of international trade (as well as production) based on the factor endowments of countries. In line with the Ricardian model of Chapter 1, trade between nations is the result of arbitrage opportunities: Prices under autarky are different, and opening up to trade allows these price differences to be exploited. In contrast to Ricardo, however, Heckscher and Ohlin describe differences in countries' endowments with factors of production as root cause of differing autarky prices for goods. Put simply, in a country that has a rich endowment with land, we expect land to be relatively cheap and thus land-intensive products to be relatively cheap as well. When trading with countries poorly endowed with land, we expect the land-abundant country to export the land-intensive good.

3.2 Model Setup

The setup of the H–O model is very similar to the 2x2 model, except that it involves two countries: Home and Foreign. Importantly, the two countries share the same production technology but differ in their endowment with

Understanding International Trade. Reto Foellmi and Stefan Legge, Oxford University Press.
 DOI: 10.1093/9780197821107.003.0004

the two factors of production. Let us assume that the Home Country is labor-abundant, while the Foreign Country is capital-abundant: $L = L^*$ and $K < K^*$, thus $L/K > L^*/K^*$. Notice that the factors of production are of equal quality in both countries. There are two goods $i \in \{1, 2\}$, and we assume good 1 to be labor-intensive. Furthermore, individuals in both countries have identical homothetic preferences.[1] This assumption is inserted for simplicity and on the principle of focusing on the endowment difference between the countries.

Further assumptions that carry over from the 2x2 model are that factors of production (i.e., labor and capital) are fully mobile across industries but not across countries. They are both fully employed, and all industries are perfectly competitive. We rule out factor intensity reversals (FIRs)—which implies that the factor price equalization (FPE) theorem holds. Finally, the model assumes that any trade between the two countries is free of trade costs.

3.3 Heckscher–Ohlin Theorem

Given this setup of the model, what pattern of trade do we expect to see between the two countries? Recall that they are identical in every aspect except that Foreign has more capital: $K < K^*$. This implies that capital is less scarce in the Foreign Country and thus cheaper. Any product using relatively large amounts of capital in production will be relatively cheap. In our setting, this implies that the relative price of the capital-intensive product (i.e., good 2) will be lower in the Foreign Country.

With relative prices under autarky being different, there is an incentive to trade once we allow the two countries to exchange goods across borders. Given that good 1 will be relatively cheap in the Home Country and good 2 relatively cheap in the Foreign Country, we can predict the pattern of trade: Home will export good 1 and import good 2. This is summarized by the H–O theorem: *Each country exports the good that uses its abundant factor intensively.*

In the real world, we can find empirical evidence in favor of this hypothesis. According to data from the World Bank, Argentina, Australia, Canada, and Ukraine all belong to the list of countries with the largest amount of arable land per person. At the same time, their share of global agricultural

[1] This implies that even though the Foreign Country is richer (it has more capital since $K < K^*$ but the same population) it consumes both goods in the same proportions as the Home Country.

exports is substantially larger than their share of all global exports. According to data from the World Bank for 2021, Argentina, for instance, had five times the world average amount of arable land per capita. The country accounted for only 0.3 percent of all global goods exports but 2.0 percent of global exports in agricultural products (Harmonized System (HS) chapters 01, 02, 04, 05, 07, 08, 10, 11, 12, and 14) according to Base pour l'Analyse du Commerce International (BACI).

To formally show that this pattern of trade arises, recall that different autarky prices are the cause of trade flows. If we can show that good 1 is relatively cheap in the Home Country, we established the pattern of trade. First, we consider the Home Country under autarky. As is shown in Figure 3.1, the country's endowment and technology determine what amounts of y_1 and y_2 the country can produce: the production possibility frontier (PPF). From among all possible combinations, it chooses the one that yields the highest utility, represented by the highest indifference curve (IC) that just touches the PPF.

Under autarky, the Home Country will produce and consume the (y_1, y_2)–combination given by point *A*, and the relative price of good 1, $p^a = p_1^a/p_2^a$, is given by the (absolute value of the) slope of the PPF at point *A*. We add the Foreign Country to this in Figure 3.2. Note that it has more capital and so can produce more of both goods (but relatively more of the capital-intensive good 2). This is reflected by the grey Foreign PPF.

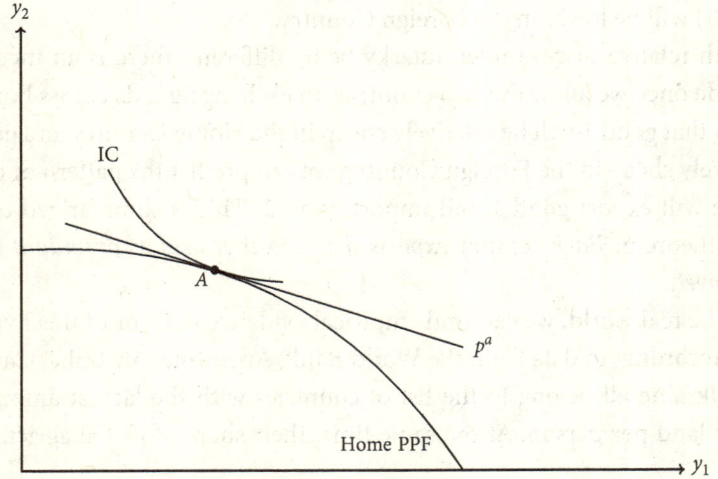

Figure 3.1 Production in the Home Country

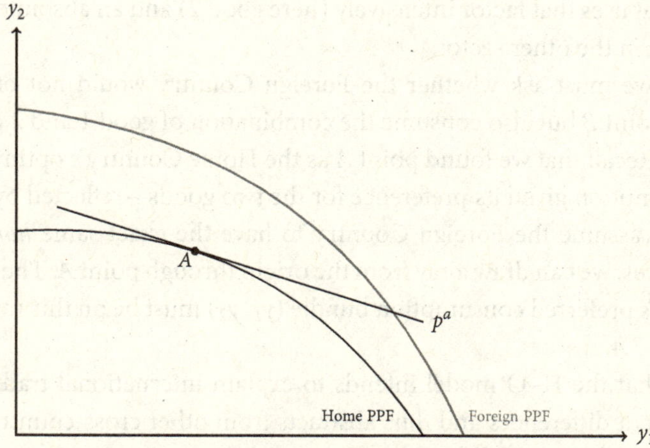

Figure 3.2 Production in Both Countries

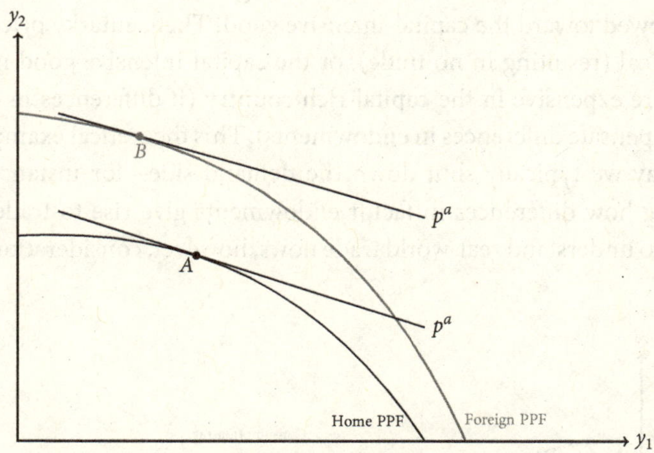

Figure 3.3 Production with Identical Relative Goods Price

To show that under autarky p^a cannot be the relative price of good 1 in the Foreign Country, let us assume that it is the price and check for a contradiction. If indeed the Foreign Country had the relative price p^a, it would choose point *B* for production, as shown in Figure 3.3. This is where the slope of the foreign PPF is equal to $-p^a$. Notice that the Rybczynski theorem predicts point *A* to be below and to the right of *B*: At constant relative goods prices, an increase in the endowment of one factor (here the Foreign Country has more capital) leads to a more than proportional expansion of output in the sector that uses that factor intensively (here good 2) and an absolute decline of output in the other sector.

Next, we must ask whether the Foreign Country would not only produce at point *B* but also consume the combination of good 1 and 2 given by point *B*. Recall that we found point *A* as the Home Country's optimal point of consumption given its preference for the two goods—reflected by the IC. Since we assume the Foreign Country to have the exact same *homothetic* preferences, we can draw a ray from the origin through point *A*. The Foreign Country's preferred consumption bundle (y_1, y_2) must be on this ray shown in Figure 3.4.

Note that the H–O model intends to explain international trade due to endowment differences and thus abstracts from other cross-country differences. If we allow for differences in demand, however, we see that capital (or labor) abundancy of a country actually refers to both supply and demand. Suppose we have two countries and the capital-rich one has preferences more skewed toward the capital-intensive good. Then, autarky prices could be identical (resulting in no trade), or the capital-intensive good might be even more expensive in the capital-rich country (if differences in demand overcompensate differences in endowments). This theoretical example illustrates why we typically shut down the demand side—for instance, when analyzing how differences in factor endowments give rise to trade. When seeking to understand real-world trade flows, however, considerations about

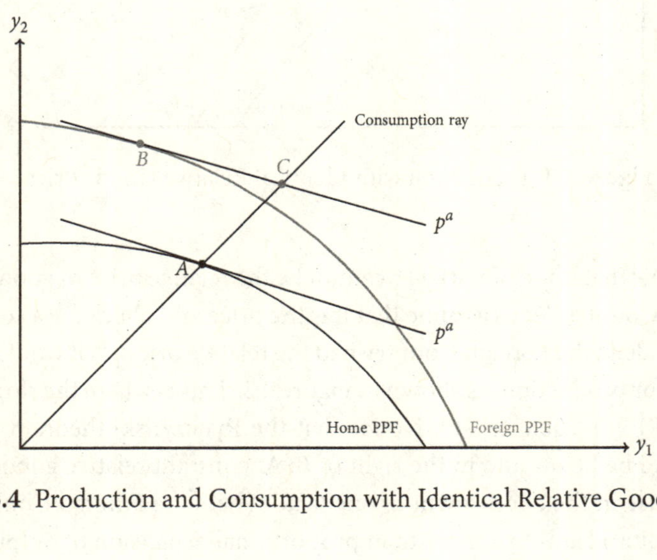

Figure 3.4 Production and Consumption with Identical Relative Goods Price

the demand side are important, especially when consumer preferences are endogenous. Over sufficiently long time periods, countries' preferences can be shaped by (natural) endowments. While in practice it is difficult to disentangle supply and demand forces, preferences for various food products could have been shaped by countries' natural endowments. In our discussion of the H–O model, however, we abstract from such cross-country differences in demand.

As Figure 3.4 illustrates, the Foreign Country would produce at point *B* (if the relative price were equal to p^a) but consume at point *C*. Under autarky, however, there cannot be a difference between the point of consumption and production. Hence, at price p^a, there would be excess demand for good 1. This will increase the price of good 1 until points *B* and *C* are identical. This proves that, under autarky, the labor-intensive good will be cheaper in the Home Country than in the Foreign Country. Therefore, when we allow for free trade, the Home Country will export good 1 and import good2.

At which free trade equilibrium price will the two countries exchange goods? Let $z(p)$ denote the excess demand for good 1 at any prevailing price p in the Home Country, while $z^*(p^*)$ denotes the excess demand for good 1 in the Foreign Country.

It follows that

- At prices below p^a, there is excess demand for good 1 in Home and Foreign.
- At prices above p^a but below p^{a*}, there is excess supply of good 1 in Home and excess demand for good 1 in Foreign.
- At prices above p^{a*}, there is excess supply of good 1 in Home and Foreign.

Because the excess demand function $z(p)$ is continuous, there must be a price p^w between p^a and p^{a*} for which world excess supply and excess demand are zero, $z(p^w) + z^*(p^w) = 0$. This is the relative price at which the two countries trade with each other. The resulting trade pattern is illustrated in Figure 3.5. Note that unlike in the Ricardian model (with linear PPF) we do not get a corner solution (i.e., no full specialization): Both countries continue to produce some positive amount of each good.

Figure 3.5 shows the trade equilibrium with p^w as the relative price of good 1 at which Home and Foreign trade. Compared to a hypothetical situation where the autarky price of Home prevailed, both countries have shifted

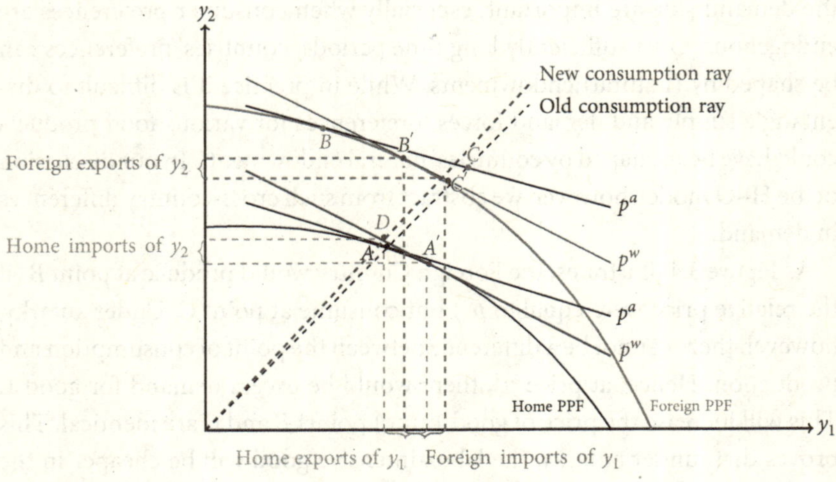

Figure 3.5 Production and Consumption in Both Countries

their consumption toward good 2. Since good 2 got relatively cheaper (p_1/p_2 increased), the consumption ray is steeper than before. With trade, Home consumes at point D and Foreign at point C. Trade is balanced in the sense that exports of one country are equivalent to imports by the other country. Furthermore, we see that both countries benefit from trade: They can consume a combination of y_1 and y_2 outside of their PPF.

3.4 Effects of Trade, Gains from Trade, and Trade Policy

The impact of international trade on production and the distributional consequences are identical to what we already found in the 2x2 model (see Chapter 2). The relative price of good 1 rises in the Home County. As a result, the factor used intensively in the production of this good (i.e., labor) will gain in real terms, while the other factor (capital) loses. Thus, there are winners and losers from international trade in the H–O model.

The overall gains from trade, as is shown in Figure 3.6, can be broken down into gains from exchange and gains from specialization. The Home Country's PPF and indifference curve under autarky (IC_1) pin down production (y_1^a and y_2^a), consumption, and welfare without trade. If the country opens up to trade but does not adjust its production (to y_1^t and y_2^t), it will still benefit from trade: Producing at point y_1^a and y_2^a, it can now trade both goods

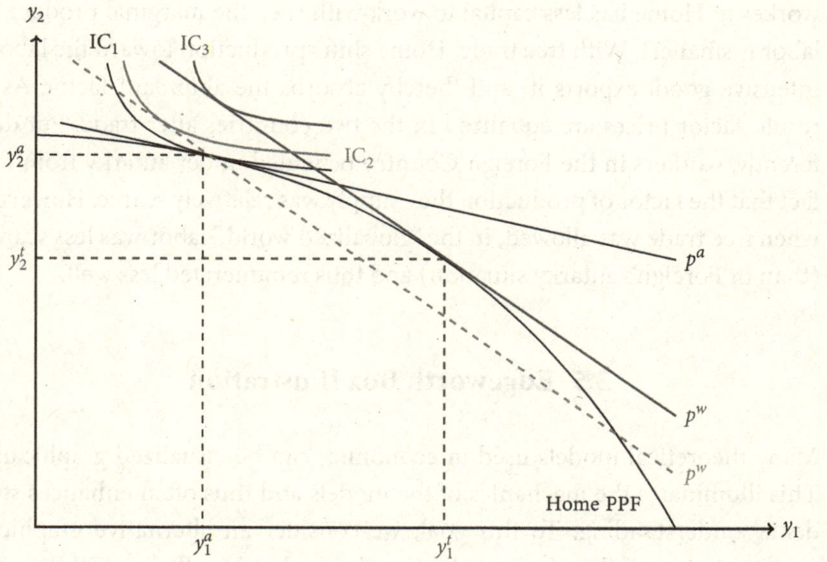

Figure 3.6 Gains from Trade Due to Exchange and Specialization

at the relative price p^w. The dashed line parallel labeled p^w goes through the point of production under autarky but has the slope p^w. Trading goods at more favorable rates allows the Home Country to reach a higher IC: IC$_2$ instead of IC$_1$. When adjusting production to y_1^t and y_2^t, however, an even higher IC (IC$_3$) is possible. Thus, the difference between IC$_2$ and IC$_3$ are the gains from specialization.

Trade policy can alter the gains from trade. As an example, we can think of the Home Country introducing an import tariff on good 2. Whether this has an effect on p^w depends on the size of the Home Country: If it is "large enough" such that its purchasing decisions matter, p^w will increase. Note how this would allow the Home Country to reach an IC higher than IC$_3$. However, the tariff also alters domestic prices in the Home Country. As a result, it will not (fully) specialize according to its comparative advantage. Therefore, the overall effects of a tariff depend on its impact on the terms of trade (p^w) as well as the domestic production distortion.

Who in the Home Country would be in favor of such protectionism? This also depends on the FPE we already studied in the 2x2 economy. In the H–O framework, wages would be lower in the Home Country's autarky equilibrium than in the Foreign Country's autarky equilibrium. This is because each worker in Home has less capital to work with (i.e., the marginal product of labor is smaller). With free trade, Home shifts production toward the labor-intensive good, exports it, and thereby absorbs the abundant factor. As a result, factor prices are equalized in the two countries after trade. Put differently, workers in the Foreign Country benefited under autarky from the fact that the factor of production they supply was relatively scarce. However, when free trade was allowed, in the "globalized world," labor was less scarce (than in Foreign's autarky situation) and thus remunerated less well.

3.5 Edgeworth Box Illustration

Many theoretical models used in economics can be visualized graphically. This illuminates the mechanics of the models and thus often enhances students' understanding. To this goal, we consider an alternative graphical representation of the H–O model based on what is called an Edgeworth box. The tool is named after Irish economist Francis Ysidro Edgeworth, refined by Italian engineer and economist Vilfredo Pareto, and popularized by the English statistician Arthur Lyon Bowley (and so sometimes called an Edgeworth–Bowley box). In essence, it is a device for illustrating the allocation of two resources, each available in a fixed total amount, between two types of use. Kelvin Lancaster (1957) discusses the H–O model by means of the Edgeworth box. Following his work, Figure 3.7 provides the basic setup. We see the Home Country, which allocates both labor and capital

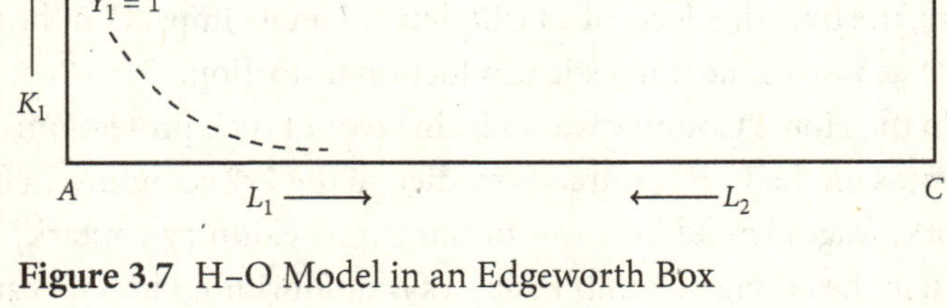

Figure 3.7 H–O Model in an Edgeworth Box

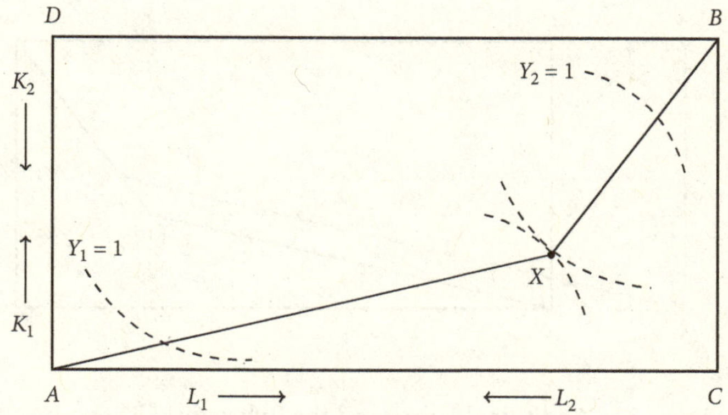

Figure 3.8 Factor Allocation in the Home Country

to two industries. The rectangle *ABCD* represents the economy with fixed total endowments. The distance from point *A* to *C* (henceforth labeled *AC*) describes the total endowment with labor, while *AD* indicates the total capital endowment. The two dashed curves illustrate isoquant lines. Given that we have homogeneous production functions (i.e., constant returns to scale), all other isoquant lines can be obtained by uniform radial expansion or contraction relative to the origin.

Notice that the slope of the isoquant lines is determined by the marginal productivity of labor and capital, which we describe by *MPL* and *MPC*, respectively. Perfect competition in the factor markets ensures that factor prices—and thus marginal productivities—are equal in both industries. Graphically, this implies that the isoquant lines of both sectors must be tangential. This is shown by point *X* in Figure 3.8.

We observe that point *X* is to the southeast of the diagonal *AB*. This indicates that industry 1 is labor-intensive. The line *AX* cuts all industry 1 isoquant lines at the same angle, such that MPL_1/MPC_1 is constant (this ratio is the tangent to the isoquant line). With constant returns to scale, the absolute values of the marginal productivities are constant along *AX*. The goods prices are given by the condition that the value marginal products and therefore the factor prices must be equalized across industries as a result of free factor mobility:

$$p_1 * MPL_1 = p_2 * MPL_2 \quad \text{and} \quad p_1 * MPC_1 = p_2 * MPC_2 \tag{3.1}$$

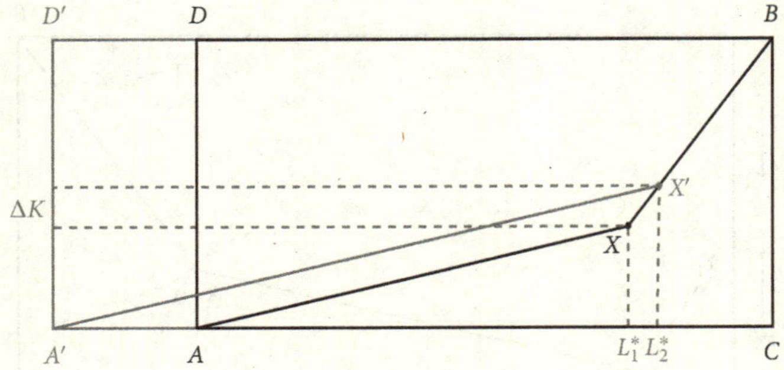

Figure 3.9 Additional Labor and the Rybczynski Theorem

This can be rewritten as

$$\frac{p_1}{p_2} = \frac{MPL_2}{MPL_1} = \frac{MPC_2}{MPC_1} \tag{3.2}$$

It is straightforward to illustrate the Rybczynski theorem using the Edgeworth box. Suppose as a result of immigration the Home Country's labor endowment grows by ΔL. We add this in Figure 3.9 on the left side. With unchanged goods prices and technology, the slope from A' to the new allocation point X' is identical to the slope of AX. All additional labor ($\Delta L = A'A$) is allocated to the labor-intensive industry, some additional capital is moved from industry 2 to industry 1 (shown by ΔK), and then some additional labor moves as well (shown by $L_1^* L_2^*$). Overall, output in the labor-intensive industry expands, and production in the capital-intensive industry shrinks.

Having solved the resource allocation problem in the Home Country, we can turn to the two-country situation. Suppose the Foreign Country has more capital but less labor, as shown by the rectangle $A'B'C'D'$ in Figure 3.10. Given that both countries use the same production technologies, the slope of AX and $A'X'$ is identical. Moreover, the marginal productivities (and thus the prices) of both factors in both industries are the same at X and at X'. The goods price ratio is also identical at X and X'.

In line with the results obtained earlier, we see that the Home Country—which is relatively labor-abundant—produces relatively more of the labor-intensive good 1. There is an incentive for the two countries to engage in international trade because they have identical preferences but produce goods 1 and 2 in different relative quantities. If trade occurs, each country

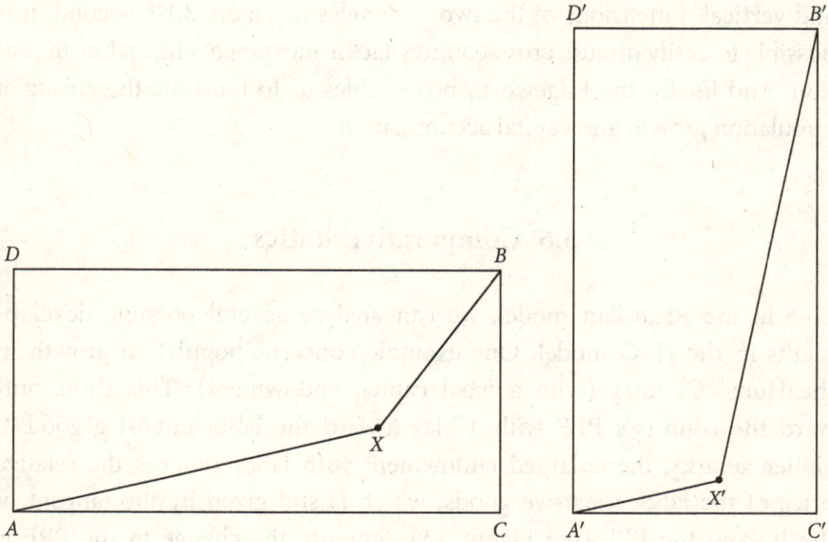

Figure 3.10 Factor Allocation in the Two Countries

will export the good that is relatively intensive in the factor with which it is abundantly endowed.

Recall that we ruled out FIRs in the model setup. This implies that good 1 is labor-intensive in both countries and at all relative factor prices. If we allow FIR, it is possible to obtain a somewhat paradoxical result, as discussed by Lancaster (1957). Suppose two countries have inverse endowments—Home has more labor but less capital (formally $L^*/K^* = (L/K)^{-1}$)—but good 1 is labor-intensive in the Home Country and capital-intensive in the Foreign Country. When the factor endowments are just reverse to each other, it is possible to construct a situation where, with identical preferences, there will be no incentive to trade since the production patterns will be identical in the two countries at all prices. As Lancaster points out, two travelers from the two countries would note that what one country calls "labor" is described as "capital" in the other. Labor in the Home Country and capital in the Foreign Country might be considered as the same factor. Of course, this paradoxical situation only arises as we ruled out cross-country factor mobility.

The Edgeworth box illustration is also suitable to analyze a range of other aspects and comparative statics. First, we can show that free trade is equivalent to merging two countries into one. For this, we add up the horizontal and vertical dimensions of the two rectangles in Figure 3.10. Second, it is possible to easily discuss cross-country factor movements like labor migration. And finally, the Edgeworth box enables us to illustrate the effects of population growth and capital accumulation.

3.6 Comparative Statics

Like in the Ricardian model, we can analyze several possible developments in the H–O model. One example concerns population growth in the Home Country (with a fixed capital endowment). This shifts outward the country's PPF with a bias toward the labor-intensive good 1. Under autarky, the enlarged endowment with labor reduces the relative price of the labor-intensive goods, which is still given by the tangent of the IC and the PPF (see Figure 3.1). Suppose the change in the PPF is such that the Home Country now produces larger amounts of both goods. Under free trade, it then carries "a larger weight" in shaping world market prices. Thus, the relative goods prices under free trade are now closer to the Home Country's autarky prices—which reduces gains from trade. Vice versa, the Foreign Country benefits from improved terms of trade as a result of Home Country's population growth. This case, to some extent, resembles the situation of immiserizing growth discussed in Chapter 2. Along the same line, we can examine other comparative statics. Instead of a growing labor force, the Home Country might build up a larger capital stock. If we alter the model's assumptions, it is also possible to study, for instance, what happens to trade volumes and gains from trade if one country develops a superior technology (which lowers labor and capital requirements for each unit of output) or a higher preference for one of the two goods.

3.7 Empirical Tests

At first glance, there seem to be plenty of real-world anecdotes that support the H–O theorem. The United States, for example, is abundant in high-skilled information technology (IT) specialists and exports many IT-related services. It is also relatively land-abundant and exports numerous land-intensive agricultural goods.

However, a more careful analysis of trade data reveals that the H–O theorem is a poor predictor of global trade patterns. This point was made early on. Wassily Leontief (1953) conducted a study of the theory that seemed to invalidate it. He noted that the United States had a lot of capital after World War II. Therefore, it should export capital-intensive products and import labor-intensive products. Instead, Leontief found that the United States exported products that used more labor than the products it imported. This finding is known as the *Leontief paradox*.

Later work by Bowen et al. (1987) studied twenty-seven countries and twelve factors of production, checking whether a nation was a net exporter of a factor of production whenever it was relatively abundantly endowed with that factor. Overall, only in 61 percent of the cases did they find that net exports and factor endowment matched. This confirmed that Leontief's paradox was not an isolated case.

Does the Leontief paradox invalidate the H–O theorem? Not really. The pattern in the data that Leontief documents is not in line with the prediction of the theorem, but recall that this theorem is derived from a model that assumes, among other things, identical technologies in all countries. Furthermore, we assumed that all labor and capital are homogeneous both within and across countries. In reality, the presence of human capital causes some labor to be different from other labor. Hence, if we find a pattern of trade that does not match a theory's prediction, this could be because the model's assumptions are wrong (or ill-suited). We can then extend the model, for example by defining the "effective factor endowment" of each country, as is discussed by Robert Feenstra and Alan Taylor (2017, p.185). Empirically, we should test the theory's prediction in a setting (or an econometric way) such that the distorting factor (i.e., differences in technology across countries) is not a confounding issue.

An important contribution to resolving the puzzle was provided by Trefler (1995). Allowing for productivity differences across countries implies that the United States, for instance, has a much larger "effective" labor supply and so should not import as much labor-abundant goods. Subsequent work by Davis and Weinstein (2001) showed that the empirical fit for the factor content of international trade improves if we drop, step by step, three assumptions of the model: (i) identical technology across countries, (ii) nations produce the same set of goods, and (iii) the absence of trade costs equalizes goods prices.

Most empirical research has focused on a variant of the H–O theorem: the so-called Heckscher–Ohlin–Vanek (HOV) theorem. The Czech American economist Jaroslav Vanek (1968) argued that the international trade of goods is an indirect (or disguised) means of trading factors of production. In this view, when a good is produced using labor and capital, its export effectively resembles an export of labor and capital. But how well does this perspective hold up to empirical tests? Davis and Weinstein (2001) write, "The HOV theorem yields a simple prediction: The net export of [factors of production] will be the difference between a country's endowment and the endowment typical in the world for a country of that size. The prediction is elegant, intuitive, and spectacularly at odds with the data." It is only when we allow for cross-country productivity differences—as in the Ricardian trade model—that we can explain a large share of global trade flows. As Costinot, Donaldson, and Komunjer (2012) write, "Empirical work on the Heckscher–Ohlin model unambiguously shows that technology matters."

3.8 Conclusion

As this chapter has shown, the H–O model is very similar to the 2x2 economy of Chapter 2. The addition of a second country illustrates how goods prices differ under autarky as a result of different factor endowments. Furthermore, we can study how goods prices equalize with free trade and the distributional consequences of this equalization. There are several important insights about international trade that we can obtain from the H–O model—in addition to those we already acquired from trade models studied in previous chapters:

- **Differences in factor endowments create an incentive for countries to trade with each other.** As discussed in this chapter, countries' autarky goods prices will differ if their relative endowments are different. In a country with abundant capital, the price of capital will be low and so the price of capital-intensive goods will be low as well. Allowing for free international trade implies the no-arbitrage condition: Goods prices equalize when opportunities for arbitrage can be fully exploited.
- **Countries gain more from trading with each other the more different their endowments.** In the extreme case that factor endowments are identical, the H–O framework provides no incentive to trade. As in the

Ricardian model of Chapter 1, we find that trade is beneficial because countries can exploit their comparative advantages. These are larger if the differences in endowments are large.

- **Small countries gain more from trade than large countries.** Suppose that in the discussion earlier in this chapter the Foreign Country was minuscule in comparison with the Home Country. It would still be the case that relative goods prices are different under autarky if the relative endowments differ. However, the free trade relative price of good 1 would basically be determined by the Home Country. Hence, we would observe a large change in the relative price of good 1 in the Foreign Country (with the associated large gains from trade) but basically no change in the relative price of good 1 for the Home Country (and thus hardly any gain).
- **There are gains from exchange and gains from specialization.** When a country opens up to trade, it can potentially exchange goods at a more favorable rate than what was possible under autarky. This is the gain from exchange. In addition, a country can benefit more from trade openness if it adjusts its production according to world market prices. This is the gain from specialization. Both gains together explain the gains from trade.
- **Trade has distributional consequences, with some individuals potentially being worse off.** If workers and capital owners are rewarded according to the scarcity of labor and capital, free trade alters the scarcity of production factors and thus the remuneration of individuals. As we saw, international trade causes the owners of scarce (abundant) factors to be worse (better) off in *real* terms.
- **With more than one factor of production, we observe no full specialization.** Standard neoclassical assumptions about the production function $F(K, L)$ imply that for all $K > 0$, $\partial F/\partial L$ approaches infinity as L approaches zero. The same holds for the marginal product of K for all $L > 0$. Because we assume such production functions in both sectors, it is optimal for each country to use some positive amount of labor and capital in both industries.

3.9 Exercises

The following exercises allow students to practice and deepen their understanding of the H–O model.

Exercise 1 Pick a country of your choice and identify its factor endowments relative to the global economy. Do the country's exports align with the H–O theorem? Why (not)?

Exercise 2 Using Figure 3.6, show the effects of (i) a small country and (ii) a large country introducing an import tariff.

Exercise 3 Using the Edgeworth box, discuss and visualize how free trade is equivalent to merging two countries into one.

Exercise 4 Consider a small open economy where the local wage rate is significantly higher than the world wage rate. Initially, the country maintains high tariffs on imports, which protect domestic industries from international competition. As a result, domestic production is focused solely on the local market, and there is no trade in goods or factors. The government is now considering full trade liberalization in goods, removing all tariffs and integrating into the world market.

(a) Using the H–O model, predict the likely pattern of trade once the economy opens up. Which sectors are likely to expand or contract?
(b) Analyze the short-run and long-run welfare consequences for workers and capital owners. Who are the likely winners and losers from trade liberalization in this setting? Use the Stolper–Samuelson theorem.
(c) How would your analysis change if there were labor mobility frictions between sectors (for example, if workers could not easily switch from one industry to another)?
(d) Suppose the government opts for partial liberalization, retaining tariffs only on labor-intensive goods. How would this affect your conclusions about welfare and sectoral changes?

4
The Specific Factors Model

4.1 Idea and Background

One crucial assumption of the Heckscher–Ohlin (H–O) model is that both factors of production—labor and capital—are fully mobile between the two industries. In some sense, this can be interpreted as a long-run perspective. Over the time span of several years or after a generation, workers can move from, say, working in the steel industry to working in the software industry. However, these processes usually take time, and factors of production are not fully mobile in the short run. This is a highly relevant aspect if we want to use trade theory to understand effects in the short-term—which is often important to judge the feasibility of trade policy reforms.

This idea was brought up by Jacob Viner, a Canadian economist, when studying the migration of workers from the rural to urban areas after the Industrial Revolution. He noted that factors of production besides labor are specific to one industry. So, while labor is mobile, the other two factors of production (the two types of capital) are immobile (i.e., sector specific). Hence, the model we analyze in this chapter is called either Specific Factors model, or the Ricardo–Viner model.

One interpretation of the Specific Factors model is that it represents a short-run version of the H–O model. We have labor as a mobile factor of production and two types of capital that are specific to one industry. An alternative interpretation is that the Specific Factors model is a trade model with two goods and three factors of production.

It will be convenient to study the implications of having some factor of production be specific to one industry in a model that contains only one country. Similar to the 2x2 model discussed earlier, we can examine the impact of international trade on this economy by altering (relative) goods prices. Thus, in what follows in this chapter, we study a 2-goods–3-factors–1-country model.

Understanding International Trade. Reto Foellmi and Stefan Legge, Oxford University Press.
 DOI: 10.1093/9780197821107.003.0005

4.2 Model Setup

Most of the assumptions of the Specific Factors model carry over from the 2x2 (or H–O) framework. We have two sectors $i \in \{1, 2\}$ in which output is given by $y_i = f_i(L_i, \overline{K}_i)$. Notice that capital is industry specific, while labor is still fully mobile between sectors.

Before we continue, we should briefly reflect on what a *specific factor* is. In car factories, for instance, companies invest in specialized robotic arms that weld car frames, install engines, or paint vehicles. In the short run, this machinery is specific to the auto industry. You cannot instantly repurpose a car-welding robot to make refrigerators or smartphones. In the long run, however, it is different: Companies can depreciate the old robots, sell them off for scrap, or invest in new flexible machinery. Notably, the same is true for labor: As Fallick (1993) as well as Kambourov and Manovskii (2009) show empirically, workers typically have industry-specific skills, and it takes them several years to switch occupations.

The economy is endowed with labor L as well as specific capital $\overline{K}_1$ and $\overline{K}_2$. Because workers are free to offer their labor in either industry, wages must be equalized across sectors:

$$w = p_1 \frac{\partial f_1(L_1, \overline{K}_1)}{\partial L_1} = p_2 \frac{\partial f_2(L_2, \overline{K}_2)}{\partial L_2} = p_1 f_{1L}(L_1, \overline{K}_1) = p_2 f_{2L}(L_2, \overline{K}_2) \quad (4.1)$$

where the last two expressions simply use a more convenient notation to express the value of the marginal product of labor. Notice that wages depend on $\overline{K}_1$ and $\overline{K}_2$, which is why two countries with identical technology but different capital endowments have different wages under free trade (i.e., there is no factor price equalization). The return to the specific factor is not necessarily equalized because of its immobility:

$$r_i = p_i \frac{\partial f_i(L_i, \overline{K}_i)}{\partial K_i} \quad (4.2)$$

We impose the standard neoclassical assumptions of perfect competition in all markets, decreasing marginal returns to one factor and constant economies of scale. This allows us to illustrate the situation as shown in Figure 4.1.

The figure is drawn such that the horizontal axis from the first origin 0_1 to the second origin 0_2 measures the total labor endowment L. Going to the

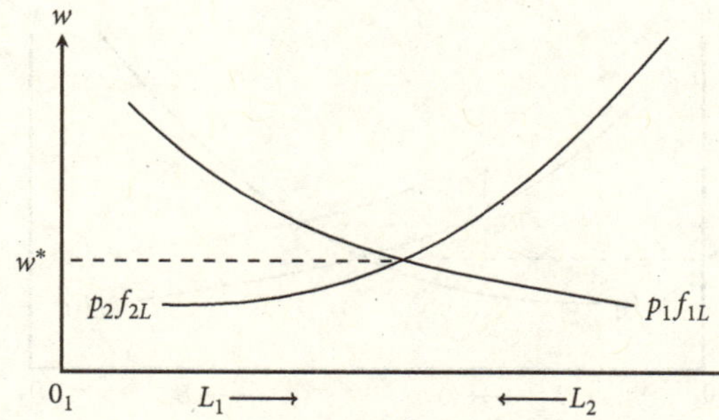

Figure 4.1 Marginal Value of Labor in Both Industries

right from 0_1, we allocate more labor to industry 1, while going from 0_2 to the left, we use more labor in the second sector. It is important to see that the downward-sloping curve p_1f_{1L} refers to origin 0_1 and simply illustrates a declining marginal product of labor. In contrast, the p_2f_{2L} curve refers to origin 0_2 and thus is drawn upward sloping. Since workers are free to move, wages in the two industries must equalize—and, accordingly, the respective marginal products of labor. The equilibrium wage w^* is found where the two marginal value lines intersect.

4.3 The Impact of International Trade

What happens to the economy if it is exposed to international trade? At this point, the reader should be familiar with the idea that we can study the impact of trade by altering goods prices (see Chapter 2). Suppose that as a result of opening up to trade, p_1 increases while p_2 remains constant. This will induce structural change such that industry 1 expands at the expense of industry 2: Workers will move to the first sector. However, unlike in the 2x2 (or H–O) model, we no longer have capital mobility. How does this alter the outcome? And how will factor returns be affected by trade?

The marginal value curve of industry 1 shifts up by $\Delta p_1 f_{1L}$, as shown by the grey arrow in Figure 4.2. We observe that as a result of the price increase, more labor is allocated to industry 1 ($L_1 \uparrow$) and less to industry 2. At the same time, the wage has increased from w^* to w'. Does this increase in the *nominal* wage imply that workers are better off in *real* terms? To answer this question, we use equation (4.1) and calculate the total derivative of w with respect to p_1:

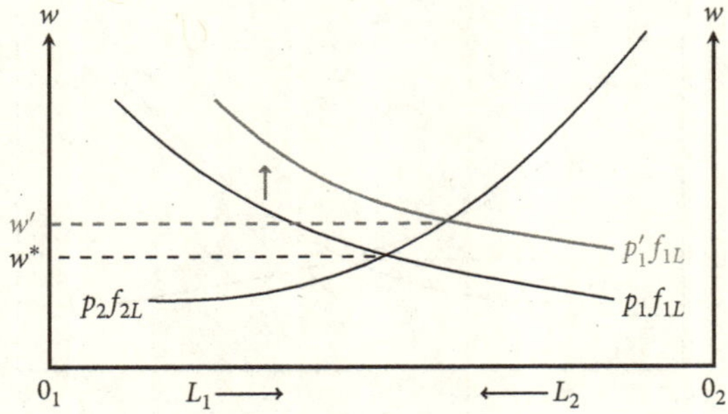

Figure 4.2 Increase in the Price of Good 1

$$\frac{dw}{dp_1} = f_{1L} + p_1 f_{1LL} \frac{dL_1}{dp_1} < f_{1L} = \frac{w}{p_1} \tag{4.3}$$

where the inequality follows from two inequalities: $f_{1LL} < 0$ and $dL_1/dp_1 > 0$. The first inequality states that the marginal product of labor (f_{1L}) is falling in the amount of labor allocated to sector 1, while the second shows that more labor is used in industry 1 if p_1 increases. It follows from equation (4.3) that $dw/dp_1 < w/p_1 \iff dw/w < dp_1/p_1$. In other words, the percent increase in the nominal wage is smaller than the percent increase in the price of good 1. Therefore, the impact of increasing the price of one good on workers' *real* return is ambiguous: They can afford more of good 2 (the price of which remained constant) but less of good 1. Thus, whether a worker is better off depends on his relative consumption of the two goods.

What about capital owners? Are they better off with trade? To answer this, we can again use the "Jones algebra" of cost shares introduced in Chapter 2. From the zero profit conditions we know that the percent change in prices of the goods is a weighted average of the change in wage and rental rate:

$$\hat{p}_1 = \theta_{1L}\hat{w} + \theta_{1K}\hat{r}_1 \tag{4.4}$$

$$\hat{p}_2 = \theta_{2L}\hat{w} + \theta_{2K}\hat{r}_2 = 0 \text{ (price unchanged)} \tag{4.5}$$

We know $\hat{p}_1 > \hat{w} > 0$. Using equation (4.4), this implies $\hat{r}_1 > \hat{p}_1 > \hat{w}$. And in equation (4.5), the fact that p_2 is unchanged and nominal wages increased implies that $\hat{r}_2 < 0$.

Numerical Example 4.1

Suppose that the price of good 1 increased by 10 percent, so that $\hat{p}_1 = 0.1$, and nominal wages increased by 5 percent ($\hat{w} = 0.05$). Given the zero-profit condition, it must be that the rental return in industry 1 increased by more than 10 percent ($\hat{r}_1 > 0.1$), because the weighted average of $\hat{w}$ and $\hat{r}_1$ must be 10 percent. And since we know that p_2 did not change ($\hat{p}_2 = 0$) but nominal wages increased by 5 percent ($\hat{w} = 0.05$), it must be that the rental return in industry 2 decreased ($\hat{r}_2 < 0$). Labor costs are up, but overall costs must remain the same to satisfy the zero-profit condition.

Summarizing the findings, we have an *altered magnification effect:*

$$\frac{\Delta r_2}{r_2} < \frac{\Delta p_2}{p_2} = 0 < \frac{\Delta w}{w} < \frac{\Delta p_1}{p_1} < \frac{\Delta r_1}{r_1} \tag{4.6}$$

An increase in the price of good 1 makes owners of capital used in sector 1 better off in real terms, while owners of the other type of capital are worse off. This is because the capital-labor ratio decreases in industry 1. Owners of capital in industry 1 have more workers using the capital (i.e., the marginal product of capital increases in industry 1). The opposite happens to capital in the second industry.

The altered magnification effect makes a clear prediction about who should support trade liberalization in the real world and who should oppose it. Is there empirical evidence to support this? Looking at the relationship between economic status and pro-trade preferences, Mayda and Rodrik (2005) provide empirical support for the Factor Endowments model. The authors explore individual-level attitudes toward trade protection using survey data from more than twenty countries. They find that pro-trade preferences are significantly and robustly correlated with an individual's level of human capital—in the manner predicted by the Factor Endowments model.

Adjustments in the Long Run

Remember that the altered magnification effect follows directly from the immobility of capital in this framework, and therefore the model can be interpreted as a short-run version of the H–O model. To connect the two

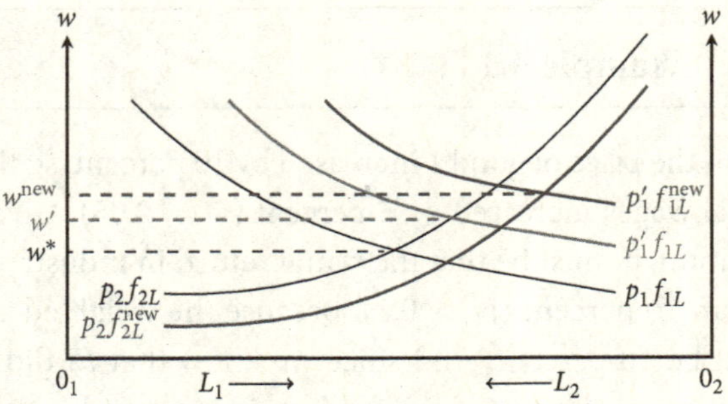

Figure 4.3 Long-Run Adjustment to an Increase in the Price of Good 1

models, let us explore the adjustment over time. We would expect that as a result of the changes to real returns, in the long run capital would flow from industry 2 to industry 1. When this happens, the marginal product of labor in industry 1, f_{1L}, increases, while it falls in the second industry. We illustrate this in Figure 4.3 with the new marginal products denoted $f_{1L}{}^{new}$ and $f_{2L}{}^{new}$.

As is shown, when capital is able to move from industry 2 to industry 1, the wage increases further—to the extent that workers are certainly better off than before p_1 increased. We get back to the original magnification effect. Capital returns between the two industries will converge, and returns will decrease in the long run if the relative price of the labor-intensive industry increases.

4.4 The Impact of Endowment Changes

In the 2x2 model, we had an equilibrium characterized by four equations in four unknowns (w, r, y_1, y_2) with four exogenous parameters (p_1, p_2, L, K). We now know what happens in the Specific Factors model if we alter the goods prices. What is left is to analyze what happens to factor returns if there is a change in factor endowments.

Suppose that because of immigration L increases by the amount ΔL. In the 2x2 model, with both factors of production fully mobile, we derived the Rybczynski theorem, which states that the labor-intensive industry expands more than proportionally, the capital-intensive industry shrinks absolutely, and wages remain unaffected.[1] How does the situation differ in the Specific

[1] Recall that in the 2x2 model, goods prices pin down unique factor prices (if there are no factor-intensity reversals) and the Rybczynski theorem holds for constant goods prices.

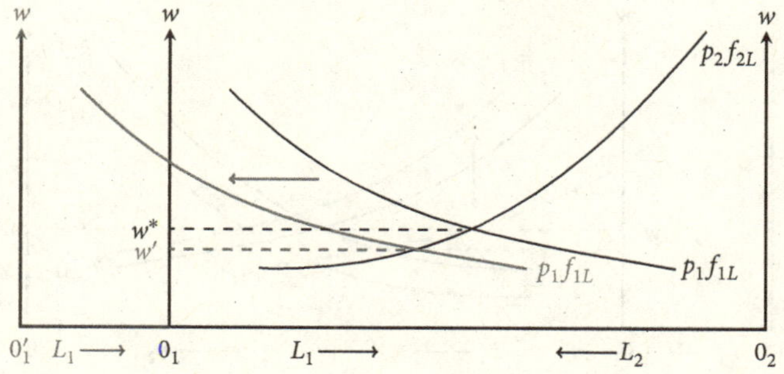

Figure 4.4 Impact of Immigration in the Specific Factors Model

Factors model? We first study the impact of migration in the diagram shown in Figure 4.4.

We illustrate the increased endowment with labor by expanding the horizontal axis (which is equal to L when going from 0_1 to 0_2). This shifts the first origin from 0_1 to $0_1'$. Note that this carries with it the p_1f_{1L} curve since it refers to the first origin. As a result of the enlarged labor force, the wage decreases from w^* to w'. Furthermore, we observe that the relative employment of labor in the two sectors (L_1/L and L_2/L) changes: The labor-intensive industry 1 will absorb more labor. However, it is no longer possible that capital moves from the capital-intensive industry to the labor-intensive industry. Hence, the marginal product of labor falls, and the wage is lower.

Again, this can be interpreted as a short-run result of immigration: In the long run, we obtain the dynamics discussed in the 2x2 model—provided that capital is eventually mobile and structural change is possible. As before, we can also examine how the economy adjusts over time. Capital will move from sector 2 to sector 1. This increases f_{1L}, thus shifting the p_1f_{1L} curve up and the p_2f_{2L} curve down. The end result is that w returns to w^* and all new labor ΔL (as well as some from industry 2; recall the Rybczynski theorem) is used in sector 1. We illustrate this in Figure 4.5.

The long-run impact of immigration shown in Figure 4.5 illustrates what we already know from the 2x2 model. All the new labor ΔL and some labor from industry 2 is used in the labor-intensive industry 1. In addition, the equilibrium wage w^* remains unchanged.

Having discussed the impact of increased labor endowment, we conclude by examining the effect of raising the endowment with one of the two types of capital. Suppose $\overline{K}_1$ increases. We see the impact in Figure 4.6.

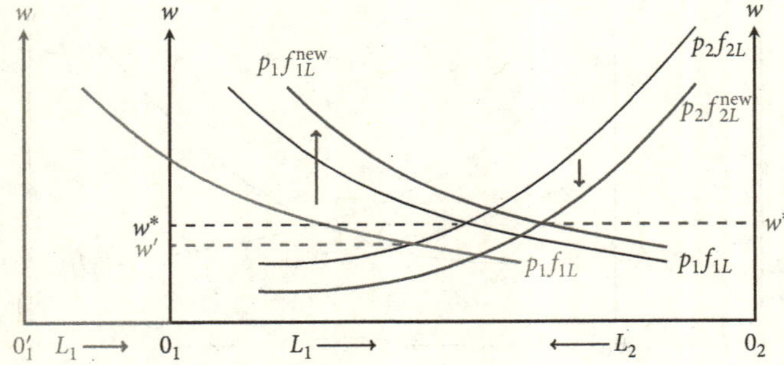

Figure 4.5 Long-Run Impact of Immigration

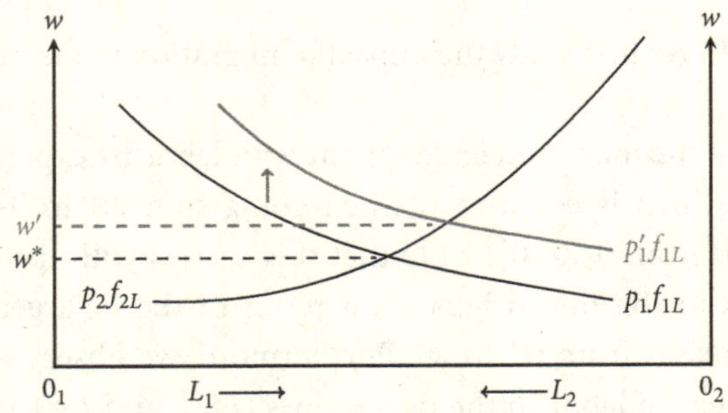

Figure 4.6 Impact of Increase in K_1 Endowment

As the marginal value product curve shifts in Figure 4.6, more labor is allocated to the labor-intensive industry 1. We observe that the impact is similar to an increase in p_1 that we discussed above: The $p_1 f_{1L}$ curve shifts up. However, now the upward shift is not due to p_1 increasing but due to the fact that the marginal product of labor in sector 1 (f_{1L}) increases in $\overline{K}_1$. As a result, wages increase in both industries. We also observe that output in industry 1 increases (as L_1 and $\bar{K}_1$ increase) and falls in industry 2. Finally, if goods prices do not change, rental rates in both industries decrease. The latter becomes clear if we recall two facts:

- The total endowment of labor L is now allocated such that L_2 is smaller (see Figure 4.6). This reduces the number of workers utilizing the capital specific to industry 2. As a result, the marginal product of capital falls in this industry and thus r_2 decreases.
- The first industry witnesses an increase in both labor and capital. We already know that the nominal wage w increased, and we recall that

goods prices are fixed ($\hat{p}_1 = 0$). Therefore, the increase in the wage must be offset by a fall in the return to capital.

To conclude, an increase in either specific factor raises the output of that industry and lowers the output of the other industry. In terms of changes to factor returns, it holds that $0 = \hat{p}_1 = \hat{p}_2 < \hat{w}$. No clear statement can be made on the relative magnitude of $\hat{r}_2$ versus $\hat{r}_1$. The owners of the specific factor in industry 1 lose directly, whereas r_2 falls because of an outflow of workers (L_2 decreases). Which capital owners lose more depends on the size of the elasticity of substitution between factors. In the case of identical Cobb–Douglas technologies, the factor intensities in both sectors depend on the p_1/p_2 ratio only; therefore, $\hat{r}_2 = \hat{r}_1$.

4.5 Conclusion

Viewed as a short-run variant of the 2x2 model, the Specific Factors model provides us with important insights to understand how trade and factor movements impact an economy. Furthermore, we learn more about the effect on factor returns. The latter are particularly important because they affect how people vote on trade or migration policies. For example, while the 2x2 model predicts that immigration will not lead to lower wages, we now see that the outcome can be very different in the short run. We summarize two key findings here:

- **The impact of international trade depends on the mobility of factors of production.** Comparing the results of the H–O and the Specific Factors model, we see that changes in goods prices have different effects on the economy, in particular on factor returns. For example, an increase in the price of the labor-intensive good (e.g., due to opening up to trade) makes workers better off in real terms in the H-O model, but not necessarily in the Specific Factors model.
- **Structural change and factor mobility are crucial for policy reforms.** There is a notable difference between the impact of an increase in the labor endowment in the 2x2 model and the Specific Factors model: Wages fall if capital is not mobile. Since policy reforms (e.g., on immigration) are often decided by whether a majority of voters benefit in the short run, this difference is crucial when judging the feasibility of reforms.

4.6 Exercises

The following exercises allow students to practice and deepen their understanding of the Specific Factors model.

Exercise 1 Show that the real wage increase in the Specific Factors model is larger if the price of good 1 increases and good 1 is labor-intensive than if industry 1 is capital-intensive.

Exercise 2 A country can produce two goods, cheese and watches, with three factors of production. While labor is used in the production of both goods, capital is used specifically in the production of watches, while land is used specifically in the production of cheese. Denote the quantities produced by Y_C and Y_W, respectively. Labor is denoted $L = L_C + L_W$, while capital and land are denoted by K and A, respectively. Production functions are Cobb–Douglas:

$$f_C(L_C, A) = (L_C \cdot A)^{1/2}$$
$$f_W(L_W, K) = (L_W \cdot K)^{1/2}$$

(a) Show that the marginal product of labor in each sector is decreasing in the amount of labor per specific factor in each sector.
(b) Suppose the Home Country is a price taker (i.e., a small open economy) and opens up to trade. Show that the resulting increase in the relative world market price $p = \frac{p_C}{p_W}$ leads to a shift of labor from watches to cheese production.
(c) What does opening up to trade mean for the return on capital? What about the return on owning land?

Exercise 3 Consider a small open economy in a Specific Factors framework with two goods. The economy initially exports good X. Suppose that part of the capital stock, which is only used in the production of good Y, is destroyed. Prices and the size of labor force remain constant. What is the impact on the following?

(a) Output of goods X and Y
(b) The real wage
(c) The real rental price of capital in industry X
(d) The quantity of good X exported

5
The Dornbusch–Fischer–Samuelson Model

5.1 Idea and Background

The classical trade models, in particular the Ricardian framework and the Heckscher–Ohlin model, provide numerous important insights into the causes and effects of international trade. Part of their success is based on the lack of complexity. Reducing the setting to just two goods, two factors of production, and two countries makes them easy to present, teach, and understand. This simplification, however, comes at a price: It is difficult, if not impossible, to bring the models to real-world data. To enable this, models must capture a much larger set of goods, factors of production, and countries. But as Chapters 5 and 6 point out, enriching the classical Ricardian model requires some elegant (mathematical) approaches.

To have more than two goods, it is useful to assume a continuum of goods instead of a specific number. It is also helpful to assume that each country randomly draws a productivity for each good. Provided that these productivities are drawn from a specific distribution, we can calculate the probability that a given country has the best technology or is the lowest-cost provider for a given good in another country. Using the law of large numbers (LLN) allows us to compute the share of goods that one country will import from another one.

The first model that uses the "trick" of having a continuum of goods is the Ricardian trade model provided by Dornbusch, Fischer, and Samuelson (1977). In this model, we go back to the familiar Ricardian trade model but have a large number (i.e., a continuum) of goods.[1]

Analyzing models with a larger number of goods (and countries) also allows us to answer whether the insights we learned in the chapters thus

[1] We discuss here the 1977 paper by Dornbusch, Fischer, and Samuelson, which follows the Ricardian approach of exploring cross-country differences in technology. In contrast, Dornbusch, Fischer, and Samuelson (1980) develop a similar model based on differences in factor endowments.

Understanding International Trade. Reto Foellmi and Stefan Legge, Oxford University Press.
 DOI: 10.1093/9780197821107.003.0006

far hold if we broaden the setting. One hint that this might not be the case can be seen in the Specific Factors model. If we interpret this as a 2x3x2 model (with three factors of production), we have already observed that factor price equalization (FPE), the Stolper–Samuelson, and the Rybczynski theorem must be adjusted if we have more than two factors. This highlights that it only required us to change one assumption of the model—the within-country free mobility of capital—and the model's predictions (e.g., for the impact of immigration on wages) changed substantially.

Will key results from the simple classical trade models hold if we have many goods? To find out, this chapter explores a Ricardian model with a large number of goods, one factor of production, and two countries.

5.2 Moving Beyond the 2x2x2 Framework

Moving beyond the 2-goods–2-factors–2-countries setup is not straightforward. In Chapter 1, we studied the basic Ricardian model with two countries, one factor of production (labor), and two goods. One example of this is to have Germany and Switzerland producing cars and watches. We can easily determine the pattern of trade as they are determined by comparative advantages. Suppose the unit labor costs are as shown in Table 5.1.

To find the comparative advantages, we perform pairwise comparisons and find that $10/5 < 10/3$. Germany has to give up $10/5 = 2$ watches to produce one car, while Switzerland would have to give up $10/3 = 3.33$ watches. Thus, Germany has lower opportunity costs for producing cars. It has a comparative advantage in the production of cars. If we allow for free trade, Germany will produce and export cars, while Switzerland will specialize in the production of watches.

Can we follow the same procedure if we have three countries and three goods? To find out, let us add France and wine to the situation, as shown in Table 5.2.

Table 5.1 Ricardian Model with Two Goods and Two Countries

	Switzerland	Germany
Cars	10	10
Watches	3	5

Table 5.2 Ricardian Model with Three Goods and Three Countries

	Switzerland	**Germany**	**France**
Cars	10	10	10
Watches	3	5	7
Wine	2	4	3

With this setting, pairwise comparisons no longer suffice. If we start with Switzerland and Germany, and cars and watches, we find that Germany should produce cars. Then the question is whether Switzerland or France should produce watches. The comparison 3/2 < 7/3 indicates that Switzerland should specialize in watches while France supplies wine. We then have Swiss watches, German cars, and French wine. Yet, if we start with a comparison of Switzerland and France, and cars and wine, 10/2 > 10/3 suggests that France should produce cars. Between Switzerland and Germany, and watches and wine, we find that Switzerland should produce wine (3/2 > 5/4). Overall, we get Swiss wine, German watches, and French cars. These two outcomes satisfy pairwise comparisons. Yet, only the first one is an equilibrium (the second one fails if we perform other comparisons such as Germany and France and watches and cars).

A discussion of the basic Ricardian model with more than two goods and countries is provided by Eaton and Kortum (2012). We see that a generalization of the basic Ricardian model to feature many goods and countries is conceptually fairly easy, but tedious. In addition, the economic insight is rather limited.

There are several approaches to address this problem. First, we could add more structure to the setting—essentially such that pairwise comparisons work again and are straightforward. Such approaches are sometimes called Ricardo–Roy models because they feature linear production functions, as in Ricardo, but more than one factor, as in Roy (1951). This is done, among others, by Arnaud Costinot (2009). A summary of these assignment models is provided by Costinot and Vogel (2015). A second approach is to replace the number of goods simply by a continuum of goods, as is done in the Dornbusch–Fischer–Samuelson (DFS) model, which we study in this chapter.

What about models featuring more than two factors of production? Usually, models of international trade do not feature a continuum of input factors, but instead retain the assumption of only one or two factors. This reduction of the dimension of factors of production is useful and can be justified even though there are many different factors of production in the real world. In many applications, it suffices to look at, for example, labor in general, instead of considering high- and low-skilled labor separately.

General Setup

In the general setup, we have $i \in \{1, ..., N\}$ goods and $j \in \{1, ..., M\}$ fully mobile factors of production. Furthermore, we assume a constant-returns-to-scale production function: $y_i = f_i(v_i)$, where $v_i = (v_{i1}, ..., v_{iM})$ is a vector of factor inputs. Denoting the vector of factor prices by w, the unit-cost functions are $c_i(w) \equiv \min\{w'v_i | f_i(v_i) \geq 1\}$. Zero-profit conditions are given by

$$p_i = c_i(w) \qquad i = 1, ..., N \tag{5.1}$$

and we further assume full employment of all resources:

$$\sum_{i=1}^{N} a_{ij}(w) y_i = V_j \qquad j = 1, ..., M \tag{5.2}$$

with V_j being the endowment of resource j. The equilibrium conditions (5.1) and (5.2) are $N + M$ equations in $N + M$ unknowns: The factor prices w_j for $j = 1, ..., M$ and the outputs y_i for $i = 1, ..., N$. For the simple $N = M = 2$ case, we obtain the system of equations discussed in Section 2.2 in Chapter 2, with four equations in four unknowns.

How does this system of $N+M$ equations that characterizes the economy's equilibrium behave? This crucially depends on the relation between N and M. We must distinguish between three cases.

Case 1: Same Number of Goods and Factors

In this case, the factor price equalization theorem holds. We have shown it for the situation with $N = M = 2$, but it generalizes to larger numbers of goods and factors. Concerning the Stolper–Samuelson model and the Rybczynski theorem, it can be shown that they hold as well. However, they are not as "strong" as in the 2x2 model: For a change in the price of each good, there will exist some factor that gains in real terms and another that loses. For an increase in the endowment of a factor, there must be a good whose output rises and another good whose output falls.

Case 2: More Factors Than Goods

As an example of this, we studied the Specific Factors model ($N = 2, M = 3$), and we already saw that the factor price equalization theorem does not hold. Furthermore, we had to modify the Stolper–Samuelson model and the Rybczynski theorem.

Case 3: More goods than factors

For this case we discuss in detail the DFS model in the present chapter. As we will see, the factor price equalization theorem holds as long as technology is identical. However, we must adjust both the Stolper-Samuelson and the Rybczynski theorem.

Extending the 2x2x2 framework we discussed in the preceding chapters is possible. However, depending on the relative number of goods and factors of production, we may or may not obtain factor price equalization. Furthermore, both the Stolper–Samuelson model and the Rybczynski theorem must be modified or hold in a weaker form. A detailed discussion is provided in the Chapter 3 of Feenstra (2016).

5.3 Model Setup

Suppose that there are two countries, Home and Foreign, with the same endowment of labor ($L = L^*$) as the only factor of production. The two countries differ in their technology (i.e., the unit labor requirements). Furthermore, we assume that there are homothetic preferences, no trade costs, and that perfect competition prevails in all markets.

In contrast to the simple (two-goods) Ricardian model that we discussed in Chapter 1, we now assume there to be many goods z on a continuous measure from zero to one: $z \in [0, 1]$. Trade across borders of these goods will occur because of technology differences. In particular, we assume the Home Country to have a comparative advantage in low-z and the Foreign Country to have a comparative advantage in high-z goods. The unit labor requirements $a(z)$ and $a^*(z)$ are such that $a^*(z)/a(z)$ is strictly decreasing in z. In other words, we sort all goods by the relative productivity advantage of the Home Country. Goods z near zero are the ones for which $A(z) \equiv a^*(z)/a(z)$ is relatively large. We illustrate this in Figure 5.1 as a downward-sloping line.

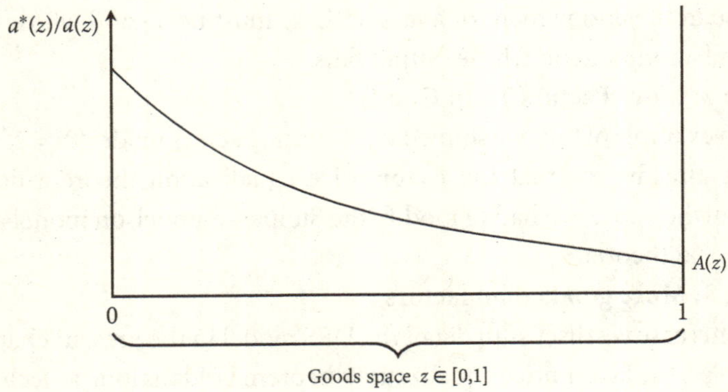

Figure 5.1 Relative Productivity of the Home Country

5.4 Free Trade Equilibrium

If we allow for free trade, what is the range of commodities that are produced by the Home Country and those produced abroad? This depends on the relative cost structure, which itself depends on wages in both countries. Let us define w and w^* as the domestic and foreign wages, respectively. The Home Country will produce all those commodities for which domestic production costs (depending on wages and unit labor requirements) are lower than foreign production costs. Accordingly, any commodity z will be produced in the Home Country if and only if $wa(z) \leq w^*a^*(z)$. With $A(z) = a^*(z)/a(z)$ from before, we obtain $w/w^* < A(z)$.

The downward-sloping $A(z)$ curve in Figure 5.2 illustrates the condition for a product being produced in the Home Country: The higher the relative wage in Home (i.e., the higher w/w^*), the smaller the range of goods z that are produced in the Home Country. Put differently, if wages in Home are very high, only those goods are produced in the Home Country for which it has a much higher productivity (i.e., a^*/a is very high).

In general, Home will produce goods for which it has a comparative advantage (i.e., goods on the left side of the continuum $z \in [0,1]$). The Foreign Country will produce goods with high values of z. However, where do we split the continuum? To find the separating good between zero and one, we must first determine autarky prices. Remember that in Chapter 1 we first derived these autarky prices and then each country bought each good from the cheaper source, either Home or Foreign.

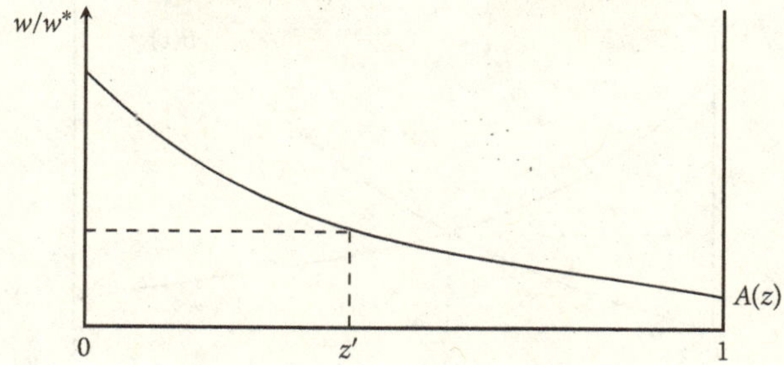

Figure 5.2 Goods Produced in Home and Foreign

In the present setting, autarky prices in Home and Foreign, $p(z)$ and $p^*(z)$, are equal to $wa(z)$ and $w^*a^*(z)$, where w and w^* are the respective wage levels. With free trade, both countries are buying each product where it is cheapest: $p(z) = p^*(z) = \min\{wa(z),\ w^*a^*(z)\}$ or

$$p(z) = \begin{matrix} wa(z) & z \in [0, z'] \\ w^*a^*(z) & z \in (z', 1] \end{matrix} \tag{5.3}$$

Equation (5.3) states that there is a marginal good z' that separates what is produced in the Home Country and what is produced abroad. This marginal good is determined by the condition $wa(z') = w^*a^*(z')$. Notice that we can rewrite this last equation and realize that it pins down relative wages $A(z')$:

$$\frac{w}{w^*} = \frac{a^*(z')}{a(z')} = A(z') \tag{5.4}$$

Goods with indices $[0, z']$ are produced in the Home Country, while the remaining goods $(z', 1]$ are produced abroad, as illustrated in Figure 5.2.

Note in Figure 5.2 that we have not imposed any restriction on whether $A(z)$ is larger or smaller than unity for any good. It could be that $A(z) > 1\ \forall z$ if the Home Country has an *absolute* advantage for all goods. For a comparison with the basic Ricardian trade model, this refers to the situation in equation (1.1) with $a_1/a_1^* < a_2/a_2^* < 1$. The reason we do not discuss whether $A(z)$ exceeds unity for none, some, or all of the goods is because it does not matter for showing the pattern of specialization and the presence of gains from trade. The intention of David Ricardo was to show that countries can benefit from trade even if they are inferior to others with respect to all goods.

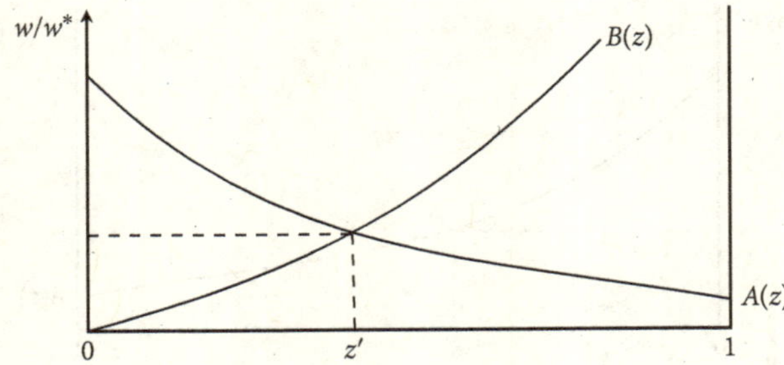

Figure 5.3 Determining the Threshold Good z'

Using the same logic, we see here that trade can be profitable for a country even when it has the better technology for every product.

Since we only have two countries, it must hold that world income and global expenditure are identical and given by $wL + w^* L^*$. Note that z' gives us the share of world income spent on Home's goods. Total spending on Home's goods is equal to $z'(wL + w^* L^*)$. If we assume balanced trade, spending on Home's goods must equal Home's income: $z'(wL + w^* L^*) = wL$. Similarly, for the Foreign Country, it must hold that $(1 - z')(wL + w^* L^*) = w^* L^*$. If we divide the two equations by each other, we obtain

$$\frac{z'(wL + w^* L^*)}{(1 - z')(wL + w^* L^*)} = \frac{wL}{w^* L^*} \Longleftrightarrow \frac{w}{w^*} = \frac{z'}{1 - z'} \frac{L^*}{L} \equiv B(z') \tag{5.5}$$

The income–spending conditions determine the upward-sloping curve $B(z)$, which we can add to the previous figure to obtain Figure 5.3.

There are two ways to interpret the $B(z)$ schedule in Figure 5.3. First, we can see it as a representation of the demand side. In this case, the function $B(z)$ is increasing in z because if the range of domestically produced goods were increased at constant relative wages, demand for domestic goods (and thus for domestic labor) would increase and lead to a higher wage in the Home Country. The intersection of $A(z)$ and $B(z)$ determines equilibrium wages and shares of goods produced in both countries. An alternative interpretation of the $B(z)$ schedule is that it illustrates the locus of trade balance equilibria: Imports are equal in value to exports. Following this interpretation, the $B(z)$ curve is upward sloping because an increase in the range of commodities (hypothetically) produced in the Home Country at constant relative wages lowers its imports and raises its exports. The resulting trade imbalance would have to be corrected by an increase in Home's relative wage, which would raise Home's import demand for goods, reduce its exports, and thus restore the trade balance.

The pattern of trade that emerges is exactly what we expected: Each country specializes according to its *comparative* advantage: Home is relatively productive in low-z goods and exports them. As discussed above, there will be trade even if $a^*(z) > a(z)\ \forall z$. The reason is that relative wages ($A(z) = w/w^*$) adjust. Finally, as in the basic Ricardian model, we find that wages are determined by *absolute* advantage. The more productive country will have a higher wage.

5.5 Gains from Trade

Having found the equilibrium under free trade, the question remains whether the two countries are better off under trade than under autarky. In the simple Ricardian model, we were able to prove this by showing that each country could reach a higher indifference curve with trade than what was possible under autarky (when the production possibility frontier was the constraining element). Here, we have to take a different approach. Suppose we have a log-utility function in both countries:

$$U = \int_0^1 \ln c(z)dz \quad \text{and} \quad U^* = \int_0^1 \ln c^*(z)dz \tag{5.6}$$

Per capita consumption under autarky is given by $c(z) = w/p(z)$ and $c^*(z) = w^*/p^*(z)$. Welfare is then given by

$$U = \int_0^1 \ln(w/p(z))dz \quad \text{and} \quad U^* = \int_0^1 \ln(w^*/p^*(z))dz \tag{5.7}$$

Under autarky, each country will purchase goods at prices that are determined by domestic wages and productivity. Hence, we have prices $p(z) = wa(z)$ and $p^*(z) = w^*a^*(z)$ that we plug into equations (5.7). This yields the utility under autarky (recall that $\ln 1/x = -\ln x$):

$$U_A = -\int_0^1 \ln a(z)dz \quad \text{and} \quad U_A^* = -\int_0^1 \ln a^*(z)dz \tag{5.8}$$

Equation (5.8) tells us that, *ceteris paribus*, individuals are better off the more productive the country is. Let us compare this utility under autarky with the situation when the two countries trade with each other. Under free trade, prices of equation (5.3) apply: $p(z) = wa(z)$ if produced in Home and $p(z) = w^*a^*(z)$ if produced abroad. Thus, we split the integrals into two parts: from 0 to z' and from z' to 1, with the latter produced in the Foreign Country under free trade.

$$U_T = -\int_0^{z'} \ln a(z)dz + \int_{z'}^1 \ln \frac{w}{w^*a^*(z)}dz \text{ and}$$

$$U_T^* = \int_0^{z'} \ln \frac{w^*}{wa(z)}dz - \int_{z'}^1 \ln a^*(z)dz \tag{5.9}$$

We find the gains from trade if we calculate $U_T - U_A$ and $U_T^* - U_A^*$. To do so, we take the difference between equations (5.9) and (5.8) and the fact that $A(z) = a^*(z)/a(z)$ and $A(z') = a^*(z')/a(z') = w/w^*$:

$$\begin{aligned} U_T - U_A &= -\int_0^{z'} \ln a(z)dz + \int_{z'}^1 \ln \frac{w}{w^*a^*(z)}dz \\ &\quad - \left[-\int_0^{z'} \ln a(z)dz - \int_{z'}^1 \ln a(z)dz \right] \\ &= \int_{z'}^1 \ln \frac{w}{w^*a^*(z)} + \ln a(z)dz \\ &= \int_{z'}^1 \ln \frac{w}{w^*}\frac{a(z)}{a^*(z)}dz = \int_{z'}^1 \ln \left[\frac{A(z')}{A(z)}\right]dz \end{aligned} \tag{5.10}$$

Notice that we find again cheaper imports to be the cause of gains from trade: The final integral shows the gains from trade for the Home Country, and it is defined over the range of goods z that the country imports from abroad. Overall, the difference between utility under trade and under autarky in the two countries is given by

$$U_T - U_A = \int_{z'}^{1} \ln\left[\frac{A(z')}{A(z)}\right] dz \quad \text{and} \quad U_T^* - U_A^* = \int_{0}^{z'} \ln\left[\frac{A(z)}{A(z')}\right] dz \qquad (5.11)$$

Both countries gain under weak conditions: First, it must be that $0 < z' < 1$ (i.e., there is any trade). Second, we must have $A(0) > A(z') > A(1)$. In other words, relative costs are not constant for all z (in which case, there would be no trade). The size of the gains from trade may be different between the two countries. This depends on the terms of trade—we can think of $A(z') = w/w^*$ as the terms of trade for the Home Country—and the magnitude of technological differences.

5.6 Comparative Statics

As in the models we discussed before, altering the model's parameters provides important insights. In what follows, changes to the countries' population and technology and changes to trade costs are examined.

Population Growth

How does the free-trade equilibrium change if the workforce grows in one country? Suppose that the Foreign Country experiences an increase in its endowment with labor such that L^*/L increases. Without any further changes, there would be an imbalance: Recall that total spending on Home's goods must equal Home's income, formally $z'(wL + w^*L^*) = wL$. With the right side of this equation unchanged, but L^* higher, there are only two ways to restore balance: z' must decrease, and w^* must fall. We illustrate the impact graphically in Figure 5.4. Notice that the equilibrium is governed by $A(z) = a^*(z)/a(z)$ and $\frac{z'}{1-z'}\frac{L^*}{L} \equiv B(z')$. With no change in technology, $A(z)$ remains unchanged, but $B(z)$ shifts up.

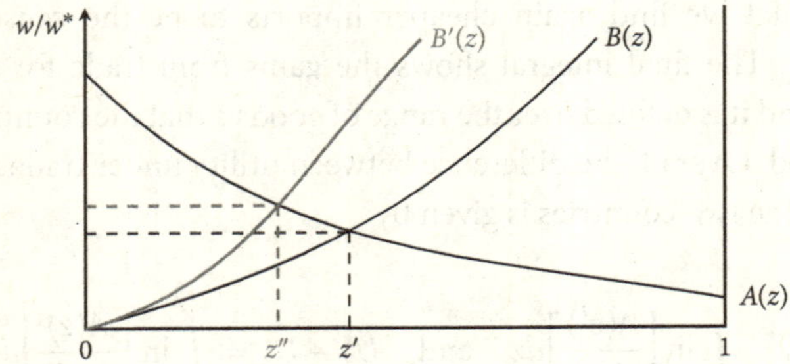

Figure 5.4 Impact of Higher Labor Endowment in the Foreign Country

The increased labor endowment in the Foreign Country causes an increase in the share of goods that are produced abroad ($z'' < z'$). We also see that Home's wages increase relative to foreign wages (i.e., w/w^* is higher). Why does this happen? The spending-equal-income condition summarized by $B(z)$ of equation (5.14) shows that a larger share of the goods will be produced by the Foreign Country. Put differently, z' falls. In turn, this implies that the marginal good (z') is one for which Foreign has a smaller comparative advantage. As a result, the terms of trade, $A(z)$, worsen for the Foreign Country. Put another way, the increase in L^* makes Foreign labor cheaper. The Home Country gains not only because its import prices go down but also because it can further specialize in activities that it is particularly good at. This good news for the Home Country comes with one caveat: Due to reduced labor costs in the Foreign Country, Home loses its competitiveness in certain sectors (from z' to z''), which move to the Foreign Country.

One interesting application of the DFS model in this regard considers the impact of many poor countries integrating into the global economy. This can be interpreted as a rise in L^*. From our analysis before, we understand the impact of this on other nations. We can also see why small rich countries need not be good in many sectors to stay rich. Following Kiminori Matsuyama (2009), "As long as there is enough world demand for the few things they are good at doing, they can maintain the high wage income. This may explain why countries like Norway and Switzerland are rich in spite that their climate and geography are not suitable for most economic activities."

Technology Improvement

Another relevant question is how Home's welfare changes if either its own productivity increases or Foreign's productivity improves. The former case implies that $a(z)$ falls—either for some or for all goods z. If the improvement concerns all products, it shifts up the $A(z)$ curve in Figure 5.3. As expected, the Home Country benefits from having improved technology: It produces a wider range of products (z' moves to the right), and its wage increases relative to the Foreign Country (w/w^*).

What if the technology improvement happens abroad? How does Home's welfare respond to productivity growth in the partner country? There are two offsetting effects. On the one hand, lower labor requirements lower prices of Foreign's exports. On the other hand, higher Foreign wages work against this gain. Matsuyama (2008) discusses this in detail, concluding that it is possible for the Home Country to lose due to a partner's productivity growth but still gain from trade overall. One real-world example for this exercise is a technology transfer from the United States to China. Consider the extreme case (which is often useful to understand comparative statics) in which $a^* > a \; \forall z$ (i.e., China has worse technology for all products) and, after a full transfer of technology, it is $a^* = a \; \forall z$. The transfer makes the two countries more similar, eventually identical, regarding technological differences. Hence, gains from trade get smaller and eventually vanish in the DFS model. If China only gets better technology for some goods (to the left of and near z'), two things happen: These goods become cheaper (prices are driven by costs), and the relative wage in China goes up. Which effect dominates for those goods is *a priori* unclear. For other goods (the ones for which China already has a comparative advantage), there is only the impact of a higher Chinese wage. Thus, the United States loses because its import prices go up. It will then produce some goods itself that it used to import from China.

Trade Costs

In our analysis of international trade in the DFS model, we assume that there are no barriers to trade. How would the situation change if there were positive trade costs? In the real world, costs of transportation, tariffs, and numerous other barriers make it costly to exchange goods between countries. We will discuss this in more detail in Chapter 6. For now, suppose we can summarize all these costs by saying that we must ship $\tau > 1$ units of a good from one country to have one unit arrive in the other country. This formulation is called iceberg trade costs because we can think of shipping an iceberg that partly melts during transportation. It was first introduced by Paul Samuelson (1954).

It is intuitive to understand what happens to the situation depicted in Figure 5.3 if we introduce trade costs: For goods near z', the cost advantage of one country over the other is very small. With sufficiently large trade costs, it is beneficial for Home (Foreign) to source goods just to the right (left) of z' domestically. The Home Country will produce goods for which domestic unit labor costs fall short of foreign unit labor costs adjusted for trade costs. Similarly, the Foreign Country produces goods for which foreign unit labor costs fall short of adjusted unit labor costs of delivered imports. We then have three groups of products:

- Goods $z \in [0, z^H]$ produced only in Home
- Goods $z \in [z^F, 1]$ produced only in Foreign
- Goods $z \in (z^F, z^H)$ non-traded and produced by both countries

If we modify the expressions of Section 5.4 and price in trade costs, we obtain the following:

- Home produces $z \in [0, z^H]$ such that $w/w^* \leq A(z) * \tau$.
- Foreign produces $z \in [z^F, 1]$ such that $w/w^* \geq A(z) * \tau$.
- Non-traded goods $z \in (z^F, z^H)$ with $A(z^F)/\tau = A(z^H) * \tau$.

In Figure 5.5, we now have two downward-sloping schedules. For any given relative wage w/w^*, the Home Country produces and exports goods to the left of the $A(z)/\tau$ schedule. Both countries produce the non-traded goods in the intermediate range from z^F to z^H, and the Foreign Country produces and exports goods in the range to the right of the $A(z) * \tau$ schedule (i.e., goods from z^H to 1).

To determine the equilibrium relative w/w^*, we turn to the trade balance equilibrium condition modified to take into account the endogenous range of non-traded goods. Both countries continue to purchase each good from where it is cheapest—including trade costs. Recall that $p(z) = wa(z)$ when

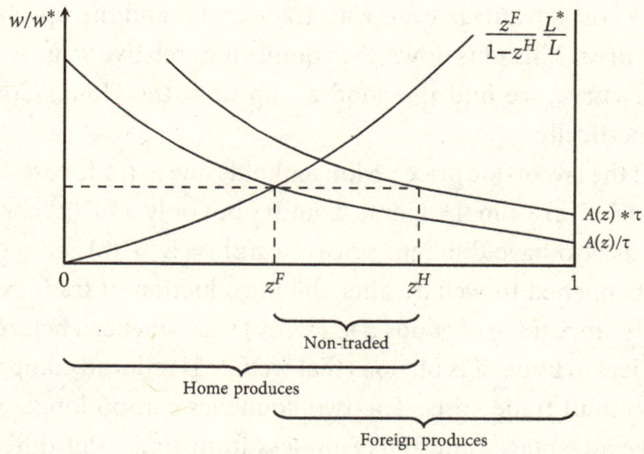

Figure 5.5 DFS Model with Trade Costs

produced in the Home Country and $p(z) = w^*a^*(z)$ when produced abroad. It follows that product z is produced

- in the Home Country and not imported if and only if
$$wa(z) \leq w^*a^*(z) * \tau.$$
- in the Foreign Country and not imported if and only if
$$wa(z) * \tau \geq w^*a^*(z).$$
- in the Home Country and exported to Foreign if and only if
$$wa(z) * \tau \leq w^*a^*(z).$$
- in the Foreign Country and exported to Home if and only if
$$wa(z) \geq w^*a^*(z) * \tau.$$

Note that the first two inequalities hold equal at $z = z^H$ and $z = z^F$, respectively. We still have world-market clearing: Total spending on a country's production must equal its income. For the Home Country, this implies $z^H(wL) + z^F(w^*L^*) = wL$, while for the Foreign Country we have $(1 - z^H)(wL) + (1 - z^F)(w^*L^*) = w^*L^*$. We use the expression for the Home Country, divide by wL, and obtain

$$z^H + z^F\frac{w^*L^*}{wL} = 1 \iff \frac{w}{w^*} = \frac{z^F}{1 - z^H}\frac{L^*}{L} \tag{5.12}$$

which gives us the upward-sloping curve shown in Figure 5.5. We now find z^F using the $A(z)/\tau$ schedule (which illustrates the products for which

Home has a cost advantage even with trade costs) and the upward-sloping "demand" curve. This pins down the equilibrium relative wage w/w^*. Using the $A(z) * \tau$ curve, we find the good z^H up until the Home Country will source domestically.

Note that the law of one price no longer holds due to trade cost: Goods $z \in [z^H, 1]$ cost $w^* a^*(z) * \tau$ in the Home Country but only $w^* a^*(z)$ abroad. Nontraded goods also have different prices: $wa(z) \neq w^* a^*(z)$ for $z \in (z^F, z^H)$. What has happened to welfare after the introduction of trade costs in the DFS model? Since trade of goods $z \in (z^F, z^H)$ was beneficial before we introduced barriers to trade, it is obvious that welfare is reduced compared to the situation without trade costs. The two countries can no longer exploit all comparative advantages and thus gain less from trade. Put differently, the removal of barriers to trade (e.g., tariff reductions or more efficient means of transportation) are welfare-improving in the DFS model.

We can bring this result from the model to the data and examine real-world trade flows. Using the Base pour l'Analyse du Commerce International (BACI) dataset from Centre for Prospective Studies and International Information (CEPII), there are about 5,000 different products (codified as six-digit Harmonized System (HS) codes). As shown in Figure 5.6, the number of goods (i.e., unique product codes) that China exports to the United States

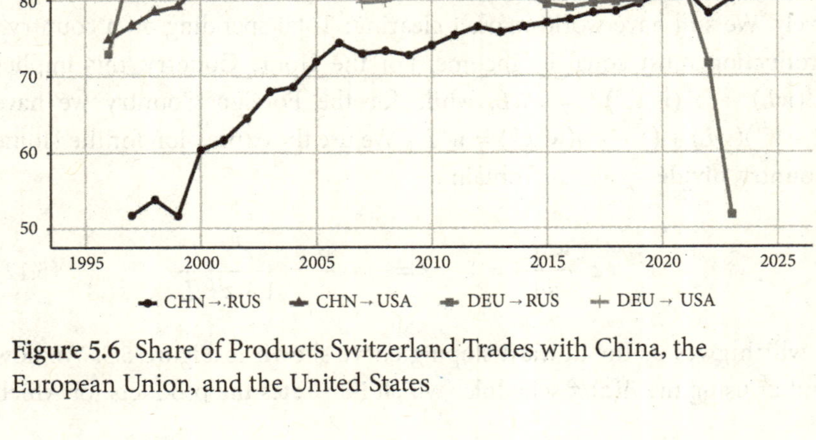

Figure 5.6 Share of Products Switzerland Trades with China, the European Union, and the United States

or Russia has increased over time. Improvements in technology and China's accession to the World Trade Organization (WTO) in 2001 reduced trade costs. In line with the DFS model, we see more goods being traded. By contrast, we can think of Germany's introduction of substantial sanctions against Russia in 2022 as large increase in trade costs. Based on the DFS model, we would expect fewer goods being exported and find exactly that in the data.

However, this little empirical exercise highlights a substantial shortcoming of the DFS model: It only features two countries. To understand real-world trade flows better, we must extend the framework to many countries. We will do this in the following chapter.

5.7 Conclusion

The DFS model of 1977 illustrates how the basic Ricardian model can be extended to feature a large number of goods. We saw that most of the insights we gained in Chapter 1 hold in this extended model. Still, there are some key new lessons:

- **Using a continuum of goods allows us to study a Ricardian model with many goods.** Extending the 2-countries–2-factors–2-goods (2x2x2) framework to many countries, factors of production and goods can cause problems. One elegant way to solve this for the number of goods in a trade model is to have a continuum of products, as shown in the DFS model.
- **Imports are the source of gains from trade.** As is shown formally in this chapter (see equation 5.10), a country benefits from trading with others by having access to goods at lower costs. Note that the latter include opportunity costs.
- **Technology transfers between countries have ambiguous welfare effects.** Suppose the Home Country is technologically more advanced than the Foreign Country. Would the Home Country be better off in this case if it shared/transferred some of its superior technology with the other country? In the DFS model, this would lower $a^*(z)$. As Matsuyama (2008) discusses in detail, this has ambiguous welfare effects for the Home Country. On the one hand, reduced labor requirements lower prices of the partner's exports. On the other hand, higher wages offset that gain. It is possible for the Home Country to lose due to the trading partner's productivity growth but still gain from trade overall.

- **Trade costs create non-traded goods and reduce gains from trade.** When exchanging goods across countries is costly, the trade of goods for which autarky price differences are small will no longer be profitable. As a result, trade costs create a range of non-traded goods and thus reduce welfare for both countries.

5.8 Exercises

The following exercises allow students to practice and deepen their understanding of the DFS model.

Exercise 1 Consider the DFS model with two countries, h and l, that differ only in the skill level of their labor $1 > r^h > r^l > 0$. There is a continuum of goods $z \in [0, 1]$. Let the constant productivity of a worker with skill level r for good z be

$$\varphi_r(z) = r^{\gamma z}, \quad \gamma > 0$$

Put differently, $1/\varphi_r(z)$ units of labor are needed in country r to produce one unit of good z.

(a) Show that $\partial^2 \ln(\varphi_r(z))/\partial r \partial z > 0$.
(b) Let the wage in country l be the numéraire ($w^l = 1$) and let $w^h > 1$. Explain briefly in words what the equilibrium price of good z is and find a formal expression.
(c) Show that in equilibrium country l will produce all goods $z \leq \bar{z}$, where $\bar{z}$ is implicitly defined as

$$\left(\frac{r^h}{r^l}\right)^{\gamma \bar{z}} = w^h$$

(d) Suppose that international trade is subject to an iceberg trade cost $\tau > 1$ such that τ units of a good need to be shipped from one country for one unit to arrive in the other country. How will this affect specialization in equilibrium and why?
(e) Will the gains from trade be higher or lower with trade costs when compared to a world of free trade? Explain briefly.

Exercise 2 Consider the DFS model. Assume the relative unit labor requirements are given by $a^*(m)/a(m) = m^{-\gamma}$, where $\gamma > 0$. The marginal good and the balanced trade condition in the DFS model read (using our standard notation)

$$\omega = \frac{w}{w^*} = m^{-\gamma} \tag{5.13}$$

$$\omega = \frac{L^*}{L} \int_0^m b^*(j)dj \Bigg/ \int_m^1 b(j)dj. \tag{5.14}$$

(a) Assume for simplicity that the preferences are symmetric across goods and countries $b^*(j) = b(j) = 1\ \forall j$. Rewrite (5.14) using that assumption.
(b) Show formally and graphically that an increase in L^*/L improves the terms of trade of the small Home Country. Explain the intuition.
(c) Assume that there are iceberg costs of $\tau > 1$ between the two countries. Argue verbally how the equilibrium looks like in this case.

6
The Eaton–Kortum Model

6.1 Idea and Background

We established differences in productivity and endowments as causes of trade. They also explain why there are gains from trade between different countries. As shown in the Chapter 5, extending the simple models to feature a large number of factors of production and more than two goods is feasible. However, several results only hold if the number of factors equals the number of goods. The (realistic) case of more goods than production factors is tricky, but the Dornbusch-Fischer-Samuelson (DFS) model, with a continuum of goods, provides an elegant generalization. In this chapter, we go a step further. We stick to the Ricardian model with one factor of production, but we extend it to feature many goods *and many countries*. Doing so allows us to understand and examine several additional aspects of international trade.

As discussed in Chapter 5, it is possible to extend the two-goods Ricardian model and have it feature an arbitrary number of countries. Gary S. Becker (1952) provided a model with a finite number of countries, while Matsuyama (1996) and Yanagawa (1996) did so with a continuum of countries. However, for a long time it remained a challenge to allow for an arbitrary number of goods and countries in a tractable way. Wilson (1980), for example, extended the DFS model to feature many dimensions, including a finite number of countries, but his model does not permit more than a local perturbation analysis. It was only with the seminal contribution of Eaton and Kortum (2002) that economists got a highly tractable model featuring many goods and many countries.

The main goal is to bring the stylized trade models closer to the data. For this, an encompassing framework should account for the following important facts:

- Trade diminishes with geographic distance.
- Goods prices vary across locations.

Understanding International Trade. Reto Foellmi and Stefan Legge, Oxford University Press.
 DOI: 10.1093/9780197821107.003.0007

- Factor rewards are far from equal across countries.
- Countries' relative productivities vary substantially across industries.
- The framework allows not just for a qualitative but a quantitative analysis.

Note that the first two points indicate that there are trade costs, and the next two points suggests that countries work with different technologies. Ricardian models capture points three and four. If we assume trade costs in DFS, points one and two can be captured too. However, all previous approaches discussed do not really allow for a quantitative analysis to take the model the real-world data, so they fall short of point five. The goal of the model by Eaton and Kortum (2002) is to provide a framework that can capture all five points. Their Ricardian model features competing forces of comparative advantage promoting trade and the barriers inhibiting it. And it operates in the multi-country, many-goods framework, thereby allowing to take the model to the data.

The point of departure is the 1977 DFS model. However, when applying DFS to many countries, there is a basic problem. For two countries 1 and 2, the model orders commodities z according to the countries' relative efficiencies $a_1(z)/a_2(z)$. This does not generalize to more than two countries, which is essential to any empirical analysis of bilateral trade. In this sense, DFS shares the problem of classical trade theories that we discussed in Chapter 5: They are intuitively appealing, give clear policy predictions, and serve as a basis for trade liberalizations. However, these models cannot be directly applied to get quantitative predictions on the impact and welfare consequences of trade policies. This is where Eaton and Kortum (2002) step in, setting up an elegant model with many countries—building on prior work by Armington (1969).

To visualize some key ideas of the Eaton–Kortum (EK) model, let us consider Figure 6.1. We see three countries (A, B, C), each of which can produce a product at different prices, P_A, P_B, and P_C. We can think of that product as cars. Selling goods from country A in country B comes at a cost of t_{AB}. This includes transportation costs, tariffs, and all other trade-related costs.

In this setup, there will be car exports from country A to B if

$$P_A * t_{AB} < P_B \quad and \quad P_A * t_{AB} < P_C * t_{CB}$$

Put differently, consumers in country B will buy cars from country A if these are cheaper, all trade-related costs taken into account, than cars from

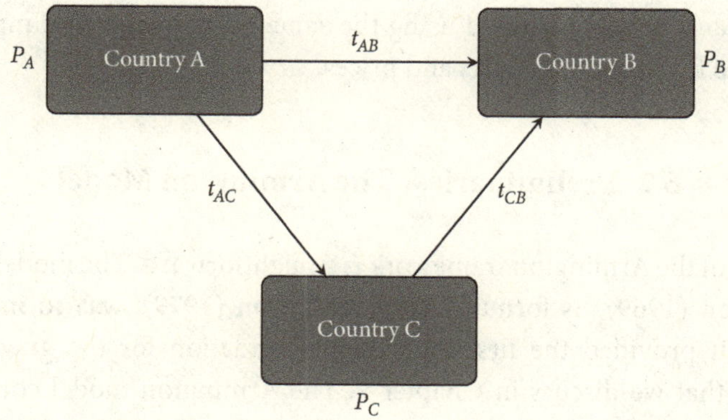

Figure 6.1 Trade Flows in a Simplified Illustration

either country B or C. This logic explains much of international trade we observe in the real world.

Notice how policy interventions can alter trade flows. First, country B could introduce a high *tariff* on cars from country A, increasing t_{AB}. In this case, we might see trade diversion in the sense that cars from country A take "a detour" through country C to then be sold in country B. Consumers in country B would suffer because cars would get more expensive ($P_A * t_{AC} * t_{CB} > P_A * t_{AB}$, as we assume direct transportation is always cheaper than indirect transportation). Notice that consumers might also find cars from country C or even domestically produced cars more attractive after the introduction of the tariffs on cars from country A. This all depends on the prices and trade costs.

Second, country A could introduce an export ban of cars as part of a *sanctions* scheme against country B. This would again raise t_{AB}. We would then expect, once again, that cars from country A could be shipped to country B via country C. Such sanctions evasion is hard to prevent if there are numerous third countries.

Third, country B could try to prevent car imports from country A by subsidizing its own car production. Such *industrial policy* would lower P_B. Whether this is a sensible policy can be debated. Many refer to the so-called infant industry argument, which claims that new or emerging industries should be temporarily protected by the government (e.g., through tariffs or subsidies) until they become competitive in the global market. We can refer to Figure 6.1 how such policy interventions can influence international trade flows.

Finally, the impact of other trade policy instruments—such as *export subsidies* or non-tariff barriers like *quotas*, *regulations*, or *local content requirements—can* be studied using the same framework. We simply need to analyze how they alter costs and prices.

6.2 Preliminaries: The Armington Model

The idea of the Armington framework is straightforward. The model by Paul Armington (1969), as formulated by Anderson (1979), was so important because it provided the first theoretical foundation for the gravity relationship that we discuss in Chapter 9. The Armington model considers a situation in which each country produces a different good and consumers have a love of variety. That is to say, they like to consume different goods from the different countries. This love of variety gives rise to international trade. As an example we can think of wine and consumers who like to have Californian, French, Italian, or many other different varieties of wine.

Preferences and Demand

Let us set up the Armington model. There are C countries. Since each country produces one distinct variety, we will index goods by their country names. Consumers in country j maximize their utility

$$U_j = \left(\sum_i q_{ij}^{(\sigma-1)/\sigma} \right)^{\sigma/(\sigma-1)}$$

where q_{ij} denotes the quantity shipped from country i to country j. The parameter σ denotes the constant elasticity of substitution between the different goods. The intuition behind this is easy to grasp when looking at the polar cases. When σ goes to infinity, the utility function is linear and the different goods are perfect substitutes. Imagine that consumers like French wine just as much as they like Californian wine. However, when σ approaches zero, goods are perfect complements and the consumer would exhibit maximal love for variety. In that case, the utility function converges to the Leontief case.[1] Income in country j is given by Y_j. For simplicity, we treat income as exogenous here. Consumers maximize the Lagrangian

[1] When consumers have a Leontief utility function, consuming a larger quantity of a single good does not increase utility, while having a larger quantity of *all* goods does.

$$\mathcal{L} = \left(\sum_i q_{ij}^{(\sigma-1)/\sigma}\right)^{\sigma/(\sigma-1)} + \lambda\left(Y_j - \sum_i p_{ij}q_{ij}\right)$$

where λ is the Lagrange multiplier and $Y_j - \sum_i p_{ij}q_{ij}$ is country j's budget constraint. Note that p_{ij} is the price of country i's good in country j, including trade costs. We will specify trade costs in subsection "Technology and Prices" below. Take the first-order conditions (FOCs) with respect to q_{ij}

$$\frac{\partial\mathcal{L}(\cdot)}{\partial q_{ij}} = \left(\sum_i q_{ij}^{(\sigma-1)/\sigma}\right)^{1/(\sigma-1)} q_{ij}^{-1/\sigma} - \lambda p_{ij} \stackrel{!}{=} 0 \tag{6.1}$$

Dividing the FOCs (6.1), we calculate the marginal rate of substitution for two goods i and v

$$\frac{q_{ij}}{q_{vj}} = \left(\frac{p_{ij}}{p_{vj}}\right)^{-\sigma}$$

Expenditure for good v is therefore given by

$$p_{vj}q_{vj} = p_{vj}^{1-\sigma}p_{ij}^{\sigma}q_{ij}$$

As this condition has to hold for every v, we can sum over v and use the budget constraint

$$Y_j = \sum_v p_{vj}q_{vj} = p_{ij}^{\sigma}q_{ij}\sum_v p_{vj}^{1-\sigma} = p_{ij}^{\sigma}q_{ij}P_j^{1-\sigma}$$

where $P_j \equiv \left(\sum_v p_{vj}^{1-\sigma}\right)^{1/(1-\sigma)}$ denotes the optimal CES price index and the weight of the different prices depends on the elasticity of substitution σ. We solve for the CES demand function

$$q_{ij} = \frac{Y_j}{P_j}\left(\frac{p_{ij}}{P_j}\right)^{-\sigma} \tag{6.2}$$

The value of trade, $X_{ij} \equiv p_{ij}q_{ij}$, is then given by

$$X_{ij} = Y_j\left(\frac{p_{ij}}{P_j}\right)^{1-\sigma} \tag{6.3}$$

It is straightforward to interpret equation (6.3). Exports of country i to country j are given by X_{ij} and depend on four variables. First, the total income of country j (Y_j): The higher, the more it will buy from all nations, including country i. Second, the price of the good from country i (p_{ij}) matters. Third, the prices of all other varieties in country j (P_j) are relevant. And fourth, it is important to what extent consumers see the different varieties as substitutes. As discussed above, this is captured by the elasticity of substitution σ. In particular, the impact of prices on the value of trade depends on the elasticity of substitution σ. If $\sigma < 1$, the price effect dominates and an increase in prices raises the value of trade. If demand is more elastic, the quantity effect dominates and total value goes down.

Technology and Prices

We assume there are many firms in one country such that markets are competitive. Labor is the only input into production. There are L_j workers in country j with a productivity of a_j and w_j as their wage. Trade is costly: If we ship good i to j, this entails *ad valorem* trade costs of τ_{ij}. Marginal costs to ship good i to j are therefore $\tau_{ij} * w_j/a_j$. In other words, if country v consumes q_{jv} units of our exported good j, this needs τ_{jv}/a_j workers. Therefore, the aggregate resource constraint reads

$$L_j = \sum_v \frac{\tau_{jv}}{a_j} q_{jv}.$$

We insert the demand function (6.2) to replace q_{jv}

$$L_j = \sum_v \frac{\tau_{jv}}{a_j} \frac{Y_v}{P_v} \left(\frac{p_{jv}}{P_v}\right)^{-\sigma}$$

Since prices equal marginal costs, we replace $p_{jv} = \tau_{jv} w_j/a_j$. We take all terms not involving v in front of the sum and get

$$L_j = \frac{1}{a_j} \left(\frac{w_j}{a_j}\right)^{-\sigma} \sum_v \left(\frac{\tau_{jv}}{P_v}\right)^{1-\sigma} Y_v$$

Total income Y_j is equal to labor income $w_j L_j$ because there are no profits. We multiply both sides of this equation by w_j and obtain

$$Y_j = w_j L_j = \left(\frac{w_j}{a_j}\right)^{1-\sigma} \sum_v \left(\frac{\tau_{jv}}{P_v}\right)^{1-\sigma} Y_v \tag{6.4}$$

Trade Volume

We insert this expression for Y_j into equation (6.3) and recall that $p_{ij} = \tau_{ij} w_i / a_i$:

$$X_{ij} = Y_j \left(\frac{\tau_{ij}}{P_j} \right)^{1-\sigma} \left(\frac{w_i}{a_i} \right)^{1-\sigma} \tag{6.5}$$

Equation (6.4) holds for every country, thus for country i as well. Hence we may solve equation (6.4) for w_i/a_i to get

$$\left(\frac{w_i}{a_i} \right)^{1-\sigma} = \frac{Y_i}{\sum_v \left(\frac{\tau_{iv}}{P_v} \right)^{1-\sigma} Y_v},$$

We insert $(w_i/a_i)^{1-\sigma}$ into equation (6.5) and solve for the volume of trade

$$X_{ij} = \frac{\left(\frac{\tau_{ij}}{P_j} \right)^{1-\sigma}}{\sum_v \left(\frac{\tau_{iv}}{P_v} \right)^{1-\sigma} Y_v} Y_i Y_j \tag{6.6}$$

The bilateral trade volumewe see on the left side of equation (6.6) depends on the product of the trade partners' gross domestic products (GDPs), $Y_i Y_j$. The Armington assumption that each country produces a different good and consumers have love for variety gives rise to a so-called gravity equation. This provides a basis for empirical testing. We will come back to this in Chapter 9. The formal structure of the Armington model serves as a basis for several recent models of trade, among them Krugman (Chapter 7), Melitz (Chapter 8), and the EK model, to which we turn our attention now.

6.3 Eaton–Kortum: Model Setup

Eaton and Kortum extend the DFS model and assume that countries receive a random draw of productivity for each of the goods in the continuum. There is a large but finite number of countries and a continuum of goods $z \in [0, 1]$. The technology features constant returns to scale and uses labor as the only input. Each household inelastically supplies one unit of labor, and perfect competition prevails in all markets.

We assume that international trade is costly and involves *ad valorem*, so-called iceberg trade costs: $\tau_{ij} \geq 1$ units of a good need to be shipped from country i (exporter) for one unit to arrive in country j (importer). We assume there are no within-country trade costs: $\tau_{ii} = 1$. What constitutes these trade costs, and what is their magnitude in the real-world? A summary study of trade costs is provided by Anderson and van Wincoop (2004), finding that the *ad valorem* tax equivalent for trade costs is about 170 percent. Their calculation includes an average tariff of 7.7 percent, transportation and time costs (equivalent to a 21.0 percent tariff), wholesale and distribution costs (55 percent), costs of different currencies (14.0 percent), differences in languages (7.0 percent), information costs (6.0 percent), and contract-enforcement costs (3.0 percent). All this adds up to $1.077 * 1.21 * 1.55 * 1.14 * 1.07 * 1.06 * 1.03 = 2.7$, which implies a 170 percent tariff equivalent. Notably, these costs are estimated with uncertainty, and other components could be added. It is important to emphasize that trade costs vary enormously across country pairs, as shown in Figure 6.2. Drawing on estimates from the ESCAP-World Bank Trade Cost Database, bilateral trade costs vary from 0.08 to 18.5, with an average close to Anderson and van Wincoop (2004). With respect to the variation in trade costs, it should be noted that they are strongly declining in a country's income level, as documented by Arvis et al. (2016).

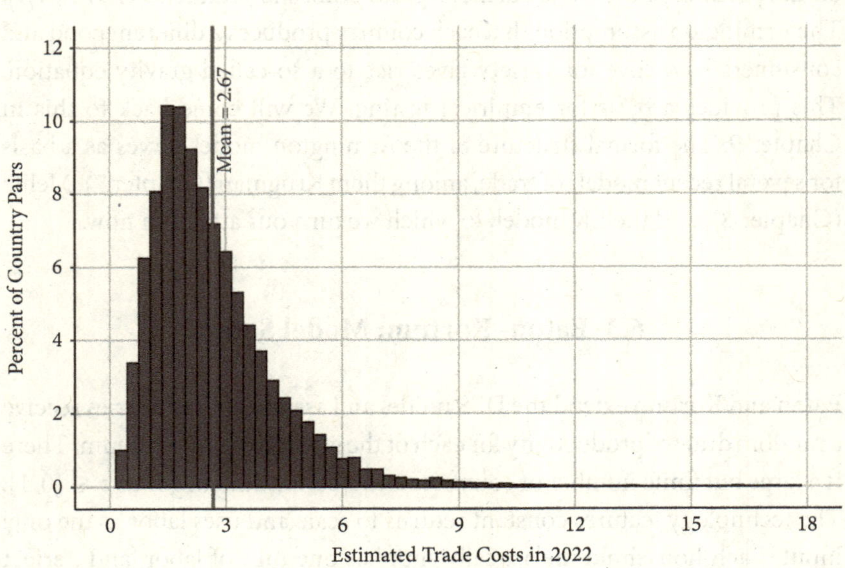

Figure 6.2 Distribution of Estimated Trade Costs in 2022

Various aspects complicate the estimation of trade costs. This includes the elasticity of trade with respect to trade costs but also cross country-differences in consumer preferences. One example for the latter is a home bias for domestically produced goods, as discussed by Holger Wolf (2000). Another one is specific preferences for goods from certain locations, like French wine or Swiss watches. Effectively, such preferences alter the elasticity of substitution between products from various countries of origin.

In the following discussion of the EK model, an important condition is that the triangle inequality $\tau_{ij} \leq \tau_{ik}\tau_{kj}$ holds for any three countries i, j, k. This implies that the cheapest way of moving goods from i to j is the direct shipment, not through k. A violation of the inequality would create an opportunity for arbitrage. There would be no direct trade between i and j; instead, all trade flows would be intermediated by country k.

Technology and Prices

Unlike in the Krugman (1980) model or the Melitz (2003) model, both of which we will study in the next chapters, an important assumption in the EK model is that every country is able to produce every good. We assume that country j's productivity in producing good z is the realization of a random variable that is drawn independently for each good. The productivity $\varphi_j(z)$ equals $1/a_j(z)$, where $a_j(z)$ denotes unit labor requirements in our previous notation. As in the DFS model, we assume perfect competition, and thus prices equal marginal costs. The latter are given by the wage times trade costs divided by productivity. Each of the N countries sources every product from the cheapest source in the world. The price for good z in country j is therefore given by

$$p_j(z) = \min_{i \in C} \{\tau_{ij} w_i a_i(z)\} = \min_{i \in C} \{\tau_{ij} w_i / \varphi_i(z)\}$$

where C denotes the set of all countries. Note that in a perfectly integrated world with $\tau_{ij} = 1$, there would be a unique world price $p(z) = \min_{i \in C} \{w_i / \varphi_i(z)\}$ for every good z. The tricky modeling question is how to find a workable expression for these prices $p_j(z)$.

To gain more structure, Eaton and Kortum assume that the productivity φ is drawn from a Fréchet distribution. The distribution function of productivity reads

$$F_i(\varphi) = e^{-S_i \varphi^{-\theta}} \qquad \text{for} \quad \varphi > 0$$

It is characterized by two parameters:

- $\theta > 1$: dispersion parameter (common across countries) $\Longrightarrow$ governs *comparative advantage*
- $S_i > 0$: location parameter, state of technology $\Longrightarrow$ governs *absolute advantage*

A higher S_i implies that a high efficiency draw is more likely. Hence, S_i reflects country i's *absolute* advantage across the continuum of goods. A lower θ generates more heterogeneity and thus creates a stronger *comparative* advantage (and force for trade against the resistance imposed by trade costs). The attractive feature of the Fréchet distribution is that the minimum or maximum of draws from a Fréchet distribution are again Fréchet distributed. As we are exactly looking for a minimum of different prices, this simplifies the analysis a lot. In addition to its useful mathematical properties, Samuel Kortum (1997) provides an economic reason for the Fréchet distribution. What we label and measure as productivity may be viewed as the "best idea" about how to produce the good. If ideas follow a Pareto distribution, it can be shown in statistical theory that the maximum of a sequence of (Pareto) random variables is Fréchet distributed, a so-called type II extreme value distribution. Figure 6.3 provides an illustration with $Pr(\varphi \leq x) = e^{-Sx^{-\theta}}$, where φ is the productivity. A smaller θ increases dispersion, as shown in the left panel of Figure 6.3. The right panel compares two countries with the same dispersion θ but different levels of absolute advantage S. The density function of the country with a higher average productivity, $S = 2$, lies to the right of the low-productivity country and has a higher mean. Since the variance is proportional to $S^{2/\theta}$, the peak of the density function is lower for $S = 2$ compared to $S = 1$. You are asked to show this in the exercises. Note that because of the Fréchet distribution, there is still a positive probability for higher productivity draws of the country with low average productivity.

It is crucial for understanding the EK model to recall the basic Ricardian logic discussed in Section 1.3 in Chapter 1 and Section 5.4 in Chapter 5. Countries specialize in the production of goods for which they have a comparative cost advantage—here it is products for which a country has drawn a high ϕ. However, if one country has an *absolute* advantage for some good z over another country, it does not follow immediately that it will export z to the other country. In the basic Ricardian trade model, the Home Country will export one good even if $a_1 < a_1^*$ and $a_2 < a_2^*$. In the

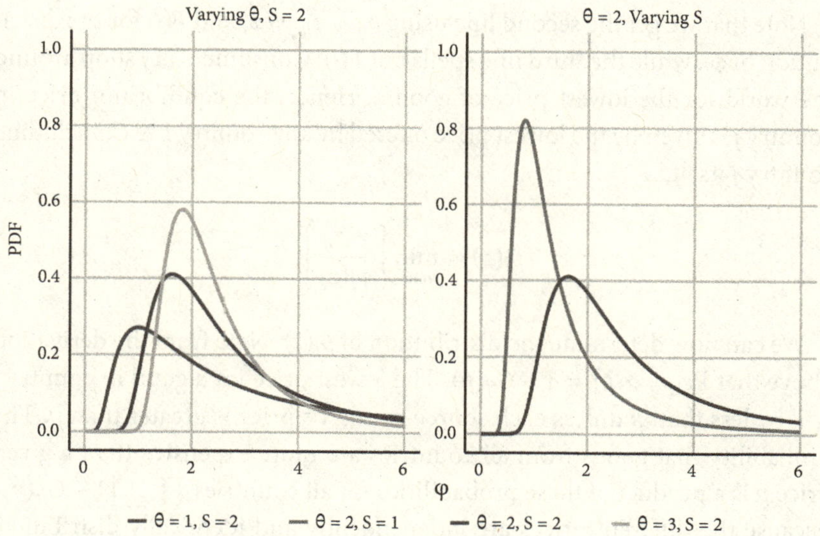

Figure 6.3 Fréchet Distributions

DFS model, the Home Country will export some goods even if $A(z) > 1$ $\forall z$. In the EK model, a country with high $S_i = 2$ (as in right-hand plot of Figure 6.3) will not necessarily export all goods with a higher productivity draw than the country with $S_i = 1$. Depending on trade costs and if the productivity for good z is close, the country with low $S_i = 1$ might be the exporter because wages are lower. If trade costs are too high, however, there might be no bilateral trade between the two countries, the countries will produce good z themselves or import it from third countries.

To determine which good from which country is the cheapest and "wins the competition," we need to know how prices are distributed. For this, we must determine the extreme value distribution. The distribution of prices of goods shipped from i to j is given by the answer to the following question: What is the probability that the price $p_{ij} = \tau_{ij} w_i / \varphi_i$ (from now on, we omit the goods index z) is smaller than or equal to the fixed value of p? This yields the distribution function $G_{ij}(p)$:

$$
\begin{aligned}
G_{ij}(p) &:= \Pr[p_{ij} \leq p] \\
&= \Pr\left[\varphi_i \geq \frac{w_i \tau_{ij}}{p}\right] = 1 - F_i(w_i \tau_{ij}/p) \\
&= 1 - e^{-S_i (w_i \tau_{ij})^{-\theta} p^{\theta}}
\end{aligned}
$$

Note that we get the second line using $p_{ij} = \tau_{ij}w_i/\varphi_i$ and $F(\cdot)$ for the distribution of φ_i, while the third line spells out $F(\cdot)$. Consumers in j shop around the world for the lowest price of good z. Hence, the equilibrium price in country j is given by the lowest price offered by any country $i \in C$, including country j itself:

$$p_j(z) = \min_{i \in C} \left\{ \frac{w_i \tau_{ij}}{\varphi_i(z)} \right\}$$

We can now determine the distribution of $p_j(z)$. Note from the derivation above that $\Pr[p_{ij} > p] = 1 - G_{ij}(p)$. The lowest price for a good in country i will be less than p unless each source country's price is greater than p. The probability that goods from all countries are more expensive than a given price p is a product of these probabilities for all countries $\prod_{i \in C} [1 - G_{ij}(p)]$ because the different prices are independently and identically distributed. The probability $G_j(p)$ that the price is lower than or equal to p reads

$$\begin{aligned}
G_j(p) :&= \Pr\left[\min_{i \in C} \{p_{ij}\} \leq p\right] \\
&= 1 - \Pr\left[\bigcap_{i \in C} p_{ij} \geq p\right] \\
&= 1 - \prod_{i \in C} [1 - G_{ij}(p)] \\
&= 1 - \prod_{i \in C} \exp\left[-S_i (w_i \tau_{ij})^{-\theta} p^{\theta}\right] \\
&= 1 - \exp\left[-p^{\theta} \sum_{i \in C} S_i (w_i \tau_{ij})^{-\theta}\right]
\end{aligned}$$

Note that e^x and $\exp(x)$ are equivalent notations. We use $\exp(x)$ to avoid expressions becoming cumbersome. To understand the last derivation, recall that $\exp[x] \exp[y] = \exp[x + y]$. We obtain a nice result: The Fréchet distribution has the convenient characteristic that a maximum of a set of draws inherits that type of distribution. We sum up

$$G_j(p) = 1 - e^{-p^{\theta} \sum_{i \in C} S_i (w_i \tau_{ij})^{-\theta}} = 1 - e^{-p^{\theta} \Phi_j}$$

The price parameter Φ_j summarizes how (i)states of technology around the world, (ii) input costs around the world, and (iii) trade barriers govern prices in each country j. This yields a useful interpretation: International trade enlarges each country's effective state of technology with technology available from other countries, discounted by input costs and trade barriers. Recall the similarity to the classical trade models where international trade allowed a country to "enlarge" its production possibility frontier. To understand Φ_j, it is illustrative to consider two extreme cases: With zero trade cost ($\tau_{ij} = 1$), Φ_j is the same everywhere and the law of one price holds for each good. However, with prohibitive trade cost ($\tau_{ij} \to \infty$), Φ_j reduces to $S_j w_j^{-\theta}$, which is country j's own technology divided by input costs.

As a next step, we calculate the probability π_{ij} that country i will be the lowest cost provider of any good z to country j. It is a *probability* because productivity for each good is random. When the price of good z from country i equals p, then the probability that this good will be the cheapest equals

$$\Pr\left[\min_{k\in C, k\neq i} \{p_{kj}\} \geq p\right] = \prod_{k\in C, k\neq i} [1 - G_{kj}(p)]$$

Put differently, the probability that country i offers the lowest price is equal to the probability that every other country has a higher price. To determine π_{ij}, we have to do this for the whole distribution of prices p. This is achieved by summing up these probabilities weighted with the density $g_{ij}(p)$. The result is as follows (we provide the derivation in the appendix at the end of this chapter):

$$\pi_{ij} = \frac{S_i (w_i \tau_{ij})^{-\theta}}{\sum_{k\in C} S_k (w_k \tau_{kj})^{-\theta}} \tag{6.7}$$

Since we have a continuous goods space, there are many different goods in this model. This allows us to work with a model featuring random draws and probabilities resulting in observable shares in equilibrium. Hence, by the law of large numbers (LLN), the probability that a good is imported equals the share of goods sourced from country i. The result is intuitive: Goods from country i are more likely to be the cheapest (i.e., the best available offer) in country j if (i)the productivity parameter S_i is large, (ii) wages w_i are low, or (iii) trade costs τ_{ij} are small. This formula explains well that imports from smaller countries can be very concentrated in a small number of goods. For instance, three-quarters of Switzerland's imports from Costa Rica in 2024 were fruits, nuts, coffee, tea, and spices. From countries with a larger economy, Switzerland sourced a much larger variety of goods.

6.4 Trade Flows and Gains from Trade

It is shown in the appendix to this chapter that the distribution of prices in j *conditional* on sourcing from country i is the same as the unconditional distribution, $G_{j|p_{ij}=p_j}(p) = G_j(p)$. More intuitively, the distribution of goods prices that country j actually buys from country i follows the same distribution $G_j(p)$.

By the LLN, this implies that the share of goods sourced from country i, π_{ij}, is equal to the share of total expenditures in j spent on goods from country i. In other words, country j's average expenditure per good does not depend on the source country. This convenient feature makes the model easy to solve, as each country sources from each country. However, as Torun (2025) argues, this is not exactly true in the data, as a large share of industry-level relationships are reported as "trade zeros," with no trade flow between two countries.

Let X_j denote total spending in country j and X_{ij} total spending on goods from i. We then have

$$\frac{X_{ij}}{X_j} = \frac{S_i(w_i\tau_{ij})^{-\theta}}{\sum_{k\in C} S_k(w_k\tau_{kj})^{-\theta}} \tag{6.8}$$

which again resembles a gravity equation (more on this in the final chapter). Like all models discussed so far, Eaton and Kortum provide a static model, implying a very long-run view of the economic situation. So, overall trade is balanced because of the budget constraint. However, as is well-known overall, deficits/surpluses can be sustained over long periods. To understand the quantitative implications on trade flows (without the aim to provide an explanation in an intertemporal model), Dekle, Eaton, and Kortum (2008) provide a quantitative model dealing with overall and bilateral imbalances. While overall trade must be balanced, the EK model is able to predict bilateral trade imbalances. For instance, when trade costs are asymmetric, there will be more exports as given in equation (6.8) from the trade partner experiencing lower exporting costs, *ceteris paribus*.

In a general structural trade model, which encompasses EK, Cunat and Zymek (2024) study the large variation in bilateral trade balances across country pairs observed in the real world. They show that bilateral trade imbalances are mainly caused by asymmetric trade costs and, to a minor degree, by sectoral expenditure and production differences (triangle trade). They document that overall deficits, like the US trade deficit, account for only a small minority of bilateral imbalances. However, asymmetries in trade frictions account for more than 80 percent of the variation in bilateral imbalances.

To evaluate the gains from international trade, we will assume that consumers have a preference for variety, as in the Armington model, characterized by constant elasticity of substitution (CES) preferences. In contrast to Armington, there is a continuum of goods, but the formula remains similar:

$$U = \left(\int_0^1 (q(z))^{\frac{\sigma-1}{\sigma}} dz \right)^{\frac{\sigma}{\sigma-1}} \tag{6.9}$$

Note the implications of this utility function: Consumers exhibit love for variety in the EK model. Under autarky, each country produces all goods domestically—even if some are produced at extreme costs and in tiny amounts. With trade, consumers do not get access to new varieties but benefit from imports of goods for which the domestic country had a bad productivity draw. We will see that trade can increase the available range of varieties (thus being a source of gains from trade) in the Krugman model in the next chapter. Unlike in the Krugman (1980) model, in the EK model not every good produced in every country is sold to country j.

The parameter σ in equation (6.9) denotes the CES. Recall that, for its interpretation, $\sigma \to 0$ corresponds to the case of perfect complements, $\sigma = 1$ is the Cobb–Douglas case (with constant expenditure shares), and $\sigma \to \infty$ (i.e., a linear utility function) is the case of perfect substitutes. We will see below that we need to have $\sigma < 1 + \theta$ in the EK model.

As in the Armington model above, to derive demand, we maximize utility subject to the budget constraint $w = \int_0^1 p(z)q(z)dz$. As a result, demand for good z reads as follows:

$$q(z) = \left(\frac{p(z)}{P}\right)^{-\sigma} Q$$

where

$$Q = \left(\int_0^1 (q(z))^{\frac{\sigma-1}{\sigma}} dz \right)^{\frac{\sigma}{\sigma-1}}$$

$$P = \left(\int_0^1 p(z)^{1-\sigma} dz \right)^{\frac{1}{1-\sigma}}$$

$$PQ = w$$

Note that w is the total nominal income of a consumer in this economy, P is the ideal price index, and Q is the real income (the quantity index) equal to utility. How is the price index P_j for country j determined? For the EK model, we can show

$$P_j = \gamma \left[\sum_{i \in C} S_i (w_i \tau_{ij})^{-\theta} \right]^{-\frac{1}{\theta}} = \gamma \Phi_j^{-1/\theta} \tag{6.10}$$

where γ is a constant term. The appendix at the end of the chapter shows that γ depends on θ and σ. The intuition follows the same logic as the discussion of Φ_j above. The price index decreases when trade costs are smaller or when there is a productivity increase (higher S_i) of a trade partner (*ceteris paribus*, wages will react as well). As an example, suppose that the productivity of a trade partner increases. This reduces costs, and because prices equal marginal costs, import prices fall. In contrast, under autarky ($\tau_{ij} \to \infty$), Φ_j reduces to $S_j w_j^{-\theta}$ and only domestic conditions are relevant.

To close the model, we assume that trade is balanced (i.e., every country has net exports equal to zero). Country j is endowed with labor L_j. Labor is the only source of income, so total spending in country j, X_j, equals $w_j L_j$. Country j spends a fraction of X_{kj}/X_j on products from country k. As discussed above, the LLN implies that this share equals $\pi_{kj} = X_{kj}/X_j$. We then obtain country j's total income as the sum of all countries' spending on goods from country j:

$$w_j L_j = \sum_{k \in C} \pi_{kj} w_k L_k, \tag{6.11}$$

where we have $X_j = w_j L_j$. This linear equation holds for every country j and allows us to solve for wages w_j where trade shares π_{kj} are given by equation (6.8).

Welfare and Trade

How much does a country benefit from international trade in the EK model? To calculate welfare $Q_j \equiv W_j^T$, recall that $Q_j = w_j/P_j$ with CES preferences. When $i = j$, equation (6.8) can be written as

$$\frac{X_{jj}}{X_j} = \frac{S_j w_j^{-\theta}}{\Phi_j}$$

$$\left(\frac{X_{jj}}{X_j}\right)^{-\frac{1}{\theta}} S_j^{\frac{1}{\theta}} = \frac{w_j}{\Phi_j^{-\frac{1}{\theta}}}$$

Since $P_j = \gamma\Phi_j^{-1/\theta}$, see equation (6.10), the welfare (or real wage) in country j with trade (T) is given by

$$W_j^T = \frac{w_j}{P_j} = \frac{1}{\gamma}\left(\frac{X_{jj}}{X_j}\right)^{-\frac{1}{\theta}} S_j^{\frac{1}{\theta}} \tag{6.12}$$

Note that X_{jj}/X_j is one minus the sum of all of country j's bilateral expenditure shares. The home share X_{jj}/X_j equals one minus the trade share. We can now gauge the gains from trade in the EK model. Let W_j^A denote the welfare of a (representative) consumer in country j under autarky, where $X_{jj} = X_j$ in equation (6.12). This implies for the gains from moving from autarky to the trade equilibrium

$$\frac{W_j^T}{W_j^A} = \left(\frac{X_{jj}}{X_j}\right)^{-\frac{1}{\theta}} \tag{6.13}$$

with only θ needed to estimate gains from trade. Intuitively, welfare gains from trade are larger the smaller the home share is—or, put differently, the larger the proportion spent on foreign goods. Similar to the DFS model, the more products are imported, the more a country benefits from higher productivity draws elsewhere and from the resulting lower costs of imported goods. Eaton and Kortum extend this intuition from DFS with two countries to the multi-country case. Furthermore, for a given home share, welfare gains are more pronounced if $1/\theta$ is larger. Recall that a lower θ is associated with more dispersion in the Fréchet distribution, and hence the exploitable comparative advantage gains are larger.

Data Example 6.1

Equation (6.13) shows that we only need two statistics to calculate the gains from trade—that is, how much higher welfare is with trade compared to autarky:

- The share of expenditure on domestic goods X_{jj}/X_j
- The price elasticity of imports θ

Home shares vary substantially across countries. According to Eaton and Kortum (2012), the share was just 35.3 percent in Switzerland in 2006 while being 53.7 percent in Germany and 73.5 percent in the United

continued

continued

States. Estimates of θ vary, but for illustration, we can use $\theta = 4$. This implies that a country that imports 25 percent of what it consumes from abroad gains about 7.5 percent in real income ($0.75^{(-1/4)} - 1$). With a home share of just 35 percent, the gain is about 30 percent. Trade shares have increased, and home shares have fallen, in almost all countries in recent decades, so substantial trade gains have been realized during that time.

Discussion and Extensions

Interestingly, the formula in equation (6.13) for the gains from trade appears in different trade models. For instance, Arkolakis, Costinot, and Rodriguez-Clare (2012) get the following formula for gains from trade in their model:

$$w'/w = (\lambda'/\lambda)^{-1/\varepsilon} \tag{6.14}$$

where w' and w denote the real income (i.e., welfare) of an economy in two different situations. The share of domestic expenditures on domestically produced goods in the two situations is given by λ' and λ, while ε denotes the price elasticity of demand for imported goods, the so-called trade elasticity. A formula like this can be obtained from the EK model (as shown above), the Krugman 1980 model, and the Melitz model we discuss in Chapter 8.

While the domestic share λ can easily be observed, the different models predict different values for ε. In the EK model, $\varepsilon = \theta$ is determined by the productivity dispersion. This is similar to the Melitz model, as we will see later. In Krugman 1980, ε is pinned down by the elasticity of substitution of the different goods. If the elasticity of substitution is low, the love of variety is very pronounced and, *ceteris paribus*, gains from trade are much larger. The handbook article by Costinot and Rodríguez-Clare (2014), Table 4.1, provides an overview of the range of welfare estimates for gains from trade. In particular, they consider a multisector extension with ε_s varying by sector. A country gains more from trade if ε_s is low and in sector s the country's own goods are a poor substitute for imported goods. Overall, Costinot and Rodríguez-Clare find that under perfect competition gains from trade are on average 15.3 percent without intermediate goods and 27.1 percent with intermediate goods. The latter concept is explained in the paragraph below. With monopolistic competition and firm heterogeneity, the gains increase to 32.2 percent and 40.0 percent, respectively. Eaton and Kortum (2012) compute the gains from international trade in manufacturing only, using a slightly augmented formula to account for the manufacturing share in final consumption and the use of manufacturing goods as intermediate inputs (i.e., as inputs used in final goods production). They use $\theta = 4$ and an extended welfare formula

$$W_j/W_j^A = \left(X_{jj}^M/X_j^M\right)^{-\alpha/(\beta\theta)}$$

where α denotes the share of total consumption spent on manufacturing and β the labor share in manufacturing costs.

The analysis of intermediate goods plays an important role in welfare considerations, as Ossa (2015) and Costinot and Rodríguez-Clare (2014) emphasize. Unlike traditional models, it is straightforward to analyze intermediate goods trade in the EK model. Imagine that intermediate goods are used to produce a final composite good with a CES production function. This composite good can be either consumed or used to produce intermediate goods (input-output loop). Firms use the goods as inputs in their production (i.e., intermediates), and consumers buy the goods directly. To get the idea, consider eggs as a simple example. They are directly consumed by households but used by many firms to produce cakes, food supplements, and the like. The formulas look very similar, the only difference to our exposition are domestic marginal costs. With intermediates, they depend not only on the wage but also on the price index of the output good (that can be used for inputs) as well. This resembles endogenous growth models à la Romer (1990), where intermediates as blueprints play an important role. We come back to the discussion of intermediate goods in the section on global value chains below.

Further extensions look at multiple sectors (as in Costinot, Donaldson, and Komunjer (2012)), or non-homothetic preferences (as in Fieler (2011) and Hepenstrick and Tarasov (2015)). The welfare formulas to determine the gains from trade look similar to the case with one sector and one input. This holds true both for the extensions with intermediate goods and multiple sectors. The log welfare change equals a weighted sum of the sectoral home shares of the different (intermediate) sectors.

Finally, the EK framework allows us to return to our discussion in Chapter 1. It is interesting to ask how domestic welfare changes if our trade partner enjoys an improvement in productivity. In most cases, this will be positive for domestic welfare as prices of imported goods go down. However, domestic producers lose market share, reducing the demand for labor. The latter decreases wages at home. Therefore, there is no general result that welfare rises uniformly. Eaton and Kortum (2002) show quantitatively, however, that the welfare changes are positive in most cases because the effect of cheaper import goods dominates. They conclude that "an improvement in a country's state of technology raises welfare almost everywhere." Generally, these arguments refer to the discussion in Chapter 1: Technological improvements affect the terms of trade. Generally, everybody gains from productivity increases. However, if the productivity increase in the Foreign Country leads to less demand for domestic products, the terms of trade of the Home Country will decrease, diminishing the overall gain in welfare because of technology advances.

6.5 Hat Algebra: A Simple Method to Quantify the Model

One of the key advantages of the EK model is that it can be taken to the data. It deals with many sectors but is still tractable. Ultimately, we are interested in what happens, quantitatively, if we change a policy parameter like, for instance, trade costs via tariffs. Taking to the data means plugging in real-world values into the model equations. Formally, we need to check how the equilibrium values of trade flows and wages change when we change exogenous variables like trade costs. Generally, such a comparative static analysis seems to be a challenging task.

To tackle this problem, international trade theory has developed a tool called hat algebra. The basic idea is to solve the EK model in changes. This has two advantages. First, the solution is much more tractable, and second, we do not need to calibrate many fundamental parameters such as productivity when we evaluate changes in trade policy. The underlying assumption is that trade policy does not have any impact on structural variables in the model. The term *hat algebra* dates back to Ronald W. Jones (1965). Therefore, it is also called Jones algebra. It refers to differentiating a model in logarithms. This implies that we look at small proportional changes, as we did in Chapter 2 when discussing the Stolper–Samuelson theorem. More recently, Dekle et al. (2008) introduced the term *exact hat algebra*. When the central equations of the model are power functions, such as CES utility, the equations are linear after taking logarithms. Hence, in such cases, the predictions are not only true for small changes but also for large deviations as well, given the constant-elasticity assumptions are valid.

Let us consider an exogenous change in trade costs. How does the equilibrium change after such a shock? Let the value of a variable x in the counterfactual equilibrium be equal to x', and let $\hat{x} := x'/x$. Using this hat notation, we can depict changes in outcomes as a function of relative trade costs, $\hat{\tau}_{ij}$, and initial expenditure levels, X_{ij}—for instance, if trade costs between China and the United States went up by 25 percent, $\hat{\tau}_{ij} = 1.25$. This value is used as an input into the model that we want to look at. In equation (6.8) above, we calculated the share of goods sourced from country i, π_{ij}, which is equal to the share of total expenditures in j spent on goods from country i. The new share π'_{ij} after the trade shocks reads

$$\pi'_{ij} = \frac{S_i(w'_i\tau'_{ij})^{-\theta}}{\sum_{k\in C} S_k(w'_k\tau'_{kj})^{-\theta}} \tag{6.15}$$

Importantly, note that wages w' change after the trade cost shock as well. In contrast, we assume that technology S_i and θ are unaffected. Using $x' = \hat{x}x$, we replace the "prime" expressions in equation (6.15). We obtain

$$\pi'_{ij} = \frac{S_i(w_i\tau_{ij})^{-\theta}(\hat{w}_i\hat{\tau}_{ij})^{-\theta}}{\sum_{k\in C} S_k(w_k\tau_{kj})^{-\theta}(\hat{w}_k\hat{\tau}_{kj})^{-\theta}}$$

Because we do not want to calibrate the technology parameters, we replace them with the existing trade shares π_{ij} (and π_{kj}), which can be observed in the data—in particular, $S_i(w_i\tau_{ij})^{-\theta} = \pi_{ij}\sum_{k\in C} S_k(w_k\tau_{kj})^{-\theta}$. The sum expressions $\sum_{k\in C} S_k(w_k\tau_{kj})^{-\theta}$ drop in the ratio, and we get

$$\pi'_{ij} = \frac{\pi_{ij}\left(\hat{w}_i\hat{\tau}_{ij}\right)^{-\theta}}{\sum_{k\in C} \pi_{kj}\left(\hat{w}_k\hat{\tau}_{kj}\right)^{-\theta}} \tag{6.16}$$

We are left to determine $\hat{w}_i$. The relative changes in wages immediately follow from the balanced trade condition (6.11). We get in "prime" notation $w'_jL_j = \sum_{k\in C} \pi'_{kj}w'_kL_k$. Since $w_jL_j = X_j$, we can replace L_j as well and rewrite the expression in hat notation:

$$\hat{w}_iX_i = \sum_{k\in C} \pi'_{ij}\hat{w}_jX_j \tag{6.17}$$

Equations (6.16) and (6.17) determine $\hat{w}_i$ and π'_{ij}. The equation system allows us to solve for the change in wages and trade shares as a function of observables, the initial trade shares π_{ij} and output levels X_i, and the relative change in trade costs. In particular, there are no fundamental technology parameters present anymore. Note further that the analysis did not rely on derivatives. This is because productivities are assumed to be Fréchet distributed. The latter implies that the trade shares are power functions of relative costs. Hence, the hat algebra is exact in the sense that it holds for large deviations as well—of course, only as long as the underlying parameters are constant. To get quantitative answers to how trade volumes (or welfare) change after we alter policy parameters, we have to solve the system numerically. There are no explicit solutions, since equations (6.16) and (6.17) are nonlinear. For readers who want to practice it further, the handbook article by Costinot and Rodriguez-Clare (2014) provides a replication package with hat algebra routines.

To summarize, hat algebra is a simplification of solution techniques that is very practical. It can be applied to all fields of economics and is not restricted to questions of international trade. For instance, hat algebra techniques are useful in problems relating to economic geography or migration. Using the basic logic outlined above, hat algebra can be used to calibrate multidimensional dynamic models of trade, such as in Caliendo et al. (2019), or on global value chains, as discussed in the subsection below. However, the method does assume that the deep model parameters are not changing in response to the shock of interest. In addition, we must always check that the underlying restrictions of fundamental parameters are still valid. Because hat algebra looks at relative changes only, conditions regarding levels could be violated with further scrutiny.

An example of the importance of fundamental parameters is the triangle inequality of trade costs, which must always hold because of cost minimization, see Foellmi et al. (2024). Formally, the triangle inequality for a trade relation reads $\tau_{ij} \leq \tau_{ik}\tau_{kj}$ for any potential intermediary country k. If we now assume that all *ad valorem* trade costs reduce by some percentage points, this inequality is violated, implying a profitable rerouting opportunity for country pair ij. To make this clear, assume that trade costs change to a factor $\gamma < 1$ (i.e., if trade costs are reduced by 10 percent $\gamma = 0.9$). Then, the new trade costs equal $\gamma\tau < \tau$, and the triangle inequality holds only if $\tau_{ij} \leq \gamma\tau_{ik}\tau_{kj}$. If γ is sufficiently small, this inequality is violated, implying a profitable rerouting opportunity for country pair ij. Foellmi et al. (2024) propose an estimation routine such that the simple hat algebra can be still applied but where the triangle inequality constraint holds. They find that the welfare impact of trade costs changes is larger than previously expected. If trade costs decrease by 25 percent, countries can reroute and exploit triangle inequality violations. The median country's real income growth increases from 19 to 30 percent.

Global Value Chains

Since the EK model can be adapted to study trade in intermediate goods, as noted above, it can be used to study the question of the international allocation of production. The decrease of communication costs with the information technology revolution (the so-called second unbundling, as Richard Baldwin (2016) called it) made it possible that the production process takes place at different locations. The communication networks allow to offshore or outsource different tasks of the production process: Production lines are set up at a different place than where design and research and development occur, and call centers or accounting units are no longer at the headquarters. The open question is to which country will the company choose to allocate the different stages of the production process, either by outsourcing or offshoring. A car may be assembled in Germany, but parts may come from Korea, relying on technology developed in the United States, while customer support is located in yet another country. This pattern is known as a global value chain (GVC), which can be interpreted as a production process broken into several tasks, or equivalently, as trade in different pieces of work.

Grossmann and Rossi-Hansberg (2008) develop a Ricardian model of trade in tasks. Building on this, Baldwin and Robert-Nicoud (2014) show that the four traditional theorems (factor price equalization, Heckscher–Ohlin, Stolper–Samuelson, and Rybczynski) hold in a framework with trade in tasks. The influential work by Caliendo et al. (2014) introduced many sectors into the EK model that we discussed in this chapter. As inputs from other sectors are used in one sector, this framework allows conveniently to study GVCs and is accessible for quantitative analysis with hat algebra. However, as the survey by Antràs and Chor (2022) notes, their elegant framework envisions production as a continuous, never-ending sequence of stages in which each step relies on inputs from previous ones in a perpetual cycle. Thus, Antràs and de Gortari (2020) develop a framework for how GVC with a discrete number of stages can be analyzed within the EK model. The idea is that the overall (i.e., chain-level) unit cost of production of the whole GVC passing different countries is a draw from a Fréchet distribution. Intuitively, as trade is costly, the location choice of a given stage in a GVC depends on the marginal cost for that stage in the country, and it depends how close the location is to the adjacent nodes of the value chain.

6.6 Trade Policy

The EK model is well suited to analyzing a whole range of trade policy interventions. It is also at the core of numerous policy studies, such as those on the economic consequences of Brexit (Dhingra et al., 2017). In what follows, we briefly illustrate how government interventions affect trade flows in the framework of the EK model. The example is taken from a real-world case that involves the European Union, China, and Egypt. Based on data from United Nations Comtrade, Table 6.1 shows the European Union's imports of glass fiber (Harmonized System (HS) code 7019).

In 2006, the European Union imported a total of \$850 million worth of glass fiber, much of it from China (country *i* henceforth). Due to the introduction of subsidies for production and export, Chinese manufacturers were then able to offer the product for a lower p_i (factory gate price). Since trade costs between China and the European Union (country *j*) did not change much, buyers of glass fiber in the European Union faced a lower $p_{ij} = p_i * \tau_{ij}$

Table 6.1 Imports of Glass Fiber by the European Union (EU-28)

Year	Imports of Glass Fiber (million USD)		
	Total	from China	from Egypt
2006	849.9	251.9	0.3
2010	1,138.3	459.6	0.1
2011	1,295.3	362.8	0.1
2012	1,175.7	365.4	0.0
2013	1,177.2	378.3	0.0
2014	1,286.7	412.5	15.0
2015	1,202.6	323.8	52.0
2016	1,286.5	346.2	57.5
2017	1,413.3	346.0	106.2
2018	1,558.7	333.8	175.4
2019	1,503.6	374.2	165.1

when purchasing the product from China. Not surprisingly, the trade data show a substantial increase in EU imports of glass fiber from China until 2010.

The increased imports of subsidized glass fiber from China displeased European manufactures, and the European Union eventually introduced an antidumping tariff. This raised τ_{ij} and let imports from China decline until 2012. In theyears after that, a Chinese company called Jushi opened in an industrial zone in Egypt. According to the *Financial Times* (February 13, 2020), Jushi said one of its rationales for going abroad was precisely to avoid EU antidumping and antisubsidy actions against production in China. With the company receiving subsidies from the Egyptian government itself and financial backing by Chinese state banks at subsidized rates, it is little surprise that the European Union's imports of glass fiber from Egypt surged until 2018. As a response and in a landmark case, the European Union introduced, in June 2020, an antisubsidy tariff of 10.9 percent on "Chinese-subsidized" glass fiber from Egypt.

6.7 Conclusion

The EK model is a Ricardian model with many goods and countries, allowing the Ricardian predictions to be taken to real-world data. The key insights are as follows:

- **Comparative advantages are driven by technology differences.** Countries receive for each good a different productivity draw from a Fréchet distribution. This generates Ricardian comparative advantages across a continuum of goods. The Fréchet assumption gives rise to tractable formulas for trade flows. This allows to quantitatively study a world with many goods and many countries.
- **Trade costs have an impact on trade flows and welfare.** While we already knew that comparative advantages due to productivity differences create gains from trade, the EK model shows that these gains are attenuated by the resistance imposed by trade costs. In particular, the EK model predicts that prices increase if tariffs are raised substantially because, in that case, domestic consumers must buy products that come from nearby but have higher costs of production.
- **We can understand the structure of bilateral trade.** The model predicts that the share of a country's imports from a trading partner falls

as trade costs with that partner rise—matching gravity-type trade patterns. The EK model predicts that firms will source from around the world, the only limit being trade costs. Therefore, many bilateral trade flows are concentrated in a narrow set of products, consistent with empirical evidence. Most of a country's trade occurs with neighboring countries because of trade costs: About 20 percent of world trade that takes place between countries that share a common border.

- **Trade diversion can occur.** When bilateral trade costs increase, trade with unaffected third countries will rise, a phenomenon known as trade diversion. This can be studied within the EK framework, as it allows for many countries. For instance, during a US–China trade war, US imports from Vietnam might surge.
- **The EK model is often used for empirical studies.** The balance of theoretical richness and empirical usability turned the EK model into a foundation for modern quantitative trade models. Using exact hat algebra, the impact of trade costs on trade flows can be estimated using initial trade shares and output levels only. Fundamental variables such as productivity do not have to be calibrated. Similarly, gains from trade can be estimated using home shares and the diffusion parameter θ.
- **There are many extensions of the EK model.** Relying on competitive assumptions, EK is the ideal benchmark model, and its setup can be applied to many extensions. For instance, the EK model allows us to discuss trade in intermediate inputs. Therefore, EK serves as a framework to study outsourcing and GVCs and to discuss a broad range of trade policy interventions.

6.8 Exercises

The following exercises allow students to practice and deepen their understanding of the EK model.

Exercise 1 In 2019, an article in the *New York Times* titled "Trump's Washing Machine Tariffs Stung Consumers While Lifting Corporate Profits"[2] discussed the impact of new US tariffs on washing machines from abroad. Using the EK model, explain why US domestic producers of washing machines would raise prices in response to these tariffs.

Exercise 2 Consider the Fréchet distribution function $F(\varphi) = e^{-S\varphi^{-\theta}}$. Assume that $\theta > 2$. Show that the mean (i.e., the expectation) is proportional to $S^{1/\theta}$ and the variance is proportional to $S^{2/\theta}$.

Exercise 3 In the EK model, for a given home share λ_{jj}, the gains from trade are higher if the dispersion parameter θ is lower and hence productivities are more dispersed."

(a) Is this statement true? Explain your answer.
(b) Explain how the dispersion parameter θ impacts the results in the model. What happens when $\theta \to \infty$ or $\theta \to 0$?

Exercise 4 Consider a world with two countries, A and B, and many goods. The countries are identical except that productivity in country A exceeds productivity in country B.

(a) In autarky, which country will have lower prices on average?
(b) Suppose the countries open up to trade. What will be the trade flows between the two countries? How does the dispersion parameter θ influence your answer in this two-country setup?
(c) The EK model assumes balanced trade. How can you reconcile this with your answer to the previous question?

[2] Please find the article here: https://www.nytimes.com/2019/04/21/business/trump-tariffs-washing-machines.html.

Appendix 6.1: Derivation of the Exporting Probability π_{ij}

Recall that $1 - G_{kj}(p) = \exp\left[-S_k\left(w_k\tau_{kj}\right)^{-\theta}p^{\theta}\right]$ and $g_{ij}(p) = dG_{ij}(p)/dp = \exp\left[-p^{\theta}S_i\left(w_i\tau_{ij}\right)^{-\theta}\right]\theta S_i\left(w_i\tau_{ij}\right)^{-\theta}p^{\theta-1}$

$$
\begin{aligned}
\pi_{ij} &= \Pr\left[p_{ij} \leq \min_{k\in C,k\neq i}\{p_{kj}\}\right] \\
&= \int_0^{\infty} \Pr\left[\min_{k\in C,k\neq i}\{p_{kj}\} \geq p\right] dG_{ij}(p) \\
&= \int_0^{\infty} \prod_{k\in C,k\neq i}\left[1 - G_{kj}(p)\right]\cdot g_{ij}(p)dp \\
&= \int_0^{\infty} \prod_{k\in C,k\neq i}\exp\left[-S_k\left(w_k\tau_{kj}\right)^{-\theta}p^{\theta}\right] g_{ij}(p)dp \\
&= \int_0^{\infty} \exp\left[-p^{\theta}\sum_{k\in C,k\neq i}S_k\left(w_k\tau_{kj}\right)^{-\theta}\right]\exp\left[-p^{\theta}S_i\left(w_i\tau_{ij}\right)^{-\theta}\right] \\
&\qquad \theta S_i\left(w_i\tau_{ij}\right)^{-\theta}p^{\theta-1}dp \\
&= S_i\left(w_i\tau_{ij}\right)^{-\theta}\int_0^{\infty}\exp\left[-p^{\theta}\left(\sum_{k\in C,k\neq i}S_k\left(w_k\tau_{kj}\right)^{-\theta} + S_i\left(w_i\tau_{ij}\right)^{-\theta}\right)\right]\theta p^{\theta-1}dp
\end{aligned}
$$

To find the anti-derivative, note that $\theta p^{\theta-1}$ is the derivative of p^{θ}. This allows to solve the integral

$$
\begin{aligned}
\pi_{ij} &= -S_i\left(w_i\tau_{ij}\right)^{-\theta}\left(\sum_{k\in C}S_k(w_k\tau_{kj})^{-\theta}\right)^{-1}\exp\left[-p^{\theta}\left(\sum_{k\in C}S_k(w_k\tau_{kj})^{-\theta}\right)\right]\Bigg|_0^{\infty} \\
&= \frac{S_i(w_i\tau_{ij})^{-\theta}}{\sum_{k\in C}S_k(w_k\tau_{kj})^{-\theta}}
\end{aligned}
$$

Appendix 6.2: Derivation of the Price Index

To derive the price index of equation (6.10), note that

$$P_j = \left(\int_0^1 p_j(z)^{1-\sigma} dz \right)^{\frac{1}{1-\sigma}}$$

$$= \left(\int_0^\infty p^{1-\sigma} g_j(p) dp \right)^{\frac{1}{1-\sigma}}$$

$$= \left(\int_0^\infty p^{1-\sigma} \exp\left[-p^\theta \Phi(j)\right] \theta\Phi(j) p^{\theta-1} dp \right)^{\frac{1}{1-\sigma}}$$

We substitute $x = \Phi(j)p^\theta$, this yields $dx = \theta p^{\theta-1}\Phi(j)dp$ and $p^{1-\sigma} = (x/\Phi(j))^{\frac{1-\sigma}{\theta}}$ The integral simplifies

$$P_j = \left(\int_0^\infty (x/\Phi(j))^{\frac{1-\sigma}{\theta}} \exp[-x]\, dx \right)^{\frac{1}{1-\sigma}}$$

$$= \Phi(j)^{-1/\theta} \left(\int_0^\infty x^{\frac{1-\sigma}{\theta}} \exp[-x]\, dx \right)^{\frac{1}{1-\sigma}}$$

The integral converges only if $\frac{1-\sigma}{\theta} > -1$ or $\sigma < 1 + \theta$ as stated above. Its value, denoted with γ above, depends on the parameters θ and σ only.

Appendix 6.3: Proof That the Price Distribution from Sourcing Country Equals the Full Price Distribution

Our aim is to derive the distribution of prices in j *conditional* on sourcing from country i. This is equal to the probability that country i is the lowest cost supplier in country j and that it has unit costs smaller or equal to the price p, divided by the probability that country i is the exporter π_{ij}.

We follow similar steps as in the appendix to derive the exporting probability. The probability that country k has higher costs than, say q, equals $1 - G_{kj}(q)$. The probability that all other countries have costs above q, is given by

$$\prod_{k \in C, k \neq i} [1 - G_{kj}(q)] = \prod_{k \in C, k \neq i} \exp\left[-S_k (w_k \tau_{kj})^{-\theta} q^\theta\right]$$

$$= \exp\left[-q^\theta \sum_{k \in C, k \neq i} S_k (w_k \tau_{kj})^{-\theta}\right]$$

The joint probability that country i is the least cost supplier in country j and that it has unit cost q smaller or equal to the price p is the sum of the probabilities that price is equal to q weighted by the density $g_{ij}(q)$. The numerator of the conditional price distribution is the integral for q running from 0 to p. The conditional distribution reads

$$\frac{1}{\pi_{ij}} \int_0^p \prod_{k \in C, k \neq i} \left[1 - G_{kj}(q)\right] \cdot g_{ij}(q) dq$$

Recall $1 - G_{kj}(p) = \exp\left[-S_k \left(w_k \tau_{kj}\right)^{-\theta} p^\theta\right]$ and $1 - G_j(p) = \exp\left[-p^\theta \sum_{i \in C} S_i(w_i \tau_{ij})^{-\theta}\right] = \exp\left[-p^\theta \Phi(j)\right]$. We insert to get

$$\begin{aligned}
&\frac{1}{\pi_{ij}} \int_0^p \prod_{k \in C, k \neq i} \left[1 - G_{kj}(q)\right] \cdot g_{ij}(q) dq \\
&= \frac{1}{\pi_{ij}} \int_0^p \exp\left[-q^\theta \sum_{k \in C, k \neq i} S_k \left(w_k \tau_{kj}\right)^{-\theta}\right] \\
&\quad \cdot \exp\left[-q^\theta S_i \left(w_i \tau_{ij}\right)^{-\theta}\right] \theta S_i \left(w_i \tau_{ij}\right)^{-\theta} q^{\theta - 1} dq \\
&= \frac{1}{\pi_{ij}} \int_0^p \exp\left[-q^\theta \sum_{k \in C} S_k \left(w_k \tau_{kj}\right)^{-\theta}\right] \cdot \theta S_i \left(w_i \tau_{ij}\right)^{-\theta} q^{\theta - 1} dq \\
&= \frac{1}{\pi_{ij}} \frac{S_i \left(w_i \tau_{ij}\right)^{-\theta}}{\sum_{i \in C} S_i (w_i \tau_{ij})^{-\theta}} \int_0^p \exp\left[-q^\theta \sum_{k \in C} S_k \left(w_k \tau_{kj}\right)^{-\theta}\right] \sum_{i \in C} S_i (w_i \tau_{ij})^{-\theta} \cdot \theta q^{\theta - 1} dq \\
&= \exp\left[-q^\theta \left(\sum_{k \in C} S_k (w_k \tau_{kj})^{-\theta}\right)\right]\Bigg|_0^p = G_j(p)
\end{aligned}$$

Note that we expanded the formula by $\sum_{i \in C} S_i(w_i \tau_{ij})^{-\theta}$ to write the expression in terms of the exporting probability π_{ij}. Furthermore, $\sum_{i \in C} S_i(w_i \tau_{ij})^{-\theta} = \sum_{k \in C} S_k \left(w_k \tau_{kj}\right)^{-\theta}$. The value of the integral is evaluated in a similar fashion as in the appendix to derive the exporting probability. To find the anti-derivative, keep in mind that $\theta q^{\theta - 1}$ is the derivative of q^θ.

We get our desired result. The distribution of prices in j *conditional* on sourcing from country i is the latter the same as the unconditional distribution.

7
The Krugman Model

7.1 Idea and Background

Classical trade theory basically argues that trade occurs because of cost differences. In such a setup, it is appropriate to assume perfect competition and constant returns to scale, as it simplifies the analysis and focuses on the main point. However, these assumptions shut down another motivation for trade: increasing returns to scale (IRS). With a larger market, firms can expand their production and lower their average costs. If a product exhibits large fixed costs, access to the world market allows it to spread the fixed costs over a large number of consumers.

When we look at the size of actual trade flows, the importance of IRS becomes even more apparent. While the previous models focus on inter-industry trade, they can explain only a minor part of the data. In reality, most trade occurs between industrialized countries. Furthermore, to a large extent, we observe intra-industry trade (i.e., two-way trade within narrowly defined industries). Contrary to the classical trade theories relying on comparative advantage, similar countries seem to trade more with each other than with more different countries. This creates a need for a theory that explains why and how similar (or even identical) countries could engage in beneficial trade.

The solution proposed by trade economists is a model featuring IRS and love of variety. These two elements lead to international trade and associated gains even between identical countries. While such ideas had been around for a long time—actually going back to Adam Smith (1776), who made the case for free trade based on IRS and not comparative advantages, as David Ricardo (1817) did—until the 1970s there was no framework able to deal with imperfect competition at a macroeconomic level. IRS are inconsistent with perfect competition: If firms have falling average costs globally, only one firm will serve the whole market for a single product. The assumption of perfect competition, an industry consisting of many price-taking suppliers, is no longer valid. This implies that we have to use a different market

Understanding International Trade. Reto Foellmi and Stefan Legge, Oxford University Press.
 DOI: 10.1093/9780197821107.003.0008

structure when seeking to explain international trade with IRS and love of variety.

Chapters 8 and 9 address this issue. First, we discuss the "new trade theory" by Paul Krugman. Subsequently, we turn to what is sometimes called the "new new trade theory" by Marc Melitz, trade models with heterogeneous firms. The models of Chapters 8 and 9 will allow for new channels of gains from international trade. In the words of Paul Krugman (1980):

> For some time now there has been considerable skepticism about the ability of comparative cost theory to explain the actual pattern of international trade. Neither the extensive trade among the industrial countries, nor the prevalence in this trade of two-way exchanges of differentiated products, make much sense in terms of standard theory.

In his earlier work published in 1979, Krugman pointed out that with two economies that have identical tastes, technologies, and endowments, there would be no reason for trade to occur and no potential gains from trade. Based on the Ricardian and Heckscher–Ohlin trade model, we might assume that most international trade takes place between countries that look very different. However, as Figure 7.1 shows, for decades, trade partners of the United States had an income level of about two-thirds the American gross domestic product (GDP) per capita.[1] For European nations, trading partners often had an income level higher than their own.

Figure 7.2 illustrates that even today, trade among rich countries accounts for a large share of global trade flows.[2] This pattern was even more striking before the rise of China and India—two countries that accounted for about 30 percent of worldwide trade in 2023 (partly because they have become more similar to rich countries). Looking at individual countries, data from the Swiss Federal Office for Customs and Border Security shows that in 2024, Switzerland's trade with the Netherlands (a total trade volume of $12.2 billion, excluding gold) was substantially larger than its trade with the entire continent of Africa (about $5.2 billion).

When Paul Krugman developed his models in the late 1970s, global trade was even more concentrated among rich countries (i.e., the Organisation for Economic Co-operation and Development (OECD) member states). This

[1] Our figure builds upon "The Hyperglobalization of Trade and Its Future" by Arvind Subramanian and Martin Kessler (*PIIE Working Papers* 13-6, 2013).

[2] The data is taken from Base pour l'Analyse du Commerce International (BACI) using OECD member countries as high-income nations.

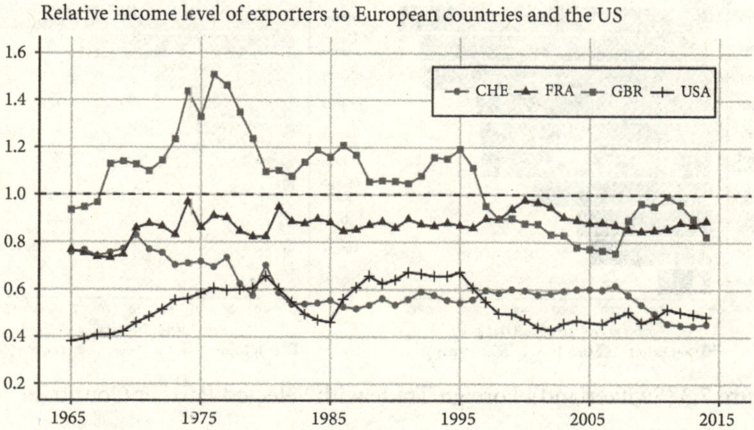

Figure 7.1 Rich Countries Largely Trade with Other Rich Countries

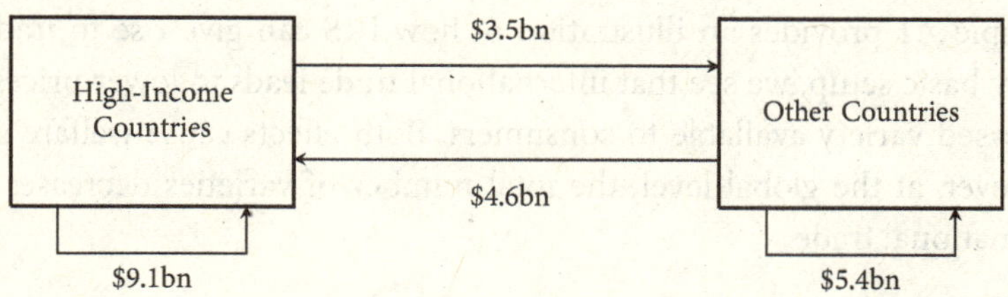

Figure 7.2 Imports by High/Low-Income Countries in 2023

motivated him and others to develop new trade theories that could explain why *similar* countries gain from the mutual exchange of goods. The central idea is that gains from trade can be achieved due to economies of scale and love of variety.

A second key observation by Krugman—as well as motivation for thinking beyond the models we have studied thus far—is that there is an enormous amount of intra-industry trade. While, for instance, the simple Ricardian trade model suggests that a country like Switzerland *only imports* some products from Germany and *only exports* some other products, the reality is very different. Figure 7.3 illustrates this point using data from the Swiss Federal Office for Customs and Border Security. The majority of products (defined here as eight-digit Harmonized System (HS) codes, excluding gold trade) are traded both ways. That is, Switzerland both imports and exports these goods from its trading partners. Expressed in terms of trade value, the plot on the right side shows that this two-way trade dominates international trade.

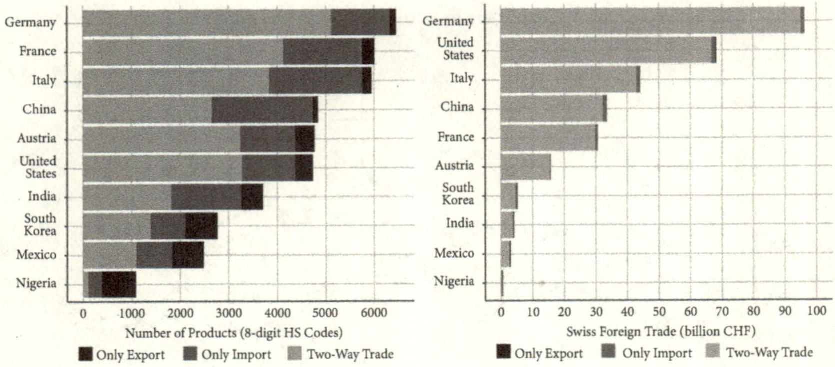

Figure 7.3 Switzerland's Foreign Trade with Selected Partner Countries

Before we turn to the discussion of the Krugman model, numerical example 7.1 provides an illustration of how IRS can give rise to trade. In a very basic setup, we see that international trade leads to lower prices and increased variety available to consumers. Both effects cause welfare gains. However, at the global level, the total number of varieties decreases with international trade.

Numerical Example 7.1

In this example, the United States and the European Union have identical technologies and demand for cars.[a] Production involves fixed costs of 5 billion and variable costs of 17,000.

- Total costs are given by $C = 5'000'000'000 + 17'000 * Q$
- Average costs are thus $AC = 5'000'000'000/Q + 17'000$

Demand for cars is given by the inverse demand function $P = 17,000 + 150/n$, with n the number of firms, while market sizes are $S_{USA} = 300$ million and $S_{EU} = 533$ million.

Without trade, the situation looks like this:

It must hold that $Q = S/n$, which we plug into the condition $AC = p$. This yields

$$(5'000'000'000 * n)/S = 150/n$$

which we can solve for

$$n = \sqrt{150S/5'000'000'000}.$$

If we plug in $S_{USA} = 300'000'000$ and $S_{EU} = 533'000'000$, we get $n_{USA} = 3$ and $n_{EU} = 4$. Using $P = 17'000 + 150/n$ from above, we get $P_{USA} = 17'050$ and $P_{EU} = 17'037.5$ The sales volume per car company is $Q_{USA} = 100$ million and $Q_{EU} = 133.25$ million. Each firm makes a profit of zero.

What happens if we allow for free trade (i.e., full market integration)?

We have $S_{new} = S_{USA} + S_{EU} = 833'000'000$. Following the calculations from above, we get $n = 5$ and $P = 17'030$. The price is lower in both countries after opening up to trade because the average costs (*AC*) have decreased. Consumers benefit from this cost reduction. Furthermore, they can now choose from five instead of three (or four in the case of the European Union) car manufacturers. Sales per car company are $Q_{World} = 166.6$ million, higher than under autarky in either the United States or the European Union. Profit of each firm remains zero.

[a] This example builds upon Exercise 3 of Chapter 8 from Krugman, Melitz, and Obstfeld (2024).

To recognize the mechanics of trade models with IRS, it is central to understand why exactly the number of varieties in the world shrinks from seven to five in numerical example 7.1. Consumer demand is such that the willingness to pay for a variety decreases in the number of available varieties. With the numbers from above, a doubling of the number of varieties reduces the markup to half its value. This is a problem because the reduced markup is no longer sufficient to pay the fixed costs. For example, if we had $3 + 4 = 7$ varieties in the world with free trade, sales per firm of 833 million/7 = 119 million at a price of 17,021.43 would not be sufficient to cover the fixed costs. Each firm would make a loss of around 3 billion. As some firms drop out of the market, losses get smaller because each remaining firm can increase its price *and* sell more cars. This happens until at $n = 5$, when firms again break even.

It is important to point out that in numerical example 7.1 the total number of varieties was reduced after allowing for free trade. This does not occur in models in which each country can produce each variety and consumer preferences are such that all varieties will be always consumed (at least in some small volumeat high prices).

There is a second crucial insight we can obtain from the numerical example: The car price falls more and the number of varieties available to consumers increases more in the smaller country (here the United States). It is again true that smaller countries benefit more from free trade than larger ones. Here it is because small countries face the problem that high fixed costs only allow a small number of firms to operate under autarky—while charging a relatively high price because they must spread the fixed costs over a small number of customers.

7.2 Model Setup (Krugman, 1979)

The model developed by Paul Krugman (1979) builds upon prior work on monopolistic competition by Edward Chamberlin (1962) and Avinash Dixit and Joseph Stiglitz (1977). We start with Krugman (1979) working with general preferences. The subsequent work of Krugman (1980), discussed in Section 7.4, works with a simplified version of preferences of the constant elasticity of substitution (CES) type. The latter rule out gains from trade because of scale effects, but allows for the integration trade costs and many countries much more easily.

As an initial step, we set up and analyze the model of Krugman (1979) with just one country under autarky. Afterward, we use this to study the effects of international trade. Consider an economy with only labor as a scarce factor of production. Many different goods can be produced using a technology that exhibits IRS. Before opening a product line, firms must pay a fixed cost. This implies that there are internal economies of scale: Costs per unit decrease with output. As a result, the market structure is characterized by monopolistic competition. Firms have a monopoly for their variety (e.g., via patent protection). The different (and differentiated) goods, also called varieties, are imperfect substitutes in the eyes of consumers. This provides firms with some price-setting power. However, in their pricing decision, firms take price setting by all other firms as given. This follows from the assumption that the total of goods produced is large. There are no market entry costs. Hence, every entrepreneur is free to enter the market by paying the fixed costs and developing a new variety. Thus, in equilibrium, industry profits will be driven down to zero. Prices are above marginal costs, but the profit margin will be just sufficient to cover the fixed cost. This is the "competition" element in the monopolistic competition.

A potential entrepreneur considers entering into business. Gauging whether this is profitable and covers the fixed costs, the entrepreneur must determine the market potential of the new variety. To do this, we need a utility function that will allow us to calculate demand and profits.

Utility and Demand

Consumers receive additively separable utilities from consumption of N goods, indexed by z, according to

$$U = \sum_{z=1}^{N} v(q_z) \tag{7.1}$$

where q_z denotes the quantity of good z. We impose the following assumptions:

- $v' > 0 > v''$
- $v(0) = 0$
- $\eta'(q) \leq 0$ where η is the demand elasticity: $\eta(q) \equiv -[v'(q)]/[q \cdot v''(q)]$ (note that Krugman (1979) assumes $\eta'(q) < 0$)
- $\exists q$ where $\eta(q) > 1$ (decreasing elasticity of substitution)

The first assumption is standard: The marginal utility is positive but decreasing. The second statement is a simple normalization. The third assumption implies that those individuals consuming more (i.e., the richer consumers) have a lower demand elasticity. Loosely speaking, richer individuals are less price sensitive, which is in line with empirical evidence. In equilibrium, the third assumption implies that markups will be lower when more firms are present in the market, which is intuitive as well. Since we allow for variable elasticity of substitution (VES), preferences are non-homothetic. They are homothetic if and only if the elasticity of substitution is constant (CES). Finally, the fourth assumption requests that there exists an elastic region of the demand curve. This is necessary in equilibrium, since a monopolist will always supply in the elastic segment of demand.

Numerical Example 7.2

Suppose the elasticity of substitution between rice and noodles equals 5. Then the consumption of rice relative to the consumption of noodles decreases by 5 percent if the price of rice relative to the price of noodles increases by 1 percent. The elasticity of substitution also provides us with information about how much consumers love variety. The higher the elasticity, the more substitutable are noodles and rice. In contrast, a low elasticity indicates that consumers perceive them as very different products—and given the utility function, love to consume both.

Equation (7.1) implies a "love of variety." But what does that mean exactly? Formally, it follows from the fact that the utility function is concave in a single good, $v''(q) < 0$. If we have to choose to spend a given amount of money on more goods but less on every single good, the gain at the extensive margin more than offsets the loss at the intensive margin, because the utility function is concave. However, it is not necessary that consumers want to consume all goods in some positive amount. This is only true whenever the marginal utility at zero consumption is infinite and therefore the reservation price is infinite. This holds for additively separable CES preferences but not necessarily for VES preferences. Consider, for instance, the quadratic utility function giving rise to linear demands that have an axis intercept and a finite reservation price.

What is an appropriate interpretation of the "goods"? Usually, the *N* goods in the model are interpreted as varieties with limited substitutability. Think of cars from different brands such as BMWs, VWs, or Toyotas. Alternatively, for other applications, the different goods represent indeed different sectors. However, in that case, the quantitative values of the elasticity of substitution would be much lower. You can replace a BMW with a Toyota much more easily than with a t-shirt, so to speak.

Consumers facing the utility function of equation (7.1) as well as an income of *y* maximize their welfare subject to their budget constraint. The welfare optimization problem of a consumer thus reads as follows:

$$\mathcal{L} = \sum_{z=1}^{N} v(q_z) + \lambda \left(y - \sum_{z=1}^{N} p_z q_z \right)$$

This implies the first-order conditions (FOCs)

$$\frac{\partial \mathcal{L}}{\partial q_z} = v'(q_z) - \lambda p_z =: 0 \quad \text{if} \quad q_z > 0 \tag{7.2}$$

The FOCs allow us to write down the demand curve as a function of the marginal utility of income λ:

$$v'(q_z) = \lambda p_z, \quad z \in \{1, ..., N\} \quad \text{if} \quad q_z > 0 \tag{7.3}$$

Equation (7.3) states that the marginal utility an individual receives from consuming the amount q_z of good z must be equal to λ times the price p_z of that good. One additional dollar raises utility by $v'(q_z)/p_z$. Hence, λ can be interpreted as the marginal utility of income. Note that, with many goods, λ does not depend on a single price p_z. The demand relation (7.3) allows us to calculate the elasticity of demand $\eta(q)$, which is done from equation (7.6) forwards below. To gain some intuition about how a demand elasticity could be derived, consider a situation with only $z \in \{1, 2\}$ goods. We would then obtain $v'(q_1)/v'(q_2) = p_1/p_2$: Consumers choose how much to consume of each variety such that relative marginal utilities equal relative goods prices.

Technology and Profits

There are L consumers in the economy. Therefore, the output of a company is given by $y_z = q_z L$ since q_z denotes the quantity consumed per capita. Labor is the only input into production. Firms need f workers to set up the product line, which represents the fixed costs. Having paid that, production takes place with a constant labor productivity of φ. The labor input as a function of output reads

$$L_z = f + \frac{y_z}{\varphi} \tag{7.4}$$

The labor input function also describes total costs (TC) as a sum of fixed costs wf and variable costs $wy_z\varphi$. To simplify the expression, we define the wage w as numéraire in what follows. The presence of fixed costs and constant marginal costs (MC $= 1/\varphi$) cause the average costs (AC $= f/y_z + 1/\varphi$) to fall with the quantity y_z produced. Figure 7.4 shows the evolution of marginal and average costs as a function of quantity. The vertical axis, labeled by the price p_z, is measured in units of the numéraire.

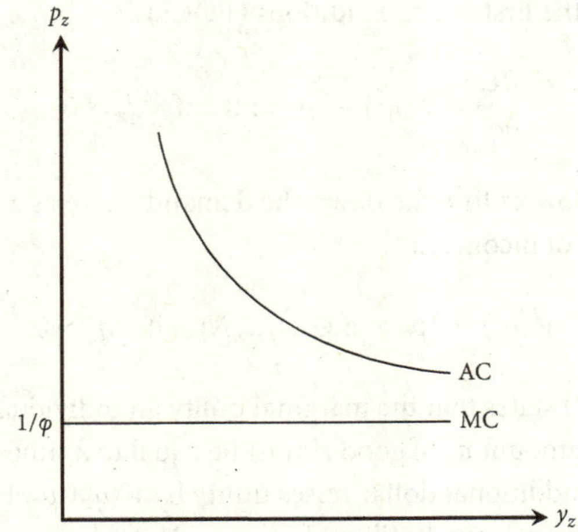

Figure 7.4 Average and Marginal Costs

The falling average costs also indicate that the opportunity costs of producing a product are not constant. Recall that differences in opportunity costs explained (i) why trade is beneficial and (ii) which pattern of trade emerges in, for example, the Ricardian model of Chapter 1. Countries export goods for which they have a lower opportunity cost. With IRS, we have another cause of cross-country differences in opportunity costs—hence another reason for international trade.

The firm producing good z is a monopolist for its good, and it chooses q_z to maximize profits given the demand expressed in equation (7.3). The profits are revenue minus fixed and variable costs, or formally

$$p_z q_z L - wf - \frac{w}{\varphi} q_z L \tag{7.5}$$

In the closed economy that we consider here, consumption equals production. The terms for revenue and variable costs are multiplied by L because q_z denotes consumption of one (representative) individual. Because there is no consumer heterogeneity, $q_z L$ is total consumption of good z in the economy.

If we had perfect competition, we could simply differentiate equation (7.5) with respect to q_z and obtain $p_z = 1/\varphi$ (i.e., price equal marginal costs). This assumes, however, that p_z is independent of q_z, an assumption that does not hold in the setting of monopolistic competition we have here. Hence, we first have to examine how p_z depends on q_z. This relationship is given by the slope of the demand curve. To calculate this slope, differentiate equation (7.3) to get

$$v''(q_z)dq_z = \lambda dp_z. \tag{7.6}$$

We assume that the producer of variety z is small and thus takes the marginal utility of income λ as given. Put differently, if the number of goods produced is large, each firm's pricing policy has a negligible impact on the marginal utility of income ($= \lambda$). In simple parlance, if there are only a handful of goods, each producer has some significant impact on how much utility consumers can obtain with additional income. But if there is a large set of varieties, each producer takes as given the alternatives consumers can choose from. Because firms can costlessly differentiate their products (the fixed costs are constant and do not depend on z), it follows that two firms will never want to produce the same product. For the same reason, each product will only be produced in one country if we allow for international trade without trade costs. Using equation (7.2) to replace λ in equation (7.6) yields

$$\frac{dp_z}{dq_z} = \frac{v''(q_z)}{\lambda} = p_z\frac{v''(q_z)}{v'(q_z)}.$$

Now we know how p_z depends on q_z. Hence, we can turn to the profit-maximization problem and get the FOC of the monopolist

$$p_z\frac{v''(q_z)}{v'(q_z)}q_zL + p_zL - \frac{1}{\varphi}L = 0.$$

After rearranging, we get the intuitive marginal revenue (MR) equals marginal cost (MC) formula

$$\underbrace{p_z\left(1 - 1/\eta(q_z)\right)}_{\text{MR}} = \underbrace{1/\varphi}_{\text{MC}} \tag{7.7}$$

where $\eta(q_z)$ denotes the elasticity of demand

$$\eta(q_z) = -\frac{d\ln(q_z)}{d\ln(p_z)} = -\left(\frac{v'(q_z)}{q_z v''(q_z)}\right)$$

The markup, the ratio of the price p_z to marginal costs $1/\varphi$, is closely linked to the elasticity of demand and equal to $\eta(q_z)/(\eta(q_z) - 1)$. Our assumption on the utility function above states that $\eta'(q) \leq 0$. The demand becomes less elastic as we move down the demand curve. Hence, in equilibrium, a higher optimal quantity q_z chosen by the monopolist is associated with a higher markup (which is our P curve in Figure 7.5 below).

Autarky Equilibrium

We first examine the equilibrium under autarky, and then discuss the trade equilibrium. Since there is free market entry and exit, to enter the market firms must pay the fixed cost f. No other barriers are assumed. Profits must be equal to zero in the long-run equilibrium:

$$p_z q_z L - f - \frac{q_z L}{\varphi} = 0 \iff p_z q_z L - \frac{q_z L}{\varphi} = wf \tag{7.9}$$

The final equilibrium condition is the resource constraint. Because there are N varieties, Nf workers are needed for setting up production of all goods, and $Ny/\varphi = NqL/\varphi$ workers for the production of the different varieties. This must be equal to the labor force L:

$$L = Nf + \frac{NqL}{\varphi} \tag{7.10}$$

The profit maximization problem is identical for all firms because each variety has the same market demand and the same costs of production. Hence, the equilibrium must be symmetric and we can simplify the notation: $p_z = p$ and $q_z = q$ for all $z \in \{1, ..., N\}$.

Furthermore, we choose w as the numéraire ($w = 1$). Taken together, we have three equilibrium equations [7.7, 7.9, 7.10] in three unknowns [p, q, N]. To solve these, note that the first two conditions are independent of the measure of goods N. Hence, we use the price-setting equation (7.7) of monopolists and the zero profit condition (7.9) to solve for p and q. The zero profit condition (7.9) states that the price is equal to average costs:

$$p_z q_z L - \frac{q_z L}{\varphi} = f \iff p = \frac{f}{qL} + \frac{1}{\varphi} \tag{7.11}$$

Since w is the numéraire, we get a Z curve, $p = AC = f/(qL) + 1/\varphi$, which is shown in Figure 7.5. The Z curve displays average costs as a function of quantity per consumer, and it is therefore falling. When a larger quantity per consumer q is produced, the fixed costs f are spread over a larger number, thus lowering average costs of production. The Z curve denotes all (p, q) combinations where price equals average costs. If the price p is above the Z curve, $p > AC$, there would be incentives to enter the market. Vice versa, below the Z curve with $p < AC$, some firms would exit the market. When the quantity q goes to infinity, the Z curve converges to the marginal cost line at value $1/\varphi$.

The price-setting equation (7.7) determines the P curve shown in Figure 7.5. A higher equilibrium quantity is associated with a less-elastic segment of the demand curve. Recall the third assumption associated with the utility function: $\eta'(q) \leq 0$. It implies that richer individuals are less price sensitive. Thus, a higher q implies a higher markup, explaining the positive slope of the P curve.[3] When the reservation price of the demand is finite (which corresponds to $v'(0)$ finite), demand is perfectly elastic at $q = 0$ and therefore markups are zero. Hence, the P curve starts at $p = 1/\varphi$ when $q = 0$.

If we are below or above the curves, the market is not in equilibrium. If prices are above the Z curve, firms would make positive profits, triggering entry of more firms. If the prices are above the P curve, a monopolist would have the incentive to increase quantity and lower the price, hence such a point is no Nash equilibrium.

The intersection of the P- and Z curve in Figure 7.5 determines both individual consumption of each good and the price of each good. We can derive an implicit solution for q using $p = \frac{1}{\varphi}\frac{\eta(q)}{\eta(q)-1}$ from equation (7.7) in equation (7.9). This provides us with the quantity in autarky q_A

$$\eta(q_A) - 1 = \frac{q_A L}{\varphi f} \tag{7.12}$$

Rearranging the resource constraint (7.10), we get the number of varieties in autarky as

$$N = \left(\frac{f}{L} + \frac{q_A}{\varphi}\right)^{-1} \tag{7.13}$$

[3] The P curve is sometimes referred to as representing demand. Thus, the positive slope might be confusing. Obviously, the demand curve is falling, but the P curve is an equilibrium relation. If the monopolist chooses to sell a higher quantity in equilibrium, the markup must be higher because demand is less elastic when q is higher.

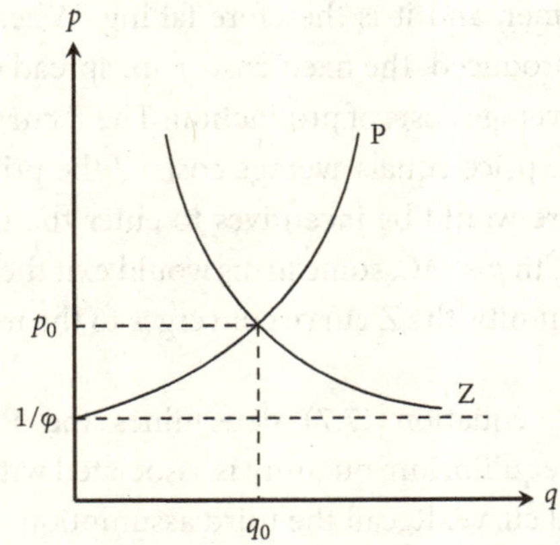

Figure 7.5 Price Setting and Costs in Equilibrium

Intuitively, the number of varieties is larger the lower fixed costs f are and the bigger market size L is. Note that a decrease in f/L increases N directly and indirectly through a fall of q_A: Equation (7.12) implies that q_A falls when f/L goes down. Lower fixed costs or a larger market size shift the Z curve in Figure 7.5 to the left. With smaller fixed costs or a larger market size (and therefore a larger output given q), it is easier to break even. Hence, the equilibrium quantity per consumer will be lower. However, N increases less than proportionally with L. To see this, we use (7.12) to get $q_A/\varphi = L/f * (\eta(q_A) - 1)$. If we insert this expression in (7.13), we get $N = L/(f\eta(q_A))$. When L increases, q_A shrinks but $\eta(q_A)$ goes up. With more firms present in the market the equilibrium, the markup $(1/\eta(q_A))$ falls. Hence, the equilibrium production of a firm $y_A = q_A L$ must be larger such that it breaks even. Using the resource constraint, this makes clear why the increase in N is smaller than the increase in L. We will make use of this insight when we discuss international trade below.

7.3 International Trade

Having solved the autarky equilibrium, it is interesting to see what will happen if this economy opens up to world trade. For simplicity, we look at full integration where trade costs go down to zero (i.e., iceberg trade costs $\tau = 1$). Let us assume $C > 1$ identical countries with equal population size L engage in free trade. Totally free trade, in some sense, is similar to "merging" the individual countries into one big country. Here, frictionless trade is equivalent to enlarging the size of the economy—more clearly, its labor force L—by the factor C such that there are CL consumers (or workers) in the integrated market. It follows that our analysis then applies equally to two different scenarios: (i) The country engages in free trade, and (ii) the country grows its workforce.

Let us denote the number of domestic goods with N_C and the consumed quantity per good q_C. The resource constraint reads $L = N_C f + N_C q_C CL/\varphi$ and states that all domestically available labor (L) is used for paying the fixed and variable costs that occur when producing the domestic varieties. We can rewrite this as

$$N_C = \left(\frac{f}{L} + \frac{q_C C}{\varphi}\right)^{-1}$$

where q_C according to equation (7.12) is given by

$$\eta(q_C) - 1 = \frac{q_C CL}{\varphi f}$$

The number of consumed varieties follows from equation (7.13) and is given by

$$CN_C = \left(\frac{f}{CL} + \frac{q_C}{\varphi}\right)^{-1}$$

Total welfare of country C is given by equation (7.1). With CN_C varieties consumed, it follows that

$$U_C = \left(\frac{f}{CL} + \frac{q_C}{\varphi}\right)^{-1} v(q_C) \tag{7.14}$$

It is insightful to consider the impact of international trade graphically. With more countries engaging in free trade, the Z curve, given by $p = f/(qCL) + 1/\varphi$, shifts to the left, as shown by the Z' curve in Figure 7.6. The P curve is unaffected since the number of consumers L does not show up in equation (7.7).

How do we reach the new equilibrium? Let us assume we move from autarky to free trade with C countries. With more countries, there are more firms in the relevant market. Assume for an instant that all firms remain active. There are C times more goods and C times more consumers. All firms

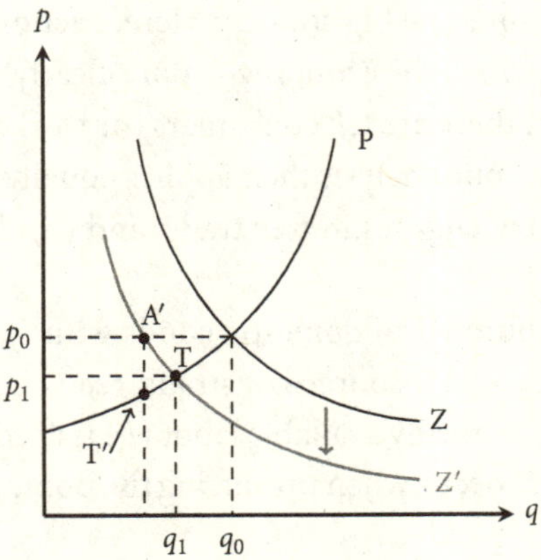

Figure 7.6 Impact of International Trade

are symmetric, and thus production and average costs per firm stays the same. In Figure 7.6, we move to point A' with quantity q_0/C and price (equal to the price/wage ratio) p_0. Graphically, we obtain the Z' curve by shifting the Z curve leftward by factor $1/C$.

However, point A' is not an equilibrium because we are above the P curve. As the quantity sold per consumer q is lower, we are in a more elastic region of the demand curve. Compared to the situation in autarky, each firm has an incentive to lower the price. This is the pro-competitive effect with more firms present. Therefore, the short-run equilibrium will be at point T'. This equilibrium only holds in the short run, because firms make losses at T' since the price is below average costs. As some firms will exit, this increases the output of surviving firms. In Figure 7.6, we move to the right and average costs go down. As there are less firms and quantity per consumer rises again, markups will rise as well (P curve) because competition is less tight. Both effects, decreasing average costs because of higher output and increasing markups, reduce losses gradually. We reach the new equilibrium in point T where firms just break even. With free trade, each surviving firm produces more, average costs are reduced, and lower markups are sustainable.

If the number of countries rises, we see from Figure 7.6 that q_C falls—the Z curve shifts further to the left—but the output per firm $y_C = q_C C$ rises, average costs fall, and so do prices. Consequently, N_C falls. Taken together, the number of varieties consumed increases, and the number of varieties produced (in each country) decreases (if $\eta'(c) < 0$). International trade reduces varieties globally but increases the number of varieties available to each consumer. Formally, we can write

$$2N^T > N > N^T$$

with N^T denoting domestic varieties with free trade and N the number of national varieties under autarky. The intuition for this result is as follows: The number of domestic varieties must fall because average costs fall, which only happens if production increases. Since those firms that remain in the market increase their output, the full employment condition ($L = N(f+y/\varphi)$) implies that some companies leave the market and their varieties disappear. Empirical evidence for this is provided by Werner Baer (1979): "In the late Sixties, the annual output of cars and trucks in eight Latin American countries was 600,000, which was produced by ninety firms (an average of 6,700 per firm)." As these countries opened up to international trade, almost all of these firms disappeared.

Welfare rises as a result of international trade. In equilibrium point T, we see that w/p is higher (i.e., p/w lower) than under autarky. While the consumption per good q_C falls, the number of varieties consumed increases. Because of declining marginal utility, consumers exhibit love for variety. In addition, with more firms present in the relevant market, there is a pro-competitive effect as markups go down. Since each surviving firms produces more, firms can exploit their scale economies better, average costs are lower, and lower markups are sustainable. Thus, welfare rises for two reasons: love for variety and economies of scale. The larger market allows sharing the fixed costs of production with a much larger number of consumers.

Formally, we see from equation (7.14) that U_C rises when the number of countries C goes up. However, there are two conflicting effects: A lower q_C decreases U_C, and the higher C increases it. To get a lower bound on the welfare increase, assume that q_C falls at the same rate as C increases such that $q_C C$ stays constant (we showed above that $q_C C$ rises when C rises, which would result in a higher utility). Let us set $q_C C$ equal to a constant a in equation (7.14). We rewrite to get

$$U_C|_{q_C C=a} = \frac{v(q_C)}{\frac{f}{a}q_C + \frac{q_C}{\varphi}} = \frac{v(q_C)}{q_C}\left(\frac{f}{a} + \frac{1}{\varphi}\right)^{-1}$$

With $v'' < 0$, it holds that $v(q_C)/q_C$ is increasing when q_C falls (this is the love for variety). Thus, welfare must increase.

As a concluding remark it is important to mention that the direction of trade—which country exports and imports which goods—cannot be determined without further structure in the model. We can, however, pin down the volume of international trade and say that each variety is produced only in one country. Furthermore, because each country adheres to its budget constraint, trade must be balanced: The value of a country's imports equals the value of exports.

Unequal Countries and Trade Costs

The Krugman (1979) model is intuitive but works in a stylized environment of two identical countries and assumes no trade costs. What happens if we extend the model to analyze a more general case where countries are nonidentical or trade costs are nonzero? The analysis is more complex, since equilibrium markups depend on the quantity sold in each market, with VES preferences. If per capita income differs between countries, we get the intuitive result that firms will set higher markups in richer markets, creating opportunities for parallel imports (Foellmi et al., 2018). When price differentiation is possible across markets, trade liberalization raises welfare for all countries. If firms are constrained in their price discrimination across markets, however, lower trade barriers might reduce welfare in the poor countries. This occurs because some firms will decide not to serve these markets altogether to avoid the threat of parallel imports.

To analyze many countries and obtain quantitative predictions, Krugman (1980) simplified the model and assumed CES preferences instead. This is less realistic on the consumer side but allows us to analyze finite trade costs and to derive simple quantitative predictions regarding welfare, similar to the EK model analyzed in Chapter 6. Thus, we discuss the Krugman model with CES preferences now.

7.4 CES Preferences (Krugman, 1980)

As discussed above, the original Krugman (1979) trade model assumed VES. This assumption makes it difficult to examine trade between nonidentical countries or situations with positive (but not infinite) trade costs. Hence, we briefly analyze how the model works with CES.

Suppose households have CES utility

$$U = \left[\int_0^N q_z^{\frac{\sigma-1}{\sigma}} \, dz \right]^{\frac{\sigma}{\sigma-1}} \quad \text{with} \quad \sigma > 1 \tag{7.15}$$

where the elasticity of demand $\eta(q) = -\frac{d\ln(q_z)}{d\ln(p_z)} = \sigma$ is constant, as can be seen in the demand function below. The elasticity of substitution (= elasticity of demand because of additive separability) must be above one, $\sigma > 1$, such that the demand function is elastic and the monopolist supplies a positive quantity. The demand function for good z reads (identical derivation to the CES utility in Eaton–Kortum)

$$q_z = \left(\frac{p_z}{P}\right)^{-\sigma} Q \tag{7.16}$$

where $P = \left[\int_0^N p_z^{1-\sigma} \, dz\right]^{\frac{1}{1-\sigma}}$ is the ideal price index and $Q = U$ the quantity index. The monopolist firms set a constant markup over marginal cost (due to CES preferences)

$$p_z = \frac{w}{\varphi} \frac{\sigma}{\sigma - 1} \tag{7.17}$$

As above, the solution is symmetric. We will therefore drop the subscript z. Free entry implies zero profits in the long run (recall that goods market clearing implies $y_z = Lq_z$).

$$\pi = y\frac{w}{\varphi}\left[\frac{\sigma}{\sigma - 1} - 1\right] - fw \stackrel{!}{=} 0 \tag{7.18}$$

This implies $y = f\varphi(\sigma - 1)$. The firm quantity y is pinned down by exogenous parameters and independent of market size and trade. The number of produced varieties, N, is the same under autarky and trade. It follows from the full employment condition, $L = N\frac{y}{\varphi} + Nf$, that

$$N = \frac{L}{f\sigma} \tag{7.19}$$

To calculate the welfare under autarky, W_A, note that the price index is given by

$$P = \left[\int_0^N p_z^{1-\sigma}\, dz\right]^{\frac{1}{1-\sigma}} = N^{\frac{1}{1-\sigma}} \frac{w}{\varphi} \frac{\sigma}{\sigma - 1}$$

using equation (7.17). We again choose $w = 1$ as the numéraire and insert the number of varieties from equation (7.19) to get

$$W_A = \frac{w}{P} = \left[\frac{L}{f\sigma}\right]^{\frac{1}{\sigma-1}} \varphi \frac{\sigma - 1}{\sigma} \tag{7.20}$$

International Trade with CES Preferences

Suppose that we have C countries. Let us denote the exporting country with i and the importer with j. The iceberg trade costs between the two countries are τ_{ij}. Note that the quantity per firm is fixed at $y = f\varphi(\sigma - 1)$ and each firm has a constant markup. We allow the productivity parameter φ and fixed costs f to vary across countries. Hence, the P curve is horizontal, while the Z curve looks identical to the one in the VES case (preferences do not enter there). In contrast to the VES case, there is no exit of firms when countries open up to trade. Because the demand is iso-elastic there are no pro-competitive effects of trade. Hence, an increase in the number of varieties when the market opens up to trade does not affect the markup of existing firms. As a result, with CES preferences, gains from trade are limited to the love-of-variety channel. This contrasts with the model featuring VES preferences discussed earlier in which there is the additional pro-competitive or scale-effect.

One benefit of the CES preferences is the possibility to determine the direction of trade. Let us calculate exports from i to j. Equation (7.17) and τ_{ij} imply for the price charged in j by firms from i:

$$p_{ij} = \frac{w_i \tau_{ij}}{\varphi_i} \frac{\sigma}{\sigma - 1} \tag{7.21}$$

The sales in j per firm from i read

$$R_{ij} = q_{ij} p_{ij} L_j = \left(\frac{p_{ij}}{P_j}\right)^{1-\sigma} w_j L_j \tag{7.22}$$

Exports from i to j equal

$$X_{ij} = N_i R_{ij} = N_i \left(\frac{p_{ij}}{P_j} \right)^{1-\sigma} w_j L_j$$

Recall that product quantities and prices within countries are symmetric in equilibrium. With balanced trade, total income in country j needs to equal total expenditures. Thus, we may write $w_j L_j = X_j$ and obtain

$$\frac{X_{ij}}{X_j} = N_i \left(\frac{p_{ij}}{P_j} \right)^{1-\sigma} \tag{7.23}$$

Using equations (7.21), (7.23), and (7.19), we get

$$\frac{X_{ij}}{X_j} = \frac{N_i \left(\frac{w_i \tau_{ij}}{\varphi_i} \right)^{1-\sigma}}{\sum_{k=1}^{C} N_k \left(\frac{w_k \tau_{kj}}{\varphi_k} \right)^{1-\sigma}} = \frac{\frac{L_i}{f_i} \left(\frac{w_i \tau_{ij}}{\varphi_i} \right)^{1-\sigma}}{\sum_{k=1}^{C} \frac{L_k}{f_k} \left(\frac{w_k \tau_{kj}}{\varphi_k} \right)^{1-\sigma}}$$

The comparative statics of exports from i to j, relative to world output, are intuitive. They increase in the ratio of the labor endowment L_i to fixed costs f_i since this ratio is proportional to the number of domestic varieties N_i. Furthermore, exports decrease in marginal costs w_i/φ_i and trade costs (recall that $\sigma > 1$).

Taking all equations for all countries together, we can solve for the different wage rates (something we do not explicitly do here but you will be asked to do so in the exercises). Intuitively, a larger size implies that the domestic price index is lower because there is a larger share of domestic products where no trade costs occur. The lower price index limits the incentive to import goods from abroad that are more expensive because of trade costs. To restore the balance of trade, the real wage at home and therefore prices must rise. Hence, there is an agglomeration effect: Larger countries have higher real wages.

An interesting observation from equation (7.23) is that the home share, λ_{jj}, is given by

$$\lambda_{jj} := \frac{X_{jj}}{X_j} = N_j \left(\frac{p_{jj}}{P_j} \right)^{1-\sigma}$$

implying for country j's price index under trade, $P_j = \left(\frac{N_j}{\lambda_{jj}}\right)^{\frac{1}{1-\sigma}} \frac{w_j}{\varphi_j} \frac{\sigma}{\sigma-1}$. The gains from trade moving from autarky to free trade are given by

$$\frac{W_T}{W_A} = \frac{\frac{w_{T_j}}{P_{T_j}}}{\frac{w_{A_j}}{P_{A_j}}} = \lambda_{jj}^{\frac{1}{1-\sigma}}$$

As in the Eaton–Kortum model (and later in Melitz model), the formula looks very similar and the home share (one minus the share of imported varieties) plays a central role. Since there are no productivity differences across countries or firms in the Krugman model, the exponent is different, however. For a given home share, welfare gains are larger the lower the elasticity of substitution σ. With CES preferences, welfare gains from trade come through increased varieties only. An additional variety has a larger impact on utility the lower the elasticity of substitution (i.e., the more differentiated the goods are). Similar to classical trade models, gains from trade are larger if cross-country differences are larger. In the new trade theory, however, it is about differences in goods (love for variety) and not primarily about differences in countries (productivity, endowments).

Discussion and Extensions

Note that we can interpret the different varieties as final consumption goods or different intermediates for one final output good. In the former case, the welfare gain accrues through increased variety for consumers, and in the latter case, it will arise through a productivity increase of firms. Broda and Weinstein (2006) study how the growth in imported varieties affected welfare in the United States between 1972 and 2001. While the number of imported varieties more than tripled during this time period, welfare, measured in GDP per capita terms, rose by 2.6 percent of GDP. Since the United States is a large economy, for other smaller countries the numbers are likely to be larger. Looking at the 1991 trade liberalization in India, Goldberg et al. (2010) show that there were substantial gains from trade because firms had better access to imported inputs. However, Hsieh et al. (2020) show that import variety gains are counteracted by domestic variety losses. We have seen this phenomenon in the VES part of this chapter, and we will come back to it in Chapter 8. On another critical note, Hummels and

Klenow (2005) estimate that the number of exported varieties does not increase proportionally with the size of the economy. They estimate that the extensive margin (i.e. the wider set of goods) contributes 60 percent to explain the larger export value of a bigger country. This is sizeable, but falls short of 100 percent, the result that we have derived with CES preferences. Hence, this finding is conflicting with the CES version of the Krugman (and Armington) model. If preferences are VES instead, a larger economy will export both more varieties (extensive margin) and more of a given variety (intensive margin).

The Krugman model also gives rise to a so-called home-market effect. An industry will settle in the market with high domestic demand because this saves trade costs (note that within-country trade costs are usually assumed to be zero). Because of scale economies, the larger industry has lower average costs, which is advantageous in international trade. Consider the following situation with two countries of identical size. In country A, a larger share of consumers prefer cars, while in country B, a larger share of consumers prefer bikes. When opening up to trade, the home-market effect suggests that the car industry will settle predominantly in country A and the bike industry will be in country B. With this argument, and quite different from the classical trade theory focusing on supply forces, the new trade theory argues that demand forces play an important role in shaping international trade, formalizing an idea framed as the Linder hypothesis. Staffan Linder (1961) argued that domestic demand shapes trade patterns and that countries with more similar demand structures would trade more with each other. Costinot et al. (2019) check whether we see a home-market effect empirically by looking at the pharmaceutical industry. They use the demographic structure of the different countries as an instrument to determine domestic demand for drugs for particular diseases. They find compelling evidence for the home-market effect. The correlation between predicted home demand and exports is positive and stronger than the correlation between home demand and imports.

Notice that the home-market effect suggests that large countries should be richer than smaller nations. Since domestic demand is a prerequisite to export, industries with scale economies concentrate in large markets. Empirically, however, we do not find a positive correlation between countries' population size and their GDP per capita levels. But as always when checking model predictions against reality, we must carefully review the model's simplifying assumptions like, for instance, zero within-country trade costs.

Moreover, the home-market effect does provide insights into why nations with a small domestic market particularly benefit from trade integration: Wealthy countries like Luxembourg and Switzerland are part of the large European market.

7.5 Conclusion

This chapter has shown how IRS and love of variety can result in intra-industry trade between identical countries. We derived several key insights.

- **Economies of scale are a basis for international trade.** The new trade theory gives rise to alternative gains from international trade. With trade, fixed costs can be shared. It is no longer necessary to "reinvent the wheel" and to duplicate fixed costs. This reduces the average costs of production. Even when there are no cost differences (technologies and endowments are identical in all countries), trade will occur because of scale economies. Since there are no technological differences, we can interpret the different goods as items within the same industry. Therefore, the Krugman model provides a neat explanation why we see so much intra-industry trade.
- **More varieties for consumption raise the welfare of consumers.** Trade makes it possible for every country to benefit from more (imported) varieties. We have seen that the welfare gains depend positively on the import share and the elasticity of substitution, a relationship that culminates in the simple gains from trade formula with CES preferences. The elasticity of substitution plays a central role as it determines how different and, therefore, how valuable new products are. Since smaller countries have a smaller home market, they benefit more from international trade and increased access to imported varieties.
- **Openness to trade can create a pro-competitive effect.** Because more firms are present in a larger market, trade creates pro-competitive effects in the VES model by Krugman (1979). More firms means that every active firm operates at a more elastic region of the demand curve, thereby reducing markups. Hence, consumers take an additional gain from lower markups and prices. While very intuitive, the quantitative importance of variable markups is an open debate. On the one hand, when estimating trade gains quantitatively, models with

constant markups seem a good approximation. Arkolakis et al. (2018) find that gains from trade liberalization predicted by models with variable markups are similar to those predicted by models with constant markups. On the other hand, the Krugman (1980) model with CES preferences predicts that the rate of variety expansion is proportional to the growth in total market size, while in the VES model it is smaller. Hummels and Klenow (2005) showed empirically that larger countries' bigger export values are explained by a wider set of goods (the extensive margin, contributing 60 percent) and larger quantities of each good (the intensive margin). Thus, the increase in varieties seems to be lower than that predicted by the CES theory. In the context of the simple Armington model, Ossa (2015) argues that the size gains from trade depend on the imports in crucial industries. While imports in the average industry do not matter too much, imports in some industries are critical to the functioning of the economy, so that a complete shutdown of international trade is very costly overall.

- **International trade increases overall efficiency but comes with risks.** Trade allows firms and countries to share the fixed costs. However, concentrating production in only a few countries requires international cooperation and reliable trade institutions. If, for example, a crucial medicine is only produced in a handful of countries, all others must be comfortable with relying on these countries. To some extent, there is a trade-off between efficiency and resilience in this case. The 2020 COVID-19 crisis elevated the importance of such concerns. In terms of the model discussed, such uncertainties would translate into higher trade costs.
- **There is a home-market effect.** Economies of scale imply that a large home market is instrumental to becoming an exporter in a particular good. For given wages, firms have an incentive to settle in the market where they face a larger domestic demand to save trade costs. Thus, Krugman provides an important reasoning for why demand factors play an important role for trade flows as well.
- **The Krugman model allows for factor movements.** As in the models we discussed in the previous chapters, the Krugman model may also be extended to study the impact of factor movements. The same gains that arise from allowing two countries to freely trade with each other could be obtained if the population of one country was allowed to migrate (at no cost) to the other. As we have seen, opening up to trade and

population growth are essentially equivalent in this model (or like in the 2x2 model, free international goods trade works as a substitute for free international factor mobility). If we assume any impediments to international trade in goods, there is an incentive for workers to move to the country with the larger labor force. The home-market effect predicts that the larger country has a higher real wage, yielding a prediction for the direction of migration flows. Initial conditions matter in a world (or model) featuring economies of scale. This line of reasoning can be extended and used to explain why we see agglomerations within countries.

- **The Krugman model offers an explanation for agglomeration effects.** Part of the success of Krugman's analysis is the fact that its logic applies to several avenues. Krugman (1991) studied agglomeration dynamics (with core and periphery) in a model of economic geography. When there are two sectors, a standard homogeneous goods sector and an innovative sector with IRS, the larger country or the densely populated region is a net exporter of the differentiated good and will attract even more resources. Another extension is firm productivity. In the basic Krugman model, firms within a country are perfectly symmetric: equal productivity, size, and export behavior. New firm data show, however, that exporters are very different from nonexporters. To capture these important facts about firm characteristics, we will expand this framework and introduce heterogeneous firms in the next chapter.

7.6 Exercises

The following exercises allow students to practice and deepen their understanding of the Krugman model.

Exercise 1 Consider a basic CES utility function like

$$U = (x_1^{1/2} + x_2^{1/2})^2$$

Show that the elasticity of substitution is constant and that CES preferences are homothetic. Discuss how realistic this mathematically convenient assumption is.

Exercise 2 Solve for the wage rates in the Krugman model with CES preferences. For simplicity, assume that there are only two countries with *ad valorem* trade costs $\tau > 1$.

Exercise 3 Consider a Krugman model of monopolistic competition with two goods. Suppose the CES utility function of consumers is given by

$$U(c_1, c_2) = \left[c_1^{\frac{\sigma-1}{\sigma}} + c_2^{\frac{\sigma-1}{\sigma}}\right]^{\frac{\sigma}{\sigma-1}}$$

We further impose $0 < (\sigma - 1)/\sigma < 1$. Consumers have an income of w and face a budget constraint given by $p_1c_1 + p_2c_2 \leq w$.

(a) Find an expression for the relative demand c_1/c_2 as a function of product prices.

(b) The elasticity of substitution is defined as $d \ln(c_1/c_2)/d \ln(p_2/p_1)$. What is the value of the elasticity of substitution for the utility function given in this exercise.

(c) Show that the demand for c_1 is given by

$$c_1 = \left(\frac{p_1}{P}\right)^{-\sigma} \cdot \frac{w}{P}$$

where $P = (p_1^{1-\sigma} + p_2^{1-\sigma})^{1/(1-\sigma)}$. Provide an intuition how p_1 and p_2 affect the optimal price index P.

Exercise 4 The production function of a monopolistically competitive firm in the Krugman model of trade reads $y(j) = a(-F + L(j))$ and is the same for all firms. The full-employment condition reads $L = N(y(j)/a + F)$ where L is total labor force and N represents the number of products. The wage rate is the numéraire. Preferences are CES, $u = \int_0^\infty v(c(j))\, dj$ where $v(c(j)) = c(j)^{\frac{\sigma-1}{\sigma}}$, and $\sigma > 1$.

(a) Show algebraically that the optimal price and quantity of a monopolist are given by

$$p(j) = \frac{\sigma}{\sigma - 1}\frac{1}{a}$$

$$y(j) = (\sigma - 1)aF$$

(b) Solve for N in autarky. How does it depend on σ and why?

(c) Assume now that the country opens up to trade with $M - 1$ countries of identical size and technology. There are no transportation costs. Use the zero profit condition to show that domestic sales per consumer are given by $c(j) = (\sigma-1)aF/M$ and total production per firm does not depend on M.

(d) Show that welfare rises when the number of countries M increases.

Exercise 5 Consider the Krugman (1980) model with monopolistic competition. Each firm requires the following labor input to produce output y_z:

$$L_z = \alpha + \frac{y_z}{\varphi}$$

Consumers have CES preferences Q, defined by equation (7.15), resulting in a demand function for good z defined by equation (7.16).

(a) Consider a closed economy first. Suppose that L households are living in the country. Let the wage be the numéraire ($w = 1$). Set up the profit maximization problem of a firm and show that it sets:

$$p = \frac{1}{\varphi}\frac{\sigma}{\sigma - 1}$$

(b) Let there be free entry. What does this imply for firm profits in equilibrium?

(c) Show that sales per firm are given by:

$$y = \alpha\varphi(\sigma - 1)$$

(d) The full employment condition reads:

$$L = NL_z = N\left[\alpha + \frac{y_z}{\varphi}\right]$$

Solve for the number of products N in autarky. How does this depend on σ and why?

(e) Suppose now that the country opens up to free trade with $M - 1$ identical countries. Show that, once again, welfare rises if the total number of countries M rises. Give a short intuitive explanation.

8
The Melitz Model

8.1 Idea and Background

The Krugman model identified a new source of gains from trade based on increasing returns to scale. International trade allows firms to expand their market size, thereby reducing their average cost of production. This rise in scale means that some domestic firms are forced to exit the market after trade liberalization; as discussed in Chapter 7, the number of domestic varieties falls. However, all firms are essentially homogeneous in productivity and the customer value of the variety that they produce. Therefore, it is indeterminate *which* firms leave the market. To explore this aspect, we need to introduce firm heterogeneity. The empirical evidence below shows that firms differ substantially in their productivity, and that exporting firms are different from non-exporters. This will introduce a new source of gains from trade: Because less-productive firms will exit the market, opening up to trade leads to reallocation of resources from less-productive to more-productive companies.

Firms within narrowly defined industries largely differ in terms of sales, employment, and productivity. Only a fraction of firms engages in exporting. This is true even for so-called export sectors. In the United States, in the year 2000, only 4 percent of all firms exported, and out of these, the top 10 percent accounted for 96 percent of total exports (Bernard et al., 2007). Table 8.1—which is taken from their paper—provides estimates from ordinary least squares regressions. The dependent variables are a firm's employment, shipments, value added per worker, and the other variables noted in the first column, all expressed in logs. The explanatory variable is a dummy variable indicating whether the firm is involved in exporting.

With the dependent variable expressed in logarithms, the coefficients can be interpreted as percentages. Hence, exporting firms have 119 percent more employment than their domestically bound counterparts. They also have 148 percent higher shipments values, 26 percent higher value added per worker, and so on. As the third column shows, these exporter premia hold

Understanding International Trade. Reto Foellmi and Stefan Legge, Oxford University Press.
 DOI: 10.1093/9780197821107.003.0009

Table 8.1 Exporter Premia in US Manufacturing, 2002

	Exporter Premia		
	(1)	(2)	(3)
Log employment	1.19	0.97	
Log shipments	1.48	1.08	0.08
Log value added per worker	0.26	0.11	0.10
Log TFP [total factor productivity]	0.02	0.03	0.05
Log wage	0.17	0.06	0.06
Log capital per worker	0.32	0.12	0.04
Log skill per worker	0.19	0.11	0.19
Additional covariates	None	Industry FE [fixed effects]	Industry FE, log employment

even when we compare firms within industries. Furthermore, they are not simply a size effect: The last column controls for employment and still documents that exporting firms are more productive and pay higher wages. Because export participation varies across industries and larger firms are more likely to export, the estimates in the last column are smaller. The observations from Table 8.1 give rise to the idea that firms participating in international trade systematically differ from those that only operate domestically.

There is further evidence on the selection effect: Trade liberalizations cause a reallocation of resources from less-productive to more-productive producers. Melitz and Redding (2014) summarize the empirical literature. Trefler (2004) finds that more-productive firms expanded following the Canada–US Free Trade Agreement. Canadian exporters even expanded their domestic activities at the cost of Canadian non-exporters. The productivity gains are substantial. The industries that have been most affected by tax cuts experienced an increase in labor productivity of up to 15 percent. Pavcnik (2002) documents that about two-thirds of the overall productivity increase after the Chilean trade liberalization is due to reallocation. These quantitative findings underline the importance of this source of gains from trade.

In the Krugman model, we saw how increasing returns and love of variety can motivate intra-industry trade and give rise to gains from trade via increasing consumption varieties (and potentially a pro-competitive effect). In that model, all firms in a given country were *homogeneous*, and trade-induced exit was random. This chapter introduces *heterogeneous* firms with the following key characteristics.

- More-productive firms earn larger profits.
- With fixed costs, only the most profitable (i.e., productive) firms export—which is consistent with the empirical evidence mentioned earlier.
- Opening up to trade implies a resource reallocation to productive firms (selection effect).

The basic idea of the model developed by Marc Melitz (2003) runs as follows. Before making an irreversible investment to enter an industry, firms face uncertainty concerning their productivity. Staying in business entails fixed operating costs (rental costs of offices, wages of personnel) that do not depend on the scale of production. Due to these costs, only firms with a high enough productivity operate profitably. Lower-productivity firms operate at a loss and exit the market. Hence, the model features a productivity cutoff such that only firms above that level continue their operation. These firms then choose whether to export. However, because exporting entails another fixed cost, only the most productive companies will find it profitable to do so. It follows that there is a second productivity cutoff, separating firms that only sell domestically from those that also engage in exporting. Ultimately, not all new firms stay in the market, and among those that do, the more-productive firms export, while the less-productive ones serve only the domestic market. This categorization of companies replicates the basic patterns we observe in the data where exporting firms are larger and more productive than non-exporting firms.

The model not only explains why certain firms participate in international trade while others do not but also identifies a new source of welfare gains from trade liberalization. The exit of the least-productive firms frees up productive resources that are employed by the most-productive firms, which gain due to additional export sales. Consequently, trade openness leads to a reallocation and an increase in an industry's average productivity. It can also increase wage inequality if there is positive assortative matching between worker skill and firm technology generating an employer-size wage premium and an exporter wage premium. A full examination of this result is provided by Sampson (2014), while Elhanan Helpman's 2008 book *Globalization and Inequality* discusses more broadly the role of globalization on rising inequality.

8.2 Model Setup

When Melitz developed his model, he drew heavily from two pieces of literature: Krugman's model of trade under monopolistic competition and increasing returns to scale and Hugo Hopenhayn's (1992a, 1992b) studies on the endogenous selection of heterogeneous firms in an industry. For the presentation here, we consider two identical countries. However, the model could be easily extended to n identical countries. We also restrict ourselves to a static model, whereas Melitz's original model is a dynamic one with continuous entry and exit of firms. The core framework is identical to the Krugman model: We assume that firms have access to an increasing returns to scale production technology using labor as the only input. The market is characterized by monopolistic competition, with entrepreneurs being free to enter the market.

The key new assumption is firm heterogeneity in productivity φ. In the model below, this takes the form of cost differences. However, we could interpret this and the differences in consumer valuations of the good they produce. Initially, entrepreneurs have to pay a fixed entry cost f_e (in terms of labor) to explore their business idea and to learn the viability of it. This fixed cost could be interpreted as capturing the setup of a firm and the associated (research and development (R&D)) costs to explore the business idea. Formally, after paying f_e, there is random draw of marginal productivity of labor φ from the distribution $G(\varphi)$. Figure 8.1. shows both the cumulative distribution function (CDF), $G(\varphi)$, as well as the probability density function (PDF), $g(\varphi)$. The cutoffs for exit, domestic production, and export will be derived and explained later in the chapter.

The idea that firms initially decide to enter the market without knowing their productivity can be justified by industry studies that document new entrants having lower average productivity and higher exit rates than incumbent firms. After learning their productivity, entrepreneurs decide whether to start producing. This requires additional fixed costs of f_d (e.g., to set up the production with plant facilities). Entrepreneurs will choose to do so if their productivity draw exceeds a cutoff productivity φ_d (where d stands for domestic). In addition, they may start producing and not only serve the domestic market but also export their output. This only happens if their productivity exceeds φ_x (with x for export) because there is a fixed cost of exporting f_x. The latter may consist of costs to set up a distribution channel in

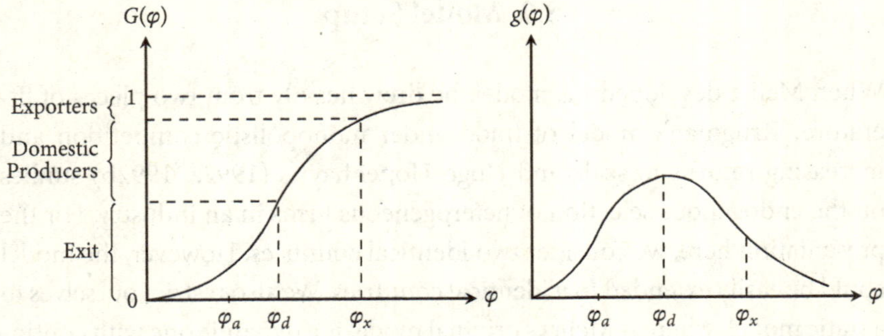

Figure 8.1 Illustrations of $G(\varphi)$ and $g(\varphi)$

the destination market, costs to adopt the foreign regulation, and marketing expenses. Finally, we assume *ad valorem* iceberg trade costs τ.

Since we add a fixed cost for foreign market entry to the *ad valorem* trade costs, it is interesting to have an idea of their magnitude. It is, however, difficult to provide a universal estimate of how large foreign entry costs are. This depends on the size and the "closeness" (e.g., language, judicial system) of the foreign market. Das, Roberts, and Tybout (2007) estimate them to be in the order of magnitude of about $400,000 on average.

Thus, while the Krugman model featured only one fixed cost, now there are three types of fixed costs: fixed entry costs f_e, fixed costs of domestic production f_d, and fixed costs of exporting f_x. Why do we introduce fixed costs of serving both the domestic and foreign market? This guarantees that only firms with sufficiently high productivity are able to make positive profits; all others exit immediately. Furthermore, there will be selection into exporting: Only firms with even higher productivity will export. Figure 8.2 summarizes the relationship graphically.

We solve the model using backward induction. As Figure 8.2 shows, markets clear at the last stage. Hence, we first determine demand and calculate profits.

Demand and Production

There is a continuum of goods indexed by ω (pronounced omega). Individuals derive utility from consuming quantities $q(\omega)$ of these goods. Their utility

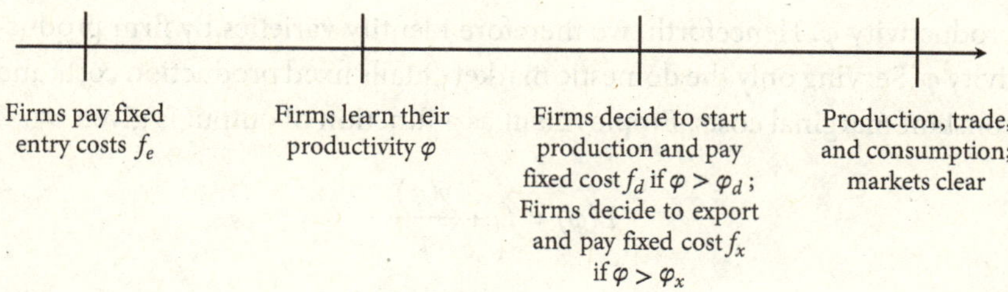

Figure 8.2 Timeline in the Melitz Model

function takes the constant elasticity of substition (CES) form, with the CES given by σ:

$$U = \left(\int_0^\infty q(\omega)^{(\sigma-1)/\sigma} d\omega \right)^{\sigma/(\sigma-1)} \quad \text{with} \quad \sigma > 1$$

Note that all goods are substitutes, but due to the functional form, every individual will consume each good—perhaps in tiny amounts and at high prices. Choosing optimal consumption, individuals face the budget constraint

$$\int_0^\infty p(\omega) q(\omega) d\omega \leq I$$

where I is the income derived from wages and dividends, arising from profits. Following Dixit and Stiglitz (1977), consumer behavior can be modeled by considering the set of varieties consumed as an aggregate good $Q \equiv U$ associated with an aggregate price P. As this chapter's appendix shows, the resulting demand for a given product ω is iso-elastic with demand elasticity σ

$$q(\omega) = \left(\frac{p(\omega)}{P} \right)^{-\sigma} Q \tag{8.1}$$

where quantity index Q equals $\left[\int_0^\infty q(\omega)^{\frac{\sigma-1}{\sigma}} d\omega \right]^{\frac{\sigma}{\sigma-1}}$ and $P = \left[\int_0^\infty p(\omega)^{1-\sigma} d\omega \right]^{\frac{1}{1-\sigma}}$ is the ideal price index. Note that total spending X (= total income I) equals PQ.

We assume there are no economies of scope, so there is no reason for a firm to produce multiple varieties. Hence, all firms specialize in distinct varieties such that there is a direct mapping of a firm's variety ω and its productivity φ. Henceforth, we therefore identify varieties by firm productivity φ. Serving only the domestic market entails fixed production costs and constant marginal costs. Employment as a function of output is given by

$$L(\varphi) = f_d + \frac{y(\varphi)}{\varphi}$$

which states that all labor employed by a firm (with productivity φ) is used to pay the fixed costs and the variable costs for producing output $y(\varphi)$. Note that a higher productivity is simply modeled as being able to produce a symmetric variety at lower marginal costs. Firms maximize their profits $\pi(\varphi) = p(\varphi)y(\varphi) - f_d - wy(\varphi)/\varphi$ by choosing the optimal price. Noting that y depends on p, we get the first-order condition: $p = w/\varphi - y/(\partial y/\partial p)$. Regardless of its productivity, each firm faces a residual demand curve with constant elasticity σ. To get $\partial y/\partial p$, we take the Marshallian demand function (8.1) and recognize that a firm's choice of p does not affect the price index P because we assume a large number of varieties. Thus, $y/(\partial y/\partial p) = -p/\sigma$. With CES demand, the monopolistic firms charge a constant markup over marginal cost

$$p(\varphi) = \frac{\sigma}{\sigma - 1} \frac{w}{\varphi}. \tag{8.2}$$

where w is the common wage that we take as numéraire and set it to 1 in what follows.

Profits

What is the profit that firms earn from serving the domestic market? They are given by revenue minus costs or, formally, $p(\varphi)y(\varphi) - L(\varphi) = \frac{1}{\sigma-1}\frac{1}{\varphi}q(\varphi) - f_d$, where we use $y(\varphi) = q(\varphi)$ (one firm serves the whole market) and equation (8.2) for the price. We determine production per firm as

$$\begin{aligned} q(\varphi) &= \left(\frac{\sigma}{\sigma - 1}\frac{1}{\varphi}\right)^{-\sigma} P^{\sigma} Q \\ &= \left(\frac{\sigma}{\sigma - 1}\right)^{-\sigma} \varphi^{\sigma} P^{\sigma-1} X \end{aligned}$$

where we use $X = PQ$ in the latter equation.

A more-productive firm (i.e., the one with a higher φ) has larger output, higher revenues, charges a lower price, and earns a higher profit than a less-productive firm. With CES demand, firms may be compared depending on their productivity ratio. The iso-elastic demand implies that a relative increase in the price leads to the same relative decrease in demand. In particular, it does not depend on the initial level of demand. Because the price is a constant markup on marginal cost, see equation (8.2), the ratios of any two firms' outputs $q(\varphi)$ and revenues $r(\varphi)$ depend on the ratio of their productivity levels.

$$\frac{q(\varphi_1)}{q(\varphi_2)} = \left(\frac{\varphi_1}{\varphi_2}\right)^{\sigma} \quad \text{and} \quad \frac{r(\varphi_1)}{r(\varphi_2)} = \left(\frac{\varphi_1}{\varphi_2}\right)^{\sigma-1}$$

Domestic profits read as follows

$$\pi_a(\varphi) = \underbrace{\left[\frac{X}{\sigma}\left(\frac{\sigma}{\sigma-1}\frac{1}{P}\right)^{1-\sigma}\right]}_{B_a}\varphi^{\sigma-1} - f_d \tag{8.3}$$

Note that for convenience in later expressions, we define the term in brackets of equation (8.3) as B_a. Firms will operate only if they can make non-negative profits, $\varphi \geq \varphi_a$. We determine the productivity threshold φ_a by calculating the zero cutoff profit (ZCP)—the point at which a firm can break even by serving the domestic market:

$$\pi_a(\varphi_a) = B_a\varphi_a^{\sigma-1} - f_d \stackrel{!}{=} 0 \tag{8.4, ZCP}$$

$$\Longleftrightarrow \quad \varphi_a^{\sigma-1} = f_d\frac{\sigma}{X}\left(\frac{\sigma}{\sigma-1}\frac{1}{P}\right)^{\sigma-1} \tag{8.5}$$

Observe from equation (8.3) that variable profits are linear in $\varphi^{\sigma-1}$, with a slope of B_a. Figure 8.3 shows this relationship graphically with more-productive firms making larger profits.

We also see in Figure 8.3 that firms that draw a productivity of zero (and enter the domestic market) have a loss equal to the fixed costs of entering the domestic market (f_d). Obviously, a firm only chooses to pay the fixed costs if it can at least break even. A firm with productivity φ_a makes zero profits.

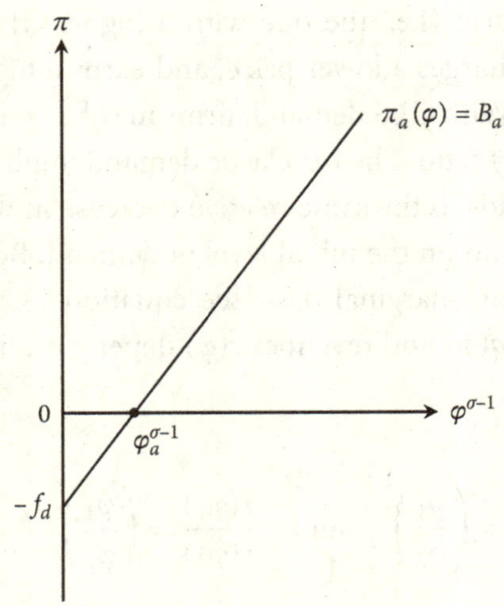

Figure 8.3: Profits and Productivity

Using this, we can simplify equation (8.3) as follows:

$$\pi_a(\varphi) = \begin{cases} \left[\left(\frac{\varphi}{\varphi_a}\right)^{\sigma-1} - 1\right] f_d & \text{if } \varphi \geq \varphi_a \\ 0 & \text{otherwise} \end{cases} \tag{8.6}$$

General equilibrium effects enter firm profits only via φ_a, which largely simplifies the analysis. We proceed by solving for this productivity threshold φ_a in terms of exogenous variables. Since all incumbent firms—except for the cutoff firm—earn positive profits, the average profit level $\bar{\pi}$ is positive. It is the expectation of future positive profits that motivates firms to consider paying the investment cost f_e, which is required for entry. If this value were negative, no firm would want to enter. At the same time, in any equilibrium where entry is unrestricted, this value cannot be positive since the mass of prospective entrants would be unbounded. Therefore, the *unconditional* expectation of profits must be equal to the entry costs f_e in equilibrium, such that potential entrepreneurs make zero profits *ex ante* (but some make positive profits *ex post*). Formally,

$$\int_0^\infty \pi_a(\varphi) g(\varphi)\, d\varphi \stackrel{!}{=} f_e \tag{8.7}$$

where $g(\varphi)$ is the density function of $G(\varphi)$, the distribution of labor productivity. It turns out to be convenient to express this in terms of the expected profits of operating firms $\bar{\pi}$—that is, the expected profits *conditional* on surviving

$$\bar{\pi}(\varphi_a) := \int_{\varphi_a}^{\infty} \pi_a(\varphi) \frac{g(\varphi)}{1 - G(\varphi_a)} \, d\varphi = \frac{f_e}{1 - G(\varphi_a)} \tag{8.8}$$

Combining equations (8.6) and (8.7) yields

$$\underbrace{\int_{\varphi_a}^{\infty} \left[\left(\frac{\varphi}{\varphi_a} \right)^{\sigma-1} - 1 \right] g(\varphi) \, d\varphi}_{J(\varphi_a)} = \frac{f_e}{f_d} \tag{8.9}$$

where we label the left side with $J(\varphi_a)$. Note that $J(\varphi_a)$ is monotonically decreasing and satisfies

$$\lim_{\varphi_a \to 0} J(\varphi_a) = \infty \qquad \text{as well as} \qquad \lim_{\varphi_a \to \infty} J(\varphi_a) = 0$$

Hence, equation (8.7) uniquely identifies an equilibrium cutoff φ_a. In turn, φ_a allows us to solve for the "demand-shifter" $B_a = \varphi_a^{1-\sigma} f_d$, which pins down the distribution of firm characteristics concerning prices, sales, and profits. The cutoff productivity φ_a depends negatively on the ratio of fixed costs f_e/f_d. While the entry fixed costs f_e accrue for sure, a relative increase in entry fixed costs must raise the probability that the business idea is successful and production takes place. Put differently, high entry fixed costs imply that, in equilibrium, the share of unsuccessful entrepreneurial bids must be lower, because they are more expensive.

Mass of Firms

All that is left is to solve is the mass of entering (M_e) and active (M_a) firms. The latter shows up in the price index P and therefore in B_a. The relationship between M_e and M_a is straightforward. Recall that firms with a productivity draw $\varphi < \varphi_a$ exit the market. Hence, M_a is simply the number of entering firms times the success probability. We get

$$M_a = M_e \left[1 - G(\varphi_a) \right] \tag{8.10}$$

Workers are employed in the production and the "business exploration" business, the latter causing the fixed entry costs f_e. The labor market clearing condition reads

$$L = M_a \left[\int_{\varphi_a}^{\infty} \frac{y(\varphi)}{\varphi} \frac{g(\varphi)}{1 - G(\varphi_a)} d\varphi + f_d \right] + M_e f_e$$

$$\overset{(8.9)}{=} M_a \left[\int_{\varphi_a}^{\infty} \frac{y(\varphi)}{\varphi} \frac{g(\varphi)}{1 - G(\varphi_a)} d\varphi + f_d + \frac{f_e}{1 - G(\varphi_a)} \right] \tag{8.11}$$

where $\frac{g(\varphi)}{1-G(\varphi_a)}$ is the density of productivity of *active* firms. Recall that firms charge a constant markup over (constant) marginal cost. This implies that *variable* profits $\pi_a(\varphi) + f_d$ are a constant fraction of revenues:

$$\pi_a(\varphi) + f_d \overset{(8.2)}{=} p(\varphi)y(\varphi) \left[1 - \frac{\sigma - 1}{\sigma} \right] = \frac{p(\varphi)y(\varphi)}{\sigma}$$

Use (8.2) and $w = 1$ as numéraire to insert for the price $p(\varphi) = \frac{\sigma}{\sigma-1} \frac{1}{\varphi}$. Using this, we have

$$\frac{p(\varphi)y(\varphi)}{\sigma} = \frac{y(\varphi)}{(\sigma - 1)\varphi}$$

We then get

$$\frac{y(\varphi)}{\varphi} = (\sigma - 1) \left[\pi_a(\varphi) + f_d \right] \tag{8.12}$$

Insert (8.12) into (8.11), use equation (8.8) to replace the integral and the last term with $\bar{\pi}(\varphi_a)$, and recall further that $\int_{\varphi_a}^{\infty} \frac{g(\varphi)}{1-G(\varphi_a)} d\varphi = 1$. Thus, we obtain

$$L = M_a \sigma \left[\bar{\pi}(\varphi_a) + f_d \right]$$

We solve for the mass of active firms M_a as

$$M_a = \frac{L}{\sigma \left[\bar{\pi}(\varphi_a) + f_d \right]} = \frac{L}{\sigma \left[\frac{f_e}{1-G(\varphi_a)} + f_d \right]} \tag{8.13}$$

Intuitively, the mass of firms is proportional to the size of the economy L. As in the Krugman model, higher fixed costs and lower profit margins (higher σ) lower the number of firms (recall that the cutoff probability φ_a depends only on the ratio of fixed costs). With higher fixed costs or lower profit margins, the average firm needs to produce more to break even. Consequently, the number of firms is lower in the aggregate.

Graphical Representation of the Autarky Equilibrium

Equation (8.4) above defines a (at least around the equilibrium) negative relationship between the cutoff productivity φ_a and the *ex ante* expected profits conditional on surviving $\bar{\pi}$ (note that $\sigma > 1$). With CES preferences, firms' sales and thus variable profits are proportional to $\varphi^{\sigma-1}$. A firm with cutoff productivity φ_a makes zero profit. For many commonly used distribution functions, profits conditional on φ_a are lower the higher the cutoff. The intuition is not easy to grasp. It follows from CES preferences and the fact that the distribution cannot have too big tails. However, if the distribution function is Pareto (a distribution function with big right tails), the ZCP curve is horizontal (starting at a minimum level of productivity φ) with CES preferences, as shown below. Using equation (8.6), the ZCP relationship reads

$$\bar{\pi} = \int_{\varphi_a}^{\infty} \left[\left(\frac{\varphi}{\varphi_a} \right)^{\sigma-1} - 1 \right] f_d \frac{g(\varphi)}{1 - G(\varphi_a)} \, d\varphi$$

Note that for φ_a approaching zero, the ZCP curve goes to infinity since the integral becomes infinitely large. The second equilibrium curve in Figure 8.4 is the free-entry condition of equation (8.7). It gives rise to a positive relationship between φ_a and the *ex ante* expected profits of producing firms $\bar{\pi}$. The higher φ_a, the lower the *ex ante* probability of surviving, $1 - G(\varphi_a)$. —hence, the higher the *ex ante* expected profits conditional on surviving $\bar{\pi}$ need to be for entrants to be able to break even in expectation. Loosely speaking, the higher the bar to be successful, the larger the expected prize must be such that you are willing to enter the game and pay f_e upfront. The FE curve reads as follows:

$$\bar{\pi} = \frac{f_e}{1 - G(\varphi_a)}$$

The intersection of the two latter equations (i.e., the ZCP and the FE curve) uniquely determines the equilibrium. Note that the size of the economy L does not appear. A change in L simply scales up this equilibrium (i.e., the mass of entering and active firms). Intuitively, with CES utility and symmetry, firm revenue is proportional to total spending but inversely proportional to the mass of varieties. We illustrate the unique equilibrium of the Melitz model in Figure 8.4.

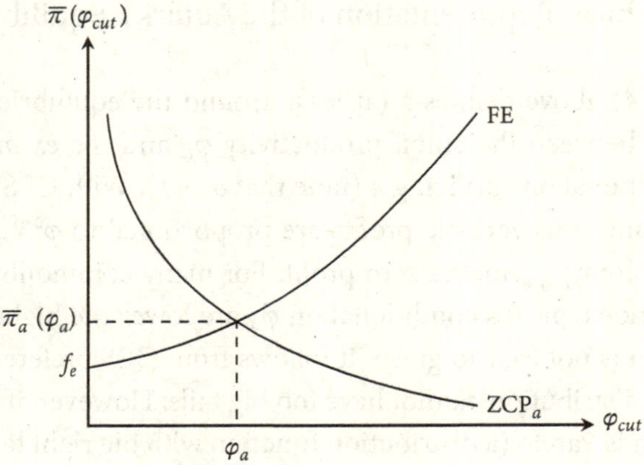

Figure 8.4: Autarky Equilibrium in the Melitz Model

8.3 Pattern of Trade

Having solved the autarky case, we can now turn to the trade equilibrium. For this, we consider two identical countries (it is easy to extend this analysis to n countries, as it is done in the Melitz (2003) paper). As mentioned above, exporting involves iceberg trade costs τ as well as a fixed cost of exporting f_x. Compared to autarky, there are two zero-profit conditions and associated cutoff values for productivity. Firms serve the domestic market (we use d for domestic, previously a for autarky) if their productivity exceeds φ_d, defined by

$$\pi_d(\varphi_d) = B_d\varphi_d^{\sigma-1} - f_d \stackrel{!}{=} 0 \tag{8.14}$$

and therefore

$$\varphi_d^{\sigma-1} = f_d\frac{\sigma}{X_d}\left(\frac{\sigma}{\sigma-1}\frac{1}{P_d}\right)^{\sigma-1} \tag{8.15}$$

Because both countries are identical, aggregate spending and the price index in the export market are the same as in the domestic market. With CES preferences, firms charge the same markup in both markets. With iceberg trade costs, domestic firms offer their goods in the export market at a price $p_x(\varphi) = \tau p_d(\varphi) = \tau\frac{\sigma}{\sigma-1}\frac{1}{\varphi}$.

Firms decide whether to enter the export market. For the most productive firms, this will be profitable. As before, however, a threshold value of productivity separates firms with high enough productivity from others. Using the same logic as in the autarky situation, we get the following cutoff for exporting:

$$\pi_x(\varphi_x) = B_x\varphi_x^{\sigma-1} - f_x \overset{!}{=} 0$$

where $B_x = \frac{X_d}{\sigma}(\frac{\sigma-1}{\sigma}\frac{P_d}{\tau})^{\sigma-1} < B_d$. The productivity cutoff φ_x reads

$$\varphi_x^{\sigma-1} = f_x\frac{\sigma}{X_d}\left(\frac{\sigma}{\sigma-1}\frac{\tau}{P_d}\right)^{\sigma-1} \tag{8.16}$$

Dividing (8.16) by (8.15), we get the following:

$$\left(\frac{\varphi_x}{\varphi_d}\right)^{\sigma-1} = \frac{f_x}{f_d}\tau^{\sigma-1} \tag{8.17}$$

Hence, whenever $f_x\tau^{\sigma-1} > f_d$ holds, only the most productive firms will export and there will be selection into exporting, in line with what we observe in real-world data. Figure 8.5 shows the profits from domestic and exporting businesses.[1] The π_x line has a slope B_x, which is smaller than B_d, the slope of the π_d schedule. The marginal costs of exporting are higher because of trade costs. This renders the export profit line flatter.

Expected unconditional profits must be equal to the fixed entry costs f_e:

$$\int_0^\infty [\pi_d(\varphi) + \pi_x(\varphi)]\, g(\varphi)\, d\varphi \overset{!}{=} f_e \tag{8.18}$$

With the function $J(\cdot)$ defined as in equation (8.9), we get the following:

$$J(\varphi_d)f_d + J(\varphi_x)f_x = f_e \tag{8.19}$$

Using equation (8.17) to substitute φ_d for φ_x uniquely determines the cutoff productivities. Due to the symmetry of countries, the relationship between φ_x and φ_d depends on exogenous variables only:

$$\varphi_x^{\sigma-1} = \frac{f_x\tau^{\sigma-1}}{f_d}\varphi_d^{\sigma-1} \tag{8.20}$$

We observe from equations (8.19) and (8.20) that the threshold productivity for serving the domestic market (not exiting the market, not exporting)

[1] Note that Figure 8.5 is based on Melitz and Redding's 2014 Chapter 1 in the *Handbook of International Economics*, Figure 1.2, while Figure 8.7 builds upon Figure 1.3 from Melitz and Redding.

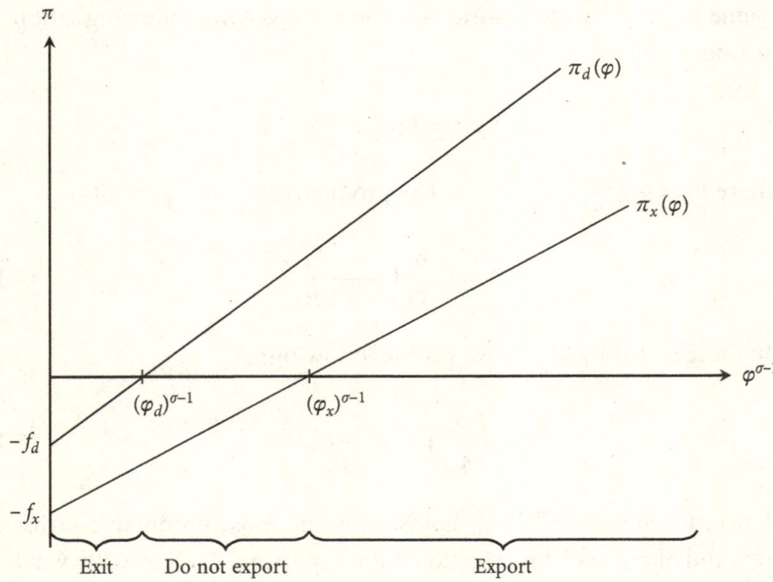

Figure 8.5: Firm Decision by Productivity

is higher than the threshold under autarky we determined before: $\varphi_d > \varphi_a$. Formally, this is because $J(\cdot)$ is monotonically decreasing. However, to understand this result more intuitively, it makes sense to consider the diagram with the FE- and the ZCP curve as in autarky. To determine the ZCP curve, we need an expression for profits from domestic and foreign business. They can be rewritten as a function of the cutoff using the same reasoning as in equation (8.6). Note that equation (8.20) implies

$$\pi_x(\varphi) = \left[\left(\frac{\varphi}{\varphi_x}\right)^{\sigma-1} - 1\right] f_x = \left[\left(\tau\frac{\varphi}{\varphi_d}\right)^{\sigma-1} \frac{f_d}{f_x} - 1\right] f_x$$

We get the following:

$$\pi_d(\varphi) = \max\left\{\left[\left(\frac{\varphi}{\varphi_d}\right)^{\sigma-1} - 1\right] f_d, 0\right\} \tag{8.21}$$

$$\pi_x(\varphi) = \max\left\{\left[\left(\tau\frac{\varphi}{\varphi_d}\right)^{\sigma-1} \frac{f_d}{f_x} - 1\right] f_x, 0\right\} \tag{8.22}$$

Profits are non-negative, since producers choose not to produce for the home or foreign market, respectively, when their productivity draws are too small. While the first summand, domestic profits, is the same as in autarky, there is a second summand, potential profits from exporting. Being successful at home, the firm may enter the exporting business, which occurs with probability

$$\Pr\left[\varphi \geq \varphi_x \,|\, \varphi \geq \varphi_d\right] = \frac{1 - G(\varphi_x)}{1 - G(\varphi_d)}$$

The average profits thus are given by

$$\bar{\pi} = \int_{\varphi_d}^{\infty} \pi_d(\varphi)\frac{g(\varphi)}{1 - G(\varphi_d)}d\varphi + \Pr\left[\varphi \geq \varphi_x \,|\, \varphi \geq \varphi_d\right]\int_{\varphi_x}^{\infty} \pi_x(\varphi)\frac{g(\varphi)}{1 - G(\varphi_x)}d\varphi$$

For a given φ_d, note that $\bar{\pi}(\varphi_d)$ is higher when compared to autarky due to profits from exporting. Hence, the ZCP schedule in Figure 8.6 shifts up. We insert equations (8.21) and (8.22) and get this:

$$\bar{\pi} = \int_{\varphi_d}^{\infty}\left[\left(\frac{\varphi}{\varphi_d}\right)^{\sigma-1} - 1\right]f_d\frac{g(\varphi)}{1 - G(\varphi_d)}\,d\varphi + \int_{\varphi_x}^{\infty}\left[\left(\frac{\varphi}{\varphi_x}\right)^{\sigma-1} - 1\right] f_x\frac{g(\varphi)}{1 - G(\varphi_d)}\,d\varphi$$

where $\varphi_x^{\sigma-1} = \dfrac{f_x\tau^{\sigma-1}}{f_d}\varphi_d^{\sigma-1}$

The free-entry relation remains unchanged. Equation (8.18) gives rise to the exact same relationship between φ_d and the expected profits conditional on surviving as under autarky (but, of course, with a different expression for these expected profits):

$$\bar{\pi} = \frac{f_e}{1 - G(\varphi_d)}$$

Finally, the mass of entering and active firms can be determined in a similar way as in the autarky equilibrium. The mass of firms that are active in the domestic market, M_d, is given by $M_d = M_e\left[1 - G(\varphi_d)\right]$, where M_e denotes the mass of entering firms. The mass of exporting firms is then simply $M_x = M_e\left[1 - G(\varphi_x)\right]$.

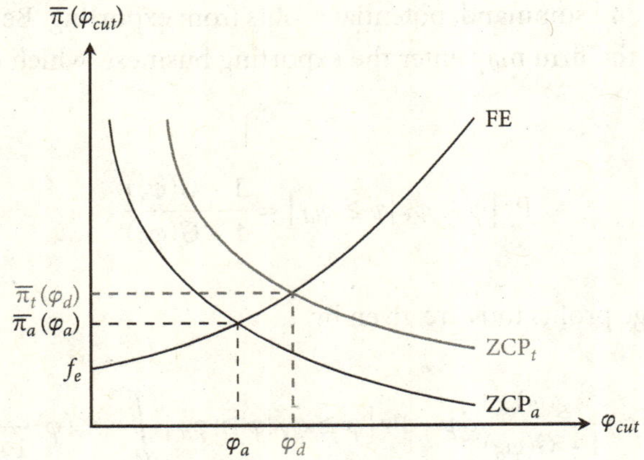

Figure 8.6: Impact of Trade in the Melitz Model

The resource constraint allows us to determine the mass of active firms (exercise 8.1 asks you to calculate it, using similar steps as in autarky).

$$L = M_d \sigma \left[\bar{\pi}(\varphi_d) + f_d \right] + M_x \sigma f_x$$

We get the following:

$$M_d = \frac{L}{\sigma \left[\frac{f_e}{1-G(\varphi_d)} + f_d + f_x \frac{1-G(\varphi_d)}{1-G(\varphi_x)} \right]} \tag{8.23}$$

The expression differs from the corresponding number of firms in autarky, see equation 8.13, only in the f_x term. The subset of exporters needs additional resources to cover the fixed costs of serving the foreign market. Comparing equations 8.13 and 8.23, we see directly that domestic variety M_d must be lower with trade compared to autarky.

We sum up the results. With selection into exporting, we have this:

$$\varphi_a < \varphi_d < \varphi_x$$

When opening up to trade, the most productive firms ($\varphi \geq \varphi_x$) are exporting, intermediate firms ($\varphi_d \leq \varphi < \varphi_x$) serve only the domestic market, while the least productive previously active firms exit the market altogether ($\varphi_a \leq \varphi < \varphi_d$).

Note that in this model, the least productive firms exit because of increased competition from highly productive domestic firms in the labor market and not because of increased competition from foreign firms in the domestic goods market. Observe from equation (8.19) that with no domestic firm exporting, we would have the same cutoff productivity as under autarky, irrespective of the import competition. Figure 8.7 shows the corresponding profits. Profits fall for low- and intermediate-productivity firms, and they rise for the group of exporters with very high productivity. Thus, international trade increases inequality in profits.

Intuitively, international trade implies that high-productive firms have the option to export. In equilibrium, expected profits $\bar{\pi}$ when successful are higher, and hence the threshold φ_d to start production will be larger. The high-productive companies grow disproportionately, driving up real wages, making it more difficult for middle-productive entrepreneurs to break even. To see that real wages rise, note that nominal labor income (labor is the only production factor, wage is the numéraire) stays constant and equals $L = X_d = X$. From equations (8.5) and (8.15), as well as $\varphi_d > \varphi_a$, it follows that the price index must decrease with trade $P_d < P_a$. Therefore, the real wage $1/P_d$ rises.

Figure 8.7 summarizes the findings and illustrates both the autarky and the free trade situation. In dotted lines, we show the profits under autarky: Firms with a productivity draw below φ_a decide not to start production and earn a zero profit. Every firm with a higher productivity serves the domestic market and earns a profit that increases with its productivity. With solid grey lines, the figure illustrates profits in the case of free trade. Firms with $\varphi_a < \varphi < \varphi_d$ stayed in the market under autarky but leave when the economy opens up to trade. Every firm with a productivity between φ_d and φ_x serves only the domestic market and those with productivity exceeding φ_x export. Notice that firms with the highest productivity gain market share, whereas others (including those that continue to serve the domestic market) lose market share.

Trade impacts welfare through various channels in the Melitz model. There are additional imported varieties but—as in the Krugman model with VES preferences—reduced domestic varieties. While the Krugman model with variable elasticity of substitution (VES) preferences (with CES preferences, there is no exit in the Krugman model) did not make any prediction about which domestic varieties would exit the market, in the Melitz model the least productive firms will exit because $\varphi_d > \varphi_a$. Hence, the cost of

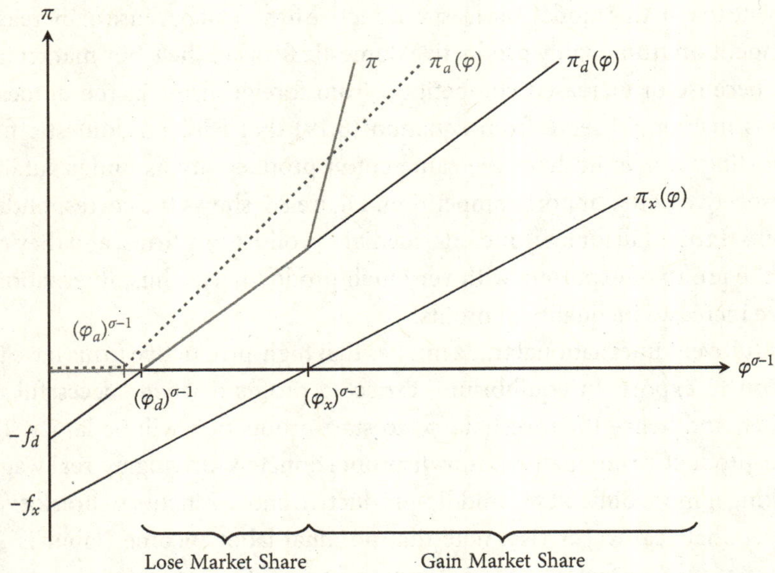

Figure 8.7 Impact on Market Shares

reduced domestic varieties is smaller. In contrast to the Krugman model, a selection effect has a positive impact on welfare: The least productive firms exit, while the most productive firms start exporting and expand their size. This structural shift in employment causes average productivity to increase. Aggregate welfare must increase since real wages rise, as shown above. The Melitz model predicts that trade liberalization increases the number of goods traded. Empirical evidence by Kehoe and Ruhl (2013) and previous studies by Evenett and Venables (2002) and Hummels and Klenow (2005) confirm that the extensive margin is an important factor in trade growth.

Welfare Gains in the Melitz Model with a Pareto Distribution

The analysis above documented clearly the intuition behind the selection effect of international trade. Similar to the Krugman and Eaton–Kortum frameworks discussed in the previous chapters, we need to make more assumptions to derive quantitative predictions on trade flows and welfare when analyzing trade with many countries. For this aim, Chaney (2008) assumed a Pareto distribution for firm-level productivities with constant parameters θ and b :

$$G(\varphi) = 1 - \left(\frac{\varphi}{b}\right)^{-\theta}, \quad \varphi \geq b, \quad \theta > \sigma - 1 > 0.$$

The nice feature of Pareto distributions is that the conditional (i.e., left-truncated) Pareto distribution is again Pareto, and expected values of power functions are easy to derive. Economically, the upper tail of many distributions is Pareto. For instance, a Pareto distribution provides a good approximation for the (upper tail) of the income or the firm size distribution. Moreover, it can be microfounded based on a theory of firm entry and exit (Arkolakis, 2016). Put simply, the right-skewed Pareto distribution helps explaining why only a few firms are productive enough to export, and why most exports are provided by only a small share of exporters, which is in line with the empirical facts. The Pareto assumption allows for a closed form of many expressions of the Melitz model and facilitates the analysis of trade among many heterogeneous countries. For instance, the ZCP condition under trade becomes

$$\bar{\pi} = \int_{\varphi_d}^{\infty} \left[\left(\frac{\varphi}{\varphi_d}\right)^{\sigma-1} - 1\right] f_d \theta \varphi_d^{\theta} \varphi^{-\theta-1} d\varphi + \int_{\varphi_x}^{\infty} \left[\left(\frac{\varphi}{\varphi_x}\right)^{\sigma-1} - 1\right]$$
$$f_x \theta \varphi_d^{\theta} \varphi^{-\theta-1} d\varphi$$

where $\varphi_x^{\sigma-1} = \dfrac{f_x \tau^{\sigma-1}}{f_d} \varphi_d^{\sigma-1}$

Calculating the value of the integrals is straightforward, the derivations are in appendix 8.2 of this chapter. We get a horizontal ZCP curve:

$$\bar{\pi} = \frac{\sigma - 1}{1 + \theta - \sigma} b^{-\theta} \left(f_d + f_x \left(\frac{f_d}{f_x}\right)^{\frac{\theta}{\sigma-1}} \tau^{-\theta} \right)$$

The FE curve implies

$$\bar{\pi} = f_e b^{-\theta} \varphi_d^{\theta}$$

Taking the expressions together, we get explicit solutions for the cutoff productivities. Chaney (2008) shows in a multi-country model with heterogeneous trade and fixed costs that bilateral trade flows from country i to j and therefore welfare gains may be calculated explicitly.

Are there gains from increased variety? The number of product varieties available to consumers changes after trade liberalization in two ways: (i) There is an increase in import varieties, (ii) but also a decrease in domestic varieties (due to market exit). The net effect is unclear, but welfare unambiguously rises because of the selection effect. Arkolakis et al. (2012) show that the welfare gains depend on the trade elasticity. Opening up to trade involves an intensive and extensive margin. The intensive margin elasticity equals $\sigma - 1$, as in the Krugman model with CES preferences. The extensive margin elasticity equals $\theta - (\sigma - 1)$ with a Pareto distribution. The welfare gains depend on the dispersion of productivities, captured by the coefficient θ. A smaller θ implies fatter tails in the Pareto distribution and more dispersion yielding, *ceteris paribus*, larger trade gains. Similar to the previous models, more dispersion (in Krugman it is more differentiation) leads to higher welfare gains. Adding the intensive and extensive margin elasticity together, the elasticity of substitution σ drops; this is due to the Pareto distribution and CES preferences. Thus the trade elasticity is governed by the selection effect only:

$$\frac{W^{j,t}}{W^{j,a}} = (\lambda^{jj})^{-\frac{1}{\theta}}$$

where λ^{jj} denotes the home share. This looks similar to the Eaton–Kortum model, where the trade elasticity depends on a productivity parameter as well. But note the difference to the CES version of the Krugman model, where only the intensive margin elasticity was relevant.

Head, Mayer, and Thoenig (2014) deliver welfare formulas in the Melitz model for a log normal productivity distribution and CES preferences. This is much more complex and requires knowledge of the different cutoff productivities across countries. Helpman, Melitz, and Rubinstein (2008) work with a bounded distribution of productivity. In that case, zero trade flows emerge, matching observations from real-world data. When the productivity distribution is bounded from above, there might be zeros in a bilateral trade pair if there are no highly productive firms.

Extensions of the Melitz Model

Multiple extensions of the Melitz model have been developed in recent years. Despite its complex structure, the model's framework is flexible enough to study additional questions regarding competition. Melitz and Ottaviano (2008) provide a framework with variable markups to discuss pro-competitive effects in the Melitz model. Market size and trade affect the toughness of competition, which then feeds back into the selection of firms. Helpman, Melitz, and Yeaple (2004) give international firms a choice whether to export or to pursue foreign direct investment (FDI) and find that the latter option is chosen only among the most productive of international firms. Arkolakis (2010) tries to better understand the foreign market entry costs. He introduces the idea that firms reach individual consumers rather than the market in its entirety. With higher initial outlay, firms reach an increasing number of consumers in a country, but market penetration costs decrease with the population size of the market. When credit markets do not work perfectly, wealth inequality and the limited access to equity are another source of firm heterogeneity. Intensified foreign competition through trade could have negative consequences for productivity, as Foellmi and Oechslin (2020) show, because firms with little equity stay small and cannot invest in R&D. Foellmi et al. (2021) provide evidence that financial constraints can hurt R&D efforts.

Dynamics in International Trade

Since the Melitz model focuses on differences between firms, it serves as an ideal framework to study differences in firm behavior over time. Our previous analysis was static, but obviously, firms need time to grow and to expand into new markets. Furthermore, questions dealing with uncertainty of trade policies cannot be answered in static models.

The review article by Alessandria et al. (2021) summarizes the empirical and theoretical literature on firm dynamics. The firm data sets mentioned in this chapter allow us to study the exporting pattern of firms and what impacts their entry and exit decisions. Typically, firms start out little and begin to export later. When firms are more mature, they are likely to stay in a foreign market even when there are negative shocks, for instance, because they have already established themselves in this market. By contrast, firms with little exporting experience are more likely to exit an exporting market. This creates a path dependence in trade relationships: The longer a firm has been exporting to a market, the more stable this export link. As a consequence, even temporary changes in trade policy can have long-lasting effects if they impact firms' tenure levels in a market. Egger et al. (2025) model at bilateral path dependence in trade, motivated by the aforementioned observations. In a dynamic Melitz framework, they assume that a firm's foreign market entry cost decreases over time with the firm's experience in a market. This has important implications for aggregate trade flows and welfare. For instance, this mechanism helps explain why we still see the Iron Curtain in international trade patterns: In the Cold War, there was only little trade between Western and Eastern Europe. Controlling for size and current trade costs, Egger et al. (2025) find substantially lower trade flows across the Iron Curtain than we would expect through the lens of standard trade models. Note that there can be other types of path dependence as well. For instance, Evenett and Venables (2002), Morales et al. (2019), and Albornoz et al. (2012) show that the probability of a firm entering a new market hinges on how similar this new destination is to destinations that the firm already served in past periods.

While we put firms dynamics in the Melitz chapter, it is important to note that dynamic aspects in international trade can also be studied using the competitive Ricardian framework, which we discussed in the Eaton–Kortum chapter. In that model, the focus lies more on the macroeconomic division of labor and less on individual firm-level decisions. Caliendo et al. (2021) study the impact on trade and welfare of the sequential labor market integration associated with the 2004 European Union Enlargement. Atkin et al. (2025) investigate how trade and growth interact when countries follow a development ladder and acquire more capabilities when more resources are devoted to complex sectors. In these models, trade can be beneficial or detrimental to long-run economic growth. The latter can occur if a country specializes in sectors with little complexity according to comparative advantage.

8.4 Conclusion

Following the empirical evidence of firm-level studies, the Melitz model provides a framework to understand why only a small share of firms become exporters. For this aim, Melitz extends the Krugman (1980) model and introduces heterogeneous firms. Besides this, we derive two key lessons.

- **A minority of firms are exporters.** Despite its richness, the Melitz model yields clear-cut and tractable predictions. The model explains many empirical observations such as the fact that only a small share of firms export and that exporters are different—they are larger and more productive. Theoretically, the model argues that import competition causes a selection effect of trade. It is therefore a central workhorse model in the international trade literature. With even more specific assumptions, a gravity equation can be derived (see Chapter 9).

- **The selection effect is another source of gains from trade.** As in the Krugman model with variable markups, there is exit of firms in the Melitz model. However, it does not work through lower markups but through higher real wages because the high-productivity firms attract a larger part of the work force. We saw in the subsection with the Pareto distribution that all gains from trade result from the selection effect. Highly productive firms become larger because they enter the exporting market, and low-productivity firms exit. This reallocation effect is the only source from gains from trade because the gains from additional import varieties and welfare losses from less domestic varieties just offset each other.

8.5 Exercises

The following exercises allow students to practice and deepen their understanding of the Melitz model.

Exercise 1 Referring to equation (8.23), show how to calculate the mass of active firms (M_d) with trade. How does the number of varieties available to the consumer change when trade costs fall?

Exercise 2 Consider the Pareto distribution assumed by Chaney (2008):

$$G(\varphi) = 1 - \left(\frac{\varphi}{b}\right)^{-\theta}, \quad \varphi \geq b, \quad \theta > \sigma - 1 > 0$$

Firms must pay a fixed cost f_x to export. Only firms with productivity $\varphi \geq \varphi_x$ find it profitable to export.

(a) Show that the share of firms that export is given by

$$\Pr(\varphi \geq \varphi_x) = \left(\frac{b}{\varphi_x}\right)^{\theta}.$$

(b) Derive the conditional expectation of productivity among exporters:

$$\mathbb{E}[\varphi \mid \varphi \geq \varphi_x]$$

(c) How does this expected exporter productivity depend on φ_x? Interpret this result in the context of trade liberalization or increasing trade barriers.

Appendix 8.1: Derivation of Demand $q(\omega)$

Individuals maximize their utility subject to the budget constraint that total expenditures must not exceed their income I. To find the optimal consumption, we first set up the Lagrangian

$$\mathcal{L} = \left(\int_0^\infty q(\omega)^{(\sigma-1)/\sigma} d\omega \right)^{\sigma/(\sigma-1)} - \lambda \left[\int_0^\infty q(\omega)p(\omega)d\omega - I \right]$$

Taking the first-order conditions (FOC), we obtain the following:

$$\frac{\partial \mathcal{L}}{\partial \omega} = 0 \Longleftrightarrow \frac{\sigma}{\sigma - 1}\frac{\sigma - 1}{\sigma} q(\omega)^{-1/\sigma} - \lambda p(\omega) = 0 \Longleftrightarrow q(\omega) = [\lambda p(\omega)]^{-\sigma}$$

If we take the FOC for two goods, ω_1 and ω_2, and divide them by each other, we have this:

$$q(\omega_1)/q(\omega_2) = [p(\omega_1)/p(\omega_2)]^{-\sigma} \quad \Longleftrightarrow \quad q(\omega_1) = q(\omega_2) * [p(\omega_1)/p(\omega_2)]^{-\sigma}$$

which we can expand by $p(\omega_1)$ and then take the integral over all goods:

$$\int_0^\infty p(\omega_1)q(\omega_1) = \int_0^\infty q(\omega_2)p(\omega_1)p(\omega_1)^{-\sigma}p(\omega_2)^{\sigma}d\omega_1$$

Note that the term on the left side is equal to total expenditure, which must be equal to the consumers income I. Thus we can write this:

$$I = q(\omega_2)p(\omega_2)^{\sigma} \int_0^\infty p(\omega_1)^{\sigma-1}d\omega_1 \quad \Longleftrightarrow \quad q(\omega_2) = \frac{Ip(\omega_2)^{-\sigma}}{\int_0^\infty p(\omega_1)d\omega_1}$$

The last expression holds in general for any good.

If we define the price index $P \equiv \left(\int_0^\infty p(\omega)^{1-\sigma} \right)^{1/(1-\sigma)}$, we get

$$q(\omega) = p(\omega)^{-\sigma}P^{\sigma-1}I = \left(\frac{p(\omega)}{P} \right)^{-\sigma} \frac{I}{P}$$

In the main text we defined $Q = \left[\int_0^\infty q(\omega)^{\frac{\sigma-1}{\sigma}} d\omega \right]^{\frac{\sigma}{\sigma-1}}$. Note that $Q = I/P \Longleftrightarrow I = QP$, which implies that the price index can be interpreted as a cost of living index. We can also plug the last expression for $q(\omega)$ into the utility function and obtain $U = I/P$. Finally, if all varieties had the same price p, they would be consumed in equal amounts q, such that $I \int_0^\infty pqd\omega$. We then have $I = npq$ as well as $q = I/(np)$. If we plug this into the utility function, we get $U = n^{1/(\sigma-1)}I/p$, a term that is increasing in n (taste for variety)—more so if σ is lower (i.e., products are more differentiated).

Appendix 8.2: Melitz with Pareto Distribution

We evaluate the integrals to get an expression for the ZCP curve when productivities follow a Pareto distribution. Recall that $\theta > \sigma - 1 > 0$:

$$
\begin{aligned}
\bar{\pi} &= \int_{\varphi_d}^{\infty} \left[\left(\frac{\varphi}{\varphi_d} \right)^{\sigma-1} - 1 \right] f_d \theta \varphi_d^{\theta} \varphi^{-\theta-1} d\varphi + \int_{\varphi_x}^{\infty} \left[\left(\frac{\varphi}{\varphi_x} \right)^{\sigma-1} - 1 \right] f_x \theta \varphi_d^{\theta} \varphi^{-\theta-1} d\varphi \\
&= \theta f_d \varphi_d^{\theta} \left[\frac{\varphi_d^{-\theta}}{\theta + 1 - \sigma} - \frac{\varphi_d^{-\theta}}{\theta} \right] + \theta f_x \varphi_d^{\theta} \left[\frac{\varphi_x^{-\theta}}{\theta + 1 - \sigma} - \frac{\varphi_x^{-\theta}}{\theta} \right] \\
&= f_d \frac{\sigma - 1}{\theta + 1 - \sigma} + f_x \varphi_d^{\theta} \varphi_x^{-\theta} \frac{\sigma - 1}{\theta + 1 - \sigma} \\
&= \frac{\sigma - 1}{1 + \theta - \sigma} \left(f_d + f_x \left(\frac{f_d}{f_x} \right)^{\frac{\theta}{\sigma-1}} \tau^{-\theta} \right)
\end{aligned}
$$

where we used $\varphi_x = \tau \left(f_x / f_d \right)^{1/(\sigma-1)} \varphi_d$.

9

The Gravity Equation

9.1 Idea and Background

One key goal of research on international trade is to understand the magnitude of bilateral trade flows. Let us consider some data from UN Comtrade for the year 2024. The United States had a total goods trade volume of about \$840 billion with Mexico, \$770 billion with Canada, \$600 billion with China, \$240 billion with Germany, and \$230 billion with Japan. Together, trade with these five countries accounted for almost two-thirds of the United States' imports and exports.

Why does the United States trade so much with these countries compared to others? Answering this question is not that difficult: Mexico and Canada are direct neighbors, and China, Germany, and Japan are the largest economies in the world other than the United States. These two variables, geographic distance and partner country gross domestic product (GDP), imply that nations trade more with countries that are close by and have a large economy. This is the key idea behind the gravity equation.

The earliest records of thinking about bilateral trade flows along this line probably go back to Ernst Georg Ravenstein, a German-English geographer who published "The Laws of Migration" in 1885. Later on, in 1962, Dutch economist Jan Tinbergen presented this idea in his book "*Shaping the World Economy: Suggestions for an International Economic Policy*". Both built on Isaac Newton's idea of gravity from physics and applied it to international trade flows.

Figure 9.1 shows two objects with masses m_1 and m_2, respectively, that are at a distance of r. The gravitational force between the two objects is proportional to the product of the two masses and inversely proportional to the square of the distance between them:

$$F_1 = F_2 = G\frac{m_1 * m_2}{r^2}$$

Understanding International Trade. Reto Foellmi and Stefan Legge, Oxford University Press.
 DOI: 10.1093/9780197821107.003.0010

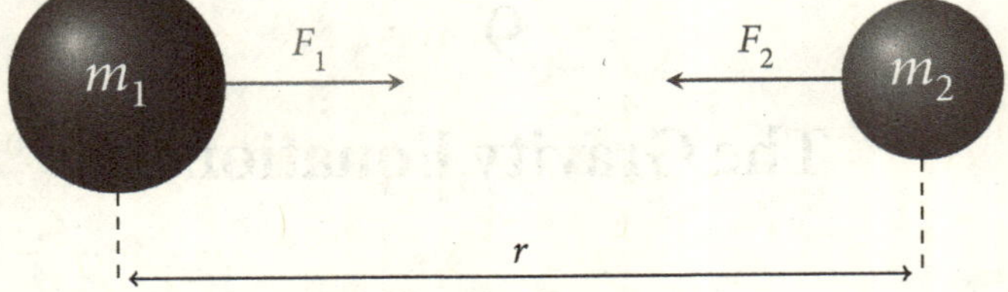

Figure 9.1 Illustration of Gravity in Physics

In a similar vein, economists think about trade flows between two countries as directly related to the size of the two countries' economies (i.e., their gross domestic products) and the geographic distance between them. Hence, the simplest gravity equation of international trade would state that country *i*'s exports to country *j* are given by

$$X_{i,j} = \frac{Y_i * Y_j}{d_{i,j}} \tag{9.1}$$

The larger either country's GDP (Y_i or Y_j) and the smaller the geographic distance ($d_{i,j}$), the larger (*ceteris paribus*) the trade flow. If we apply this simple formula to the statistics presented at the beginning of this chapter, we immediately understand why Mexico, Canada, and China are by far America's most important trading partners: They are either a direct geographic neighbor or have the second-largest economy in the world.

For all the similarity between gravity in physics and in international trade, there is one interesting difference: In physics, the simple gravity equation only holds for two objects, and a closed form solution to the general *n*-body problem has not yet been achieved (see the so-called *many-body theory*). In economics, we can obtain a closed-form solution even with many countries due to constant elasticity of substitution (CES) preferences.

9.2 Stylized Facts

Let us take a look at another country's international trade. Switzerland is a small open economy in the center of Europe and thus well suited to illustrate the gravity equation in practice. Based on data from the Swiss Federal Office for Customs and Border Security (FOCBS), Table 9.1 shows Switzerland's top-fifteen trading partners according to their share of Swiss foreign trade in 2024.

Table 9.1 Shares of Swiss Foreign Goods Trade (without gold) in 2024

Rank	Country	Share	Rank	Country	Share	Rank	Country	Share
1	Germany	18.9	6	France	5.9	11	UK	2.4
2	United States	13.2	7	Austria	3.1	12	Belgium	1.5
3	Slovenia	8.8	8	Spain	2.7	13	Poland	1.2
4	Italy	8.7	9	Japan	2.5	14	Singapore	1.2
5	China	6.6	10	Netherlands	2.4	15	Hong Kong	1.1

Table 9.1 supports the gravity equation very well. Most of Switzerland's key trading partners are in Europe, and those that are not are large economies like the United States, China, and Japan. Economists have presented numerous illustrations to show the usefulness of the gravity equation. One particularly nice presentation was carried out by Head and Mayer in their 2014 chapter *Gravity Equations: Workhorse, Toolkit, and Cookbook.* They use Japan's trade flows with European countries to test the gravity equation's ability to explain magnitudes of imports and exports. The idea is that Japan's geographic distance to (and trade relationship with) all European countries is more or less similar. Hence, partner countries' GDP alone should explain most of the variation. The two plots in Figure 9.2 provide strong support for the gravity equation. Both Japan's 2024 exports and imports strongly correlate with European partner countries' GDP. The estimated coefficients are 1.11 and 1.44 (according to theory the estimated coefficients should be close to unity), while the adjusted-R^2 is given by 0.85 and 0.84, respectively.

To illustrate the relationship between geographic distance and bilateral trade flows, we can consider Switzerland's exports to all countries in the world (divided by the GDP of the partner country). The plot in Figure 9.3 shows a statistically significant ($t = -3.3$) negative relationship between geographic distance and bilateral trade flows—despite the variation around the line.

The next logical step in understanding the variation shown in the plot of Swiss exports is to explore which group of countries systematically differs from the regression line. For instance, we can examine those that are above the line. They include, among others, countries with which Switzerland has a direct border (Germany, Austria, France, and Italy), countries that speak the same languages, and nations that signed a free trade agreement (FTA) with Switzerland (e.g., Chile or Jordan). These observations point out additional

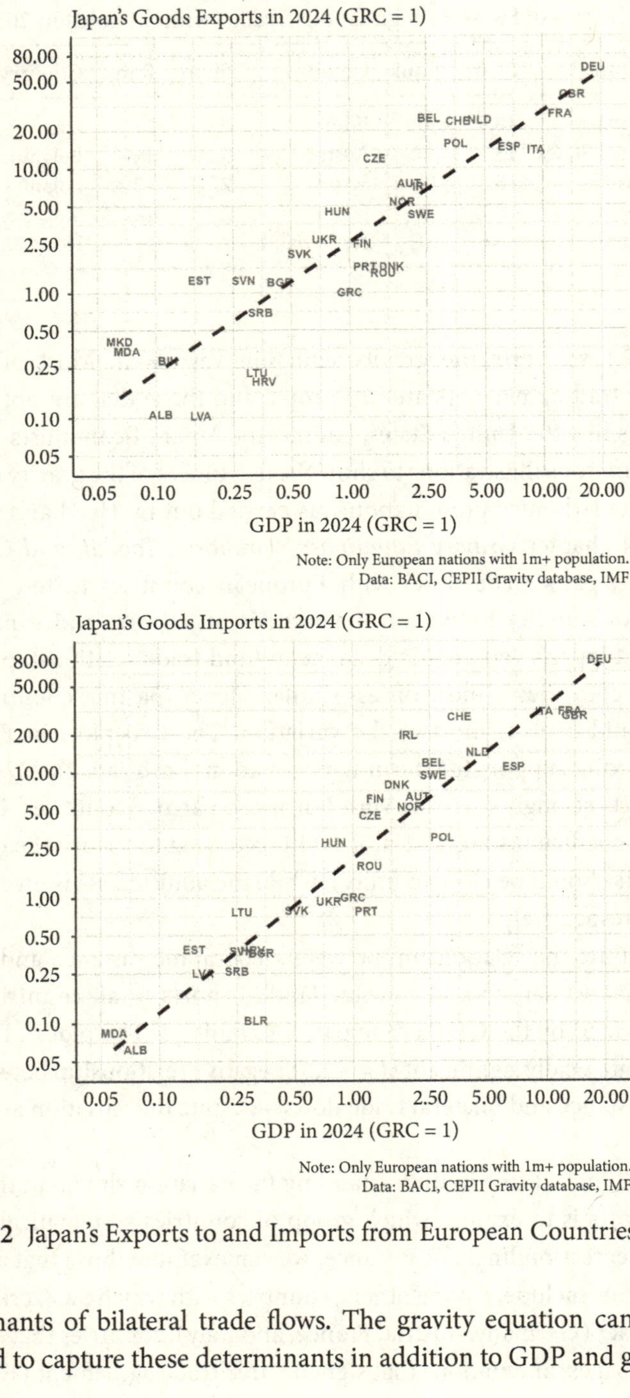

Figure 9.2 Japan's Exports to and Imports from European Countries by GDP

determinants of bilateral trade flows. The gravity equation can easily be extended to capture these determinants in addition to GDP and geographic distance.

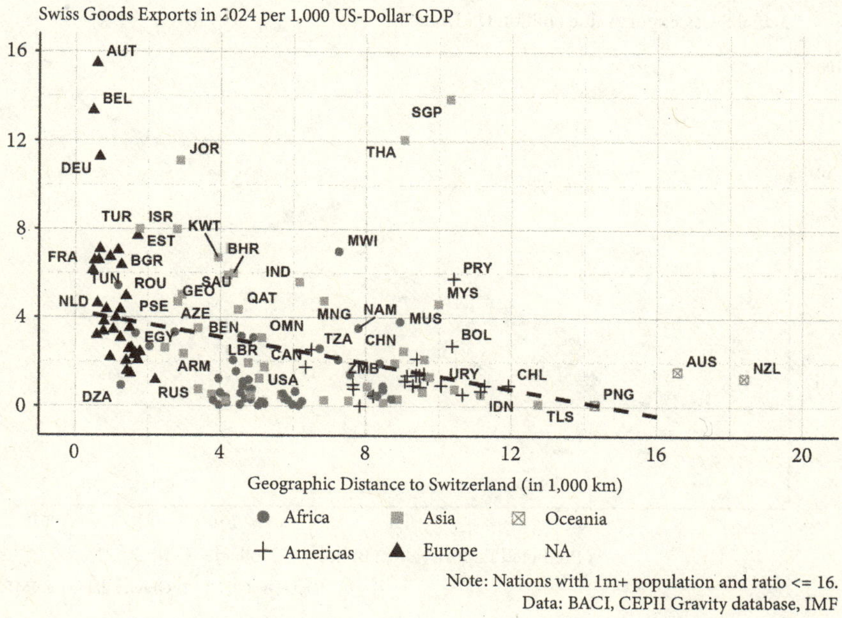

Figure 9.3 Switzerland's Exports Against Distance to Partner Countries

But already with partner countries' GDP and population, as well as the bilateral geographic distance, we can predict Switzerland's trade volumes very well. In Figure 9.4, we see for all countries the expected trade volume with Switzerland—based on its GDP, population, and geographic distance to Switzerland (reduced form of equation 9.6 below)—as well as the actual trade volume in 2024. This very simple gravity model can account for about 87 percent of the variation in the data. The main deviating nations shown in Figure 9.4 are India, Hong Kong, and Singapore because of gold exports, as well as Slovenia due to chemical and pharmaceutical exports.

Geographic Distance as a Proxy Variable

Thus far in the chapter we documented that geographic distance between two countries is a powerful predictor of bilateral trade flows. In addition, we saw that other factors like a direct border or FTAs play a key role. This warrants a brief discussion.

Using again the analogy from physics, the gravitational force between two objects is reduced by the distance between them. In a similar way, all

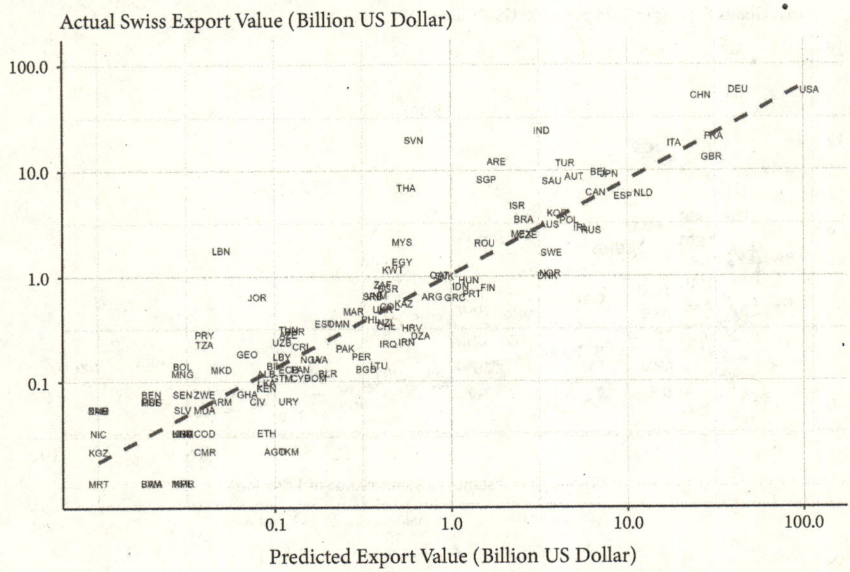

Data: BACI, CEPII Gravity database, IMF

Figure 9.4 Switzerland's Predicted and Actual Trade Flows

obstacles to bilateral trade reduce observed trade. Geographic distance turns out to be such an obstacle to trade, but not just because transportation costs increase with distance. It is straightforward to show empirically that bilateral geographic distance correlates with bilateral differences in official languages, culture, trust, and many other variables important for trade. According to the Centre d'Études Prospectives et d'Informations Internationales (CEPII) Gravity Database, for example, countries with a common official language have a shorter average geographic distance than country pairs that share no common language.

When we do not include these variables (e.g., common currency) in a regression of trade flows on distance, much of their impact will be "picked up" by the estimated coefficient on geographic distance. Plenty of empirical studies have examined the *individual* impact of such determinants of bilateral trade. Melitz (2008), for example, documents that language plays an important role in gravity models and explores the channels through which a common language promotes bilateral trade. Similarly, Baier and Bergstrand (2007) analyze whether FTAs actually increase members' bilateral trade flows, pointing out the endogeneity of FTAs. While they find large positive effects, more recent work by Baier, Yotov, and Zylkin (2019) highlights the large variation of the effect. Numerous other studies examine additional barriers to or facilitators of international trade.

This includes common currencies (Rose and van Wincoop, 2001) as well as colonial ties (Head, Mayer, and Ries, 2010).

Empirically, one problem is to disentangle the impact of the various factors that potentially affect international trade flows. One way to separate and identify mechanisms is to compare the estimated effect across groups of products. For instance, researchers have distinguished differentiated and homogeneous products (first suggested by Rauch, 1999) to carve out the mechanisms through which selected factors impact trade.

9.3 Theoretical Foundation

For decades, the gravity equation was little more than a neat tool for explaining empirical patterns of trade flows. The strong explanatory power discussed above was well known—both for explaining between-country trade flows as well as within-country trade.[1] However, the gravity equation lacked a solid theoretical foundation: It was not derived from any existing trade model. This was problematic for two reasons: First, we do not know the exact form of the "correct" gravity equation without a model. Should the relationship between trade flows and countries' GDP be log linear? Do we expect trade flows to linearly decline with geographic distance? These are not some abstract questions but of first-order importance if we want to interpret estimated coefficients. The example of the so-called McCallum border effect (see later in this chapter) provides an illustration of this. The second reason we would like to have a gravity equation based on theory is that this would allow us to understand the causal mechanisms: *Why* does the gravity equation perform so well empirically?

Somewhat ironically, trade economists intensified their research on the gravity equation and found the importance of barriers to trade (distance, language, etc.) at a time when many journalists and consultants described a "borderless, flat world" and even talked about the "Death of Distance" (the title of a book published by Frances Cairncross in 1997). In 2005, Thomas L. Friedman published *The World Is Flat*, describing ten so-called flatteners that he saw as leveling the global playing field. Among these he listed the fall of the Berlin wall, the rise of computer software, supply chains, and outsourcing. Many of these aspects have been examined in a large and growing body of empirical research. In contrast to these narratives, the

[1] Crozet and Koenig (2010) provide an illustration of the share of French firms in each region that participate in trade with neighboring countries. Their plots show that the share is usually highest in the French regions close to the partner country (Belgium, Germany, Italy, Spain, and Switzerland).

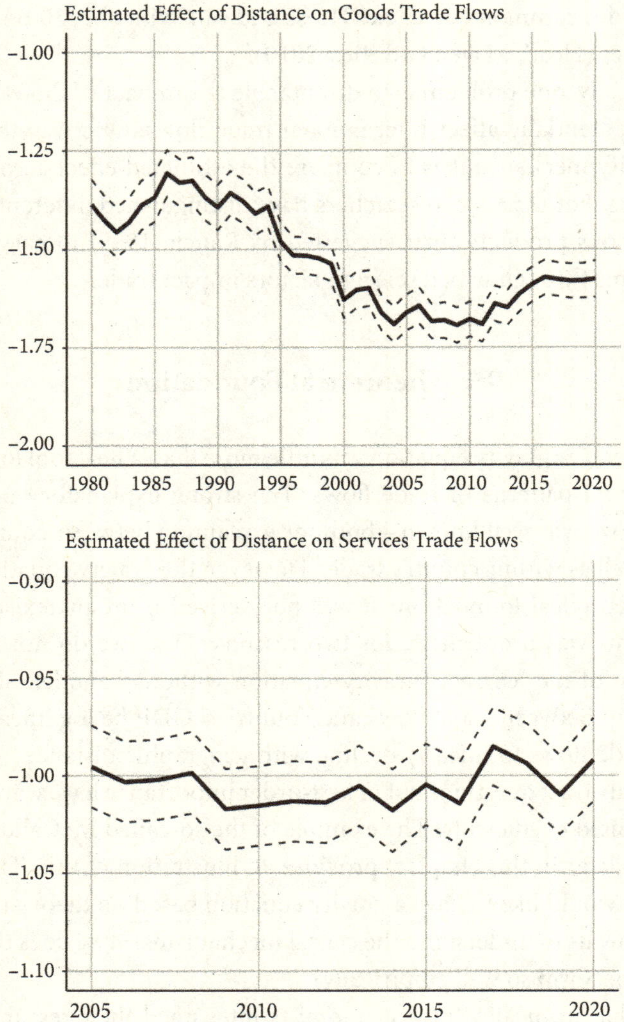

Figure 9.5 Estimated Coefficient on Geographic Distance with Gravity Model

estimated effect of geographic distance on bilateral trade has remained persistently high, for both goods and services trade, as shown in Figure 9.5. The solid line shows the point estimate for geographic distance from an annual regression of bilateral trade on geographic distance and origin as well as destination fixed effects. The dashed lines indicate a 95 percent confidence interval.

This stability of the estimated effect of geographic distance on international trade has been dubbed "distance puzzle" by Disdier and

Head (2008). Actually, new technology should have reduced the importance of geographic distance, making the world flatter. If we account for the fact that the composition of countries and products changes, the "mystery of the missing globalization" disappears; the relative weight of poorer countries and products with higher trade costs increases over time. In addition, when new technology facilitates trade with distant countries, it also facilitates trade with countries closer by. At each point of time, the effect of distance on international trade between a given pair of countries is estimated relative to the effect of distance on international trade for another pair of countries, a method that uses national *and* international production. What Figure 9.5 shows is the *relative* effect of geographic distance on bilateral trade flows.

But how can we establish the gravity equation theoretically? The first to offer a theoretical economic foundation for the gravity equation was James E. Anderson (1979). However, it was not before the late 1990s and early 2000s, with contributions by Eaton and Kortum (2002) as well as Anderson and van Wincoop (2003), that trade economists developed a successful foundation for the gravity equation. Most recently, Arkolakis, Costinot, and Rodriguez-Clare (2012), as well as Allen, Arkolakis, and Takahashi (2020), showed that a large set of trade models generate a gravity equation. This is an advantage because it implies policy advice based on the gravity model does not depend on particular assumptions. It is robust with respect to trade theories.

Deriving the Gravity Equation

In what follows, we outline the steps necessary to derive a gravity equation. There are numerous variations of gravity equations and we showed different variants in the several chapters of this book, most notably in Chapter 6, Section 6.4. To have a simple, but general framework, we follow the one introduced by Anderson and van Wincoop (2003). This approach is most accessible because it takes prices as given. Richer trade models like Eaton–Kortum identify the economic forces that cause prices to differ across countries. Let q_{ij} be consumption by consumers in region j of goods from region i. We assume CES preferences and consumers in region j to maximize their utility

$$\left(\sum_i \beta_i^{(1-\sigma)/\sigma} c_{ij}^{(\sigma-1)/\sigma}\right)^{\sigma/(\sigma-1)} \quad \text{subject to the budget constraint} \quad \sum_i p_{ij} c_{ij} = y_j$$

where $\sigma > 1$ is the elasticity of substitution between goods from different regions and β denotes the preference of consumers for goods from region i. An easy derivation of the gravity equation uses the expenditure minimization problem. Specifically, we minimize expenditures $\sum_i p_{ij} c_{ij}$ for a given consumption bundle C_j. To do this, we set up the Lagrangian

$$\mathcal{L}(\cdot) = \sum_i p_{ij} c_{ij} + P_j \left(C_j - \left(\sum_i \beta_i^{(1-\sigma)/\sigma} c_{ij}^{(\sigma-1)/\sigma} \right)^{\sigma/(\sigma-1)} \right)$$

where P_j is the Lagrange multiplier. Take the first-order conditions (FOCs) with respect to c_{ij}:

$$\frac{\partial \mathcal{L}(\cdot)}{\partial c_{ij}} = p_{ij} - P_j \left(\sum_i \beta_i^{(1-\sigma)/\sigma} c_{ij}^{(\sigma-1)/\sigma} \right)^{\sigma/(\sigma-1)-1} \beta_i^{(1-\sigma)/\sigma} c_{ij}^{-1/\sigma} \stackrel{!}{=} 0$$

$$\Longleftrightarrow c_{ij} p_{ij} = P_j C_j^{1/\sigma} \beta_i^{(1-\sigma)/\sigma} c_{ij}^{(\sigma-1)/\sigma}$$

where the second step uses $C_j = \left(\sum_i \beta_i^{(1-\sigma)/\sigma} c_{ij}^{(\sigma-1)/\sigma} \right)^{\sigma/(\sigma-1)}$.

As this condition has to hold for every i, we can sum over i to get this:

$$\begin{aligned} \sum_i p_{ij} c_{ij} &= P_j C_j^{1/\sigma} \sum_i \beta_i^{(1-\sigma)/\sigma} c_{ij}^{(\sigma-1)/\sigma} \\ &= P_j C_j \end{aligned} \qquad (9.2)$$

where the second step again uses the expression for C_j stated above. With this condition, we can express P_j in terms of β_i's and p_i's. We rewrite the FOC as follows:

$$\begin{aligned} p_{ij} &= P_j C_j^{1/\sigma} \beta_i^{(1-\sigma)/\sigma} c_{ij}^{-1/\sigma} \\ \Longleftrightarrow p_{ij} c_{ij} &= P_j^{\sigma} C_j (\beta_i p_{ij})^{1-\sigma} \\ \Longrightarrow \sum_i p_{ij} c_{ij} &= P_j^{\sigma} C_j \sum_i (\beta_i p_{ij})^{1-\sigma} \\ \stackrel{(9.2)}{\Longrightarrow} P_j &= \left(\sum_i (\beta_i p_{ij})^{1-\sigma} \right)^{1/(1-\sigma)} \end{aligned}$$

Recall that P_j denotes the (ideal) consumer price index of j. Moreover, for a given budget y_j, we must have this:

$$y_j = \sum_i p_{ij}c_{ij} \overset{(9.2)}{=} P_jC_j$$

We can now reuse the FOC to write this:

$$\begin{aligned} c_{ij}p_{ij} &= P_jC_j^{1/\sigma}\beta_i^{(1-\sigma)/\sigma}c_{ij}^{(\sigma-1)/\sigma} \\ &= y_j^{1/\sigma}\left(\frac{\beta_i}{P_j}\right)^{(1-\sigma)/\sigma}c_{ij}^{(\sigma-1)/\sigma} \end{aligned}$$

Use $x_{ij} = p_{ij}c_{ij}$ and $p_{ij} = t_{ij}p_i$ to get the (nominal) demand for region i goods by consumers in region j

$$x_{ij} = \left(\frac{\beta_i p_i t_{ij}}{P_j}\right)^{(1-\sigma)} y_j \tag{9.3}$$

as shown by Anderson and van Wincoop (2003, p.175). To derive equation (9) of the paper by Anderson and Van Wincoop (2003, p.175), define

$$\begin{aligned} y^W &\equiv \sum_j y_j \\ \theta_j &\equiv y_j/y^W \\ \Pi_i &\equiv \left(\sum_j (t_{ij}/P_j)^{1-\sigma}\theta_j\right)^{1/(1-\sigma)} \end{aligned}$$

Moreover, market clearing implies

$$\begin{aligned} y_i &= \sum_j x_{ij} \\ &= (\beta_i p_i)^{1-\sigma}\sum_j (t_{ij}/P_j)^{1-\sigma}y_j \\ &= (\beta_i p_i)^{1-\sigma}y^W\Pi_i^{1-\sigma} \end{aligned} \tag{9.4}$$

using the definition of Π_i. Rewrite equation (9.3) as

$$(\beta_i p_i)^{(1-\sigma)} = x_{ij}\left(\frac{t_{ij}}{P_j}\right)^{(\sigma-1)} y_j^{-1}$$

and plug this condition into equation (9.4) to receive the gravity equation:

$$x_{ij} = \frac{y_i y_j}{y^W}\left(\frac{t_{ij}}{\Pi_i P_j}\right)^{1-\sigma} \quad (9.5)$$

This last expression describes a gravity equation with trade between countries i and j as a function of, among other factors, the two countries' GDP (y_i, y_j) as well as bilateral trade costs (t_{ij}). Note that the first fraction ($y_i y_j / y^W$) can be interpreted as what would happen if there were no trade barriers ($t_{ij} = 1$). Country j obtains a fraction of goods from any country j (including itself) according to country js share of the global economy. The other fraction in equation (9.5) describes trade costs (t_{ij}) relative to outward and inward multilateral resistance. The term Π_i is an index of outward trade costs, while P_j describes an index of inward trade costs.

What exactly are those multilateral resistance terms and how can they be interpreted? Considering the equations above, we see that both Π_i and P_j depend on all bilateral resistances t_{ij}. If trade barriers with all trading partners increase, the resistance terms become larger. The gravity equation states that trade between countries i and j depends on the bilateral trade barrier relative to the product of their multilateral resistance indices. It is intuitive to see why higher multilateral resistance of the importing country j increases its trade with country i: For any given bilateral trade cost between i and j, higher barriers between country j and other nations reduce the relative price of goods from i and thus raise imports from country i. The same is true if the multilateral resistance of the exporting country increases. Intuitively, we see this in the context of what economists call trade diversion: Trade costs between countries i and j (that is t_{ij}) also affect trade between i and k (X_{ik}). If, for instance, countries i and j sign an FTA, country i will source more from j and less from k.

Interpreting the Gravity Equation

If we take a closer look at equations (9.3) and (9.5), there are several key observations. Expenditure in j on goods from i, x_{ij}, is as follows:

- Proportional to country j's total income y_j. All else equal, larger/richer countries consume more of all varieties.
- Inversely related to the (trade-cost-including) prices of varieties from i to destination j, $p_{ij} = p_i t_{ij}$. This *law of demand* shows that factory-gate prices (p_i) as well as trade costs (t_{ij}) matter.
- Directly related to P_j. All else equal, the relatively more expensive the rest of the varieties in the world are, the more consumers in j will substitute away from them and toward the goods from country i.
- Increasing in j's preference for i's variety, β_i.
- Contingent on σ. A higher elasticity of substitution magnifies the trade diversion effects from the more expensive products to the cheaper ones.

The results might be more intuitive if we consider a specific country pair. For Switzerland, we learn from a structurally derived gravity equation that Swiss imports from a partner country like China are determined by numerous factors:

- If Switzerland's economy becomes larger, *ceteris paribus*, imports from China will increase.
- If production costs and thus factory-gate prices in China go up, Swiss imports from China will decrease. The same happens if bilateral trade costs t_{ij} increase (e.g., due to canceling an FTA).
- If textiles from Bangladesh become more expensive, Switzerland will buy more textiles from China (instead of from Bangladesh).
- Rising demand for Chinese food increases Swiss imports from China.
- The more price-sensitive Swiss consumers are, the larger are the effects of the third point.

The final equation (9.5) contains on the right side two terms: a size term and a trade costs term. We see that in the absence of trade frictions $t_{ij} = 1$, the expenditure share on goods from any particular country is equal to the share of production of the source country in the global economy. Iceberg trade costs t_{ij} are approximated by various geographic and trade policy variables.

The term P_j is the inward multilateral resistance term—that is, j's ease of market access (see Anderson and van Wincoop, 2003). The term Π_i is the exporter i's ease of market access.

9.4 Estimating the Gravity Equation

Provided that a gravity equation like equation (9.5) governs bilateral trade flows in each period t, we can use its multiplicative nature and log-linearize it, add a constant (for y^W), and add an additive error term $\varepsilon_{ij,t}$:

$$\begin{aligned} \ln x_{ij,t} &= \ln y_{j,t} + \ln y_{i,t} + (1-\sigma)\ln t_{ij,t} \\ &\quad - (1-\sigma)\ln P_{j,t} - (1-\sigma)\ln \Pi_{i,t} + \varepsilon_{ij,t} \end{aligned} \tag{9.6}$$

This is the most popular version of the empirical gravity equation. It has been used by hundreds of papers studying the effects of geography, demographics, trade agreements, export subsidies, World Trade Organization (WTO) membership, currency unions, foreign aid, immigration, foreign direct investment, cultural ties, trust, reputation, and many other variables in international trade.

Theory and best practice based on numerous contributions to the literature substantially help researchers today in estimating a gravity equation. Among those contributions is the study by John McCallum (1995) raising the so-called border puzzle: Estimates by McCallum suggested that the US–Canadian border was a major barrier to trade. In 1988, trade between Canadian provinces was estimated to be 22 times (2,200 percent) the trade between US states and Canadian provinces.[2] Put differently, the border is such a barrier to trade that Canadian regions trade much more among themselves than with regions in the United States. This remained a puzzling result for several years until Anderson and van Wincoop (2003) solved it.

Two factors contribute to making McCallum's *ceteris paribus* ratio of interprovincial to Canada–US trade so large. First, his estimate is based on a regression with omitted variables, the multilateral resistance terms (P_j and Π_i) we see in equation (9.5). Second, the magnitude of the estimated border effect reflects the small size of the Canadian economy. When Anderson

[2] The estimated coefficient on a dummy variable for both regions being in the same country is about 3.09, which translates into a factor of $e^{3.09} \approx 22$ since the dependent variable is the logarithm of inter-regional trade.

and van Wincoop estimated McCallum's regression with US data, they found that trade between US states is only a factor 1.5 times the trade between US states and Canadian provinces.[3] Correcting for both issues, Anderson and van Wincoop find that national borders reduce trade between industrialized countries by moderate amounts of 20–50 percent. This is still a substantial border effect. It reflects that several barriers to trade indeed increase if there is a border between two regions. Among those barriers are transportation costs, tariffs and non-tariff barriers, legal and regulatory costs, contractual frictions, market entry barriers, or language and cultural differences.

The inclusion of country-fixed effects in equation (9.6) not only reflects the multilateral resistance terms but also accounts for time-fixed differences in national preferences (which have constant effects on trade flows). It is well known that consumer preferences partially explain imports. The population of the United Kingdom, for example, has a rather strong preference for tea. Trade statistics from UN Comtrade for the year 2023 indicate that France and the United Kingdom—both have a similar population size and GDP—imported coffee and tea from abroad. However, France imported \$3.3 billion worth of coffee (Harmonized (HS) code 0901) and only \$148 million worth of tea (HS code 0902). In contrast, UK imports show \$1.3 billion worth of coffee and \$310 million worth of tea. Thus, France imports more than twice as much coffee but less than half as much tea compared to the United Kingdom. The inclusion of country-fixed effects helps to account for such aspects.

Data Sources

Estimating a gravity equation requires data on bilateral trade flows (ideally at the product level) as well as information on countries and their non-trade-related relationships. The primary source for trade data is UN Comtrade. For researchers, the Centre d'Études Prospectives et d'Informations Internationales (CEPII) provides two very useful data

[3] Anderson and van Wincoop (2003) write, "The intuition is simple in the context of the model. Even a moderate barrier between Canada and the rest of the world has a large effect on multilateral resistance of the provinces because Canada is a small open economy that trades a lot with the rest of the world (particularly the United States). This significantly raises interprovincial trade, by a factor 6 based on our estimated model. In contrast, the multilateral resistance of U.S. states is much less affected by a border barrier since it does not affect the barrier between a state and the rest of the large U.S. economy. Therefore trade between the states is not much increased by border barriers."

sources: First, the CEPII Gravity Database by Conte et al. (2022), and second, for historical data from 1827–2016, TRADHIST by Fouquin and Hugot (2016).

Numerous other researchers have provided databases for econometric research. Recently, Gurevich and Herman (2018) made the Dynamic Gravity Dataset available. It covers country characteristics and relationships between two trading partners for the period 1948–2019. Furthermore, Borchert, Larch, Shikher, and Yotov (*International Economics*, 2021) provided the "International Trade and Production Database," which contains international and domestic trade for 243 countries, 170 industries, and 17 years.

For information on tariffs, the standard source is the WTO and its Tariff & Trade Data platform. Researchers, however, will find it useful to also employ data collections such as the Global Tariff Database (GTD) provided by Feodora Teti (2024).

Zero Trade Flows

When estimating equation (9.6), researchers usually employ origin- and destination-country fixed effects for the multilateral resistance terms. While this provides an easy solution, taking the log of bilateral trade flows is harder to deal with: It is impossible when such flows are zero. This becomes an issue especially when using disaggregated data (at the two-/four-/six-digit HS commodity-code level) that contains a vast amount of zeros. We document the magnitude of the problem in Table 9.2. For Switzerland's foreign trade in 2024 with five nations (Canada, China, Germany, Kenya, and the United States), the table indicates the share of products with positive trade volumes. We distinguish between four different levels of product aggregation. The statistics indicate that Switzerland trades all two-digit products with countries like China, Germany, and the United States. However, while almost 90 percent of all eight-digit products (the most disaggregated data) are traded with Switzerland, only 11.9 percent of such goods are traded with Kenya. This result restates an earlier finding by Baldwin and Harrigan (2011): Real GDP per worker in the destination country is a significant determinant of zeros in trade data.

The presence of zero trade flows again shows the limits of the analogy with gravity in physics where the gravitational force is never zero between

Table 9.2 Share of Products with Positive Trade Flows in Swiss Data for 2024

Level of Aggregation	Canada	China	Germany	Kenya	US
HS two-digit	99.0	100.0	100.0	76.0	100.0
HS four-digit	72.7	92.0	97.6	31.6	91.8
HS six-digit	49.2	79.4	93.1	15.0	77.4
HS eight-digit	39.1	64.6	86.2	11.9	63.4

two objects. Bilateral trade flows, in contrast, can and often are indeed zero. Trade economists distinguish between the extensive and intensive margin of trade. The former describes whether a product is traded at all, while the latter indicates the volume of trade. Empirically, there is robust evidence that larger countries have a greater extensive margin of imports and exports (see, for example, Hummels and Klenow (2005)).[4]

Most statistical software simply drops all these zero trade flows from the analysis when taking logs. However, this removes valuable information about the *extensive* margin of trade—whether there is any trade at all—and only keeps the *intensive* margin (i.e., how much is actually traded conditional on there being trade). The standard approach to dealing with this issue was provided by Santos Silva and Tenreyro (2006). Their research argues that the gravity equation should be estimated in the multiplicative form using a Poisson pseudo-maximum-likelihood (PPML) estimator. Besides being consistent in the presence of heteroskedasticity, this method also provides a natural way of dealing with zero values of the dependent variable. Several questions about this estimator and its implementation are discussed on the accompanying website *The Log of Gravity*.

9.5 Conclusion

In this chapter, we reviewed a key workhorse tool of modern international trade research: the gravity equation. The utilization of this tool is facilitated by several contributions such as Yotov, Piermartini, Monteiro, and Larch's 2016 *Advanced Guide to Trade Policy Analysis: The Structural Gravity Model*. Real-world applications range from estimating the impact of Brexit on trade

[4] Based on this observation, Feenstra (2010, p.108) argues that larger countries effectively face higher export and lower import prices, after being adjusted for the variety of each. This suggests that larger countries enjoy the greatest gains due to variety.

between the United Kingdom and other countries, the likely impact of joining the Euro zone, and the consequences of the China–US trade dispute.

When evaluating such policy questions, trade theory combined with the econometric implementation of the gravity equation can provide useful guidance. Consider the situation in which Swiss policymakers evaluate a hypothetical FTA with the United States. What would be the likely effects of such an agreement? Trade theory can be used to make informed predictions about the impact on (i) bilateral trade, (ii) firms in the United States and Switzerland, (iii) workers in both countries, (iv) product prices, and (v) varieties available to consumers. To the extent that a Swiss–American trade agreement reduces bilateral trade costs, we would expect all the effects of lower trade costs discussed in earlier chapters. Furthermore, using data on Swiss trade flows and FTAs signed in the past, the gravity equation can provide us with a sense of magnitude of the effects the theory predicts. Let us summarize the key insights:

- **Bilateral trade flows are directly related to countries' GDP as well as bilateral trade costs.** Nations trade more with other countries if these are larger in economic size (GDP), geographically close, share a common language, or use the same currency. Several additional variables that capture bilateral trade costs can be used in the gravity equation to estimate how much they affect trade.
- **The gravity model enables testing trade barriers' effect.** We can plug in numerous variables into the gravity model and empirically estimate their impact of bilateral trade flows. This includes, among others, bilateral trade agreements or sharing a common religion.
- **Basically all trade models predict a gravity equation.** As discussed on the previous pages, for decades the gravity equation lacked a theoretical foundation. With numerous contributions in the past two decades, this shortcoming has been resolved.
- **Estimating a gravity equation must address numerous econometric issues.** This includes addressing the multilateral resistance terms as well as dealing with zero trade flows. Again, a large and still growing body of economic research provides helpful guidance.

9.6 Exercises

The following exercises allow students to practice and deepen their understanding of the gravity equation.

Exercise 1 Download data on international trade flows, country-specific values like GDP, and country-pair values like geographic distance. One example is "the CEPII Gravity Database".

(a) Estimate a gravity equation using insights from Section 9.4 in this chapter.
(b) Are your estimates in line with what we discussed in this chapter?
(c) Besides countries' GDP and the bilateral geographic distance, which variables should we consider?

Exercise 2 Consider the gravity equation (9.5) derived in this chapter in a setting with two countries, *A* and *B*.

(a) Discuss through which channels technological progress in country *A* may impact trading patterns.
(b) Is there a way through which exports of country *A* may decrease as a consequence of the resulting increase in productivity?

Exercise 3 Suppose we have data on trade among German states and Swiss cantons. The following table shows the regression output of a gravity model.

Dependent Variable: Value of Exports	
$\ln Y^i$	1.11***
	(0.02)
$\ln Y^j$	1.01***
	(0.03)
Border effect	18.03***
Swiss cantons	(5.02)
Border effect	2.09***
German states	(0.34)
$\ln d^{ij}$	−1.29***
	(0.34)
R^2	0.134
Observations	1,722

Note that $\ln Y^i$ is the importer's GDP, $\ln Y^j$ is the exporter's GDP, and $\ln d^{ij}$ is the geographic distance between states/cantons *i* and *j*. Standard errors are shown in parentheses.

a) What effect do you expect for the coefficient on $\ln Y^i$ using the gravity theory covered in this chapter? Is this borne out in the data here?
b) Why is the border effect higher for Swiss cantons than for German states?
c) Suppose the correct regression model also includes a variable for ruggedness that captures how irregular the terrain between *i* and *j* is. This variable is positively correlated with geographic distance. What does this imply for the coefficient on distance in the regression table above?

Acknowledgments

As with every contribution in research and teaching, this book rests on the shoulders of giants. While teaching international trade at the University of St. Gallen, we had the privilege to discuss ideas and models with numerous excellent students. Furthermore, we benefited from various textbooks and other teaching material provided by scholars of the field. Of particular relevance for our textbook was Robert C. Feenstra's 2015 *Advanced International Trade: Theory and Evidence* (2nd edition), a book that is highly recommended to advanced students of international trade. In addition and as more easily accessible resources, we recommend the books *International Trade* (5th edition), published in 2021 by Robert C. Feenstra and Alan M. Taylor, as well as *International Economics* (12th edition, 2024) by Paul R. Krugman, Maurice Obstfeld, and Marc Melitz.

For their excellent contributions to the International Trade course at the University of St. Gallen and for their highly valuable support in writing this manuscript and developing exercises, we thank Marino Bucher, Björn Hartmann, Ulrich Schetter, Lukas Schmid, and David Torun.

We also want to express our gratitude to the editor and anonymous referees for their excellent suggestions for improving the manuscript.

Bibliography

Acemoglu, Daron. 2002. "Directed Technical Change." *Review of Economic Studies*, 69(4): 781–809.

Albornoz, Facundo, Héctor F Calvo Pardo, Gregory Corcos, and Emanuel Ornelas. 2012. "Sequential Exporting." *Journal of International Economics*, 88(1): 17–31.

Alessandria, George, Costas Arkolakis, and Kim J. Ruhl. 2021. "Firm Dynamics and Trade." *Annual Review of Economics*, 13(): 253–280.

Allen, Treb, Costas Arkolakis, and Yuta Takahashi. 2020. "Universal Gravity." *Journal of Political Economy*, 128(2): 393–433.

Anderson, James E. 1979. "A Theoretical Foundation for the Gravity Equation." *American Economic Review*, 69(1): 106–116.

Anderson, James E., and Eric van Wincoop. 2003. "Gravity with Gravitas: A Solution to the Border Puzzle." *American Economic Review*, 93(1): 170–192.

Anderson, James E., and Eric van Wincoop. 2004. "Trade Costs." *Journal of Economic Literature*, 42(3): 691–751.

Antràs, Pol, and Alonso de Gortari. 2020. "On the Geography of Global Value Chains." *Econometrica*, 88(4): 1553–1598.

Antràs, Pol, and Davin Chor. 2022. "Chapter 5 - Global Value Chains." In *Handbook of International Economics: International Trade, Volume 5*, ed. Gita Gopinath, Elhanan Helpman, and Kenneth Rogoff, 297–376. Elsevier.

Arkolakis, Costas. 2010. "Market Penetration Costs and the New Consumers Margin in International Trade." *Journal of Political Economy*, 118(6): 1151–1199.

Arkolakis, Costas, Arnaud Costinot, and Andrés Rodríguez-Clare. 2012. "New Trade Models, Same Old Gains?" *American Economic Review*, 102(1): 94–130.

Arkolakis, Costas, Arnaud Costinot, Dave Donaldson, and Andrés Rodríguez-Clare. 2018. "The Elusive Pro-Competitive Effects of Trade." *Review of Economic Studies*, 86(1): 46–80.

Armington, Paul S. 1969. "A Theory of Demand for Products Distinguished by Place of Production." *IMF Staff Papers*, 16(1): 159–178.

Arvis, Jean-François, Yann Duval, Ben Shepherd, Chorthip Utoktham, and Anasuya Raj. 2016. "Trade Costs in the Developing World: 1996–2010." *World Trade Review*, 15(3): 451–474.

Atkin, David, Arnaud Costinot, and Masao Fukui. 2025. "Globalization and the Ladder of Development: Pushed to the Top or Held at the Bottom?" *Review of Economic Studies*, forthcoming.

Autor, David H., David Dorn, and Gordon H. Hanson. 2013. "The China Syndrome: Local Labor Market Effects of Import Competition in the United States." *American Economic Review*, 103(6): 2121–2168.

Baer, Werner. 1972. "Import Substitution and Industrialization in Latin America: Experiences and Interpretations." *Latin American Research Review*, 7(1): 95–122.

Baicker, Katherine, and Marit M. Rehavi. 2004. "Policy Watch: Trade Adjustment Assistance." *Journal of Economic Perspectives*, 18(2): 239–255.

Baier, Scott L., and Jeffrey H. Bergstrand. 2007. "Do Free Trade Agreements Actually Increase Members' International Trade?" *Journal of International Economics*, 71(1): 72–95.

Baier, Scott L., Yoto V. Yotov, and Thomas Zylkin. 2019. "On the Widely Differing Effects of Free Trade Agreements." *Journal of International Economics*, 116: 206–226.

Balassa, Bela. 1963. "An Empirical Demonstration of Classical Comparative Cost Theory." *Review of Economics and Statistics*, 45(3): 231–238.

Balassa, Bela. 1965. "Trade Liberalisation and 'Revealed' Comparative Advantage." *The Manchester School*, 33(2): 99–123.

Baldwin, Richard. 2016. *The Great Convergence: Information Technology and the Bew Globalization*. Harvard University Press.

Baldwin, Richard, and Frédéric Robert-Nicoud. 2014. "Trade-in-Goods and Trade-in-Tasks: An Integrating Framework." *Journal of International Economics*, 92(1): 51–62.

Baldwin, Richard, and James Harrigan. 2011. "Zeros, Quality, and Space: Trade Theory and Trade Evidence." *American Economic Journal: Microeconomics*, 3(2): 60–88.

Becker, Gary S. 1952. "A Note on Multi-Country Trade." *American Economic Review*, 42(4): 558–568.

Benmelech, Efraim, Nittai K. Bergman, and Hyunseob Kim. 2022. "Strong Employers and Weak Employees: How Does Employer Concentration Affect Wages?" *Journal of Human Resources*, 57(S): S200–S250.

Bernard, Andrew B., J. Bradford Jensen, Stephen J. Redding, and Peter K. Schott. 2007. "Firms in International Trade." *Journal of Economic Perspectives*, 21(3): 105–130.

Bhagwati, Jagdish. 1958. "Immiserizing Growth: A Geometrical Note." *Review of Economic Studies*, 25(3): 201–205.

Borchert, Ingo, Mario Larch, Serge Shikher, and Yoto V. Yotov. 2021. "The International Trade and Production Database for Estimation (ITPD-E)." *International Economics* 166: 140–166.

Bowen, Harry P., Edward E. Leamer, and Leo Sveikauskas. 2001. "Multicountry, Multifactor Tests of the Factor Abundance Theory." *American Economic Review*, 77(5): 791–809.

Broda, Christian, and David E. Weinstein. 2006. "Globalization and the Gains from Variety." *Quarterly Journal of Economics*, 121(2): 541–585.

Cai, Jie, and Andrey Stoyanov. 2016. "Population Aging and Comparative Advantage." *Journal of International Economics*, 102: 1–21.

Caliendo, Lorenzo, and Fernando Parro. 2014. "Estimates of the Trade and Welfare Effects of NAFTA." *Review of Economic Studies*, 82(1): 1–44.

Caliendo, Lorenzo, Luca David Opromolla, Fernando Parro, and Alessandro Sforza. 2021. "Goods and Factor Market Integration: A Quantitative Assessment of the EU Enlargement." *Journal of Political Economy*, 129(12): 3491–3545.

Caliendo, Lorenzo, Maximiliano Dvorkin, and Fernando Parro. 2019. "Trade and Labor Market Dynamics: General Equilibrium Analysis of the China Trade Shock." *Econometrica*, 87(3): 741–835.

Chamberlin, Edward. 1962. *The Theory of Monopolistic Competition: A Re-orientation of the Theory of Value*. 8th edition, Harvard University Press.

Chaney, Thomas. 2008. "Distorted Gravity: The Intensive and Extensive Margins of International Trade." *American Economic Review*, 94(4): 1707–1721.

Coe, David T., and Elhanan Helpman. 1995. "International R & D Spillovers." *European Economic Review*, 39(5): 859–887.

Conte, Maddalena, Pierre Cotterlaz, and Thierry Mayer. 2022. "The CEPII Gravity Database." *CEPII Working Paper No. 2022-05.*

Costinot, Arnaud. 2009. "An Elementary Theory of Comparative Advantage." *Econometrica*, 77(4): 1165–1192.

Costinot, Arnaud, and Andrés Rodríguez-Clare. 2014. "Trade Theory with Numbers: Quantifying the Consequences of Globalization." In *Handbook of International Economics.* Vol. 4, 197–261. Elsevier.

Costinot, Arnaud, and Jonathan Vogel. 2015. "Beyond Ricardo: Assignment Models in International Trade." *Annual Review of Economics*, 7(1): 31–62.

Costinot, Arnaud, Dave Donaldson, and Ivana Komunjer. 2012. "What Goods Do Countries Trade? A Quantitative Exploration of Ricardo's Ideas." *Review of Economic Studies*, 79(2): 581–608.

Costinot, Arnaud, Dave Donaldson, Margaret Kyle, and Heidi Williams. 2019. "The More We Die, The More We Sell? A Simple Test of the Home-Market Effect." *Quarterly Journal of Economics*, 134(2): 843–894.

Crozet, Matthieu, and Pamela Koenig. 2010. "Structural gravity equations with intensive and extensive margins." *Canadian Journal of Economics/Revue canadienne d'économique*, 43: 41–62.

Cuñat, Alejandro, and Robert Zymek. 2024. "Bilateral Trade Imbalances." *Review of Economic Studies*, 91(3): 1537–1583.

Das, Sanghamitra, Mark J. Roberts, and James R. Tybout. 2007. "Market Entry Costs, Producer Heterogeneity, and Export Dynamics." *Econometrica*, 75(3): 837–873.

Davis, Donald R., and David E. Weinstein. 2001. "An Account of Global Factor Trade." *American Economic Review*, 91(5): 1423–1453.

Deardorff, Alan V. 1984. "Testing Trade Theories and Predicting Trade Flows." *Handbook of International Economics*, 1: 467–517.

Dekle, Robert, Jonathan Eaton, and Samuel Kortum. 2008. "Global Rebalancing with Gravity: Measuring the Burden of Adjustment." *IMF Staff Papers*, 55(3): 511–540.

Dhingra, Swati, Hanwei Huang, Gianmarco Ottaviano, João Paulo Pessoa, Thomas Sampson, and John Van Reenen. 2017. "The Costs and Benefits of Leaving the EU: Trade Effects." *Economic Policy*, 32(92): 651–705.

Disdier, Anne-Célia and Keith Head. 2008. "The Puzzling Persistence of the Distance Effect on Bilateral Trade," *The Review of Economics and Statistics*, 90(1): 37–48.

Dixit, Avinash K., and Joseph E. Stiglitz. 1977. "Monopolistic Competition and Optimum Product Diversity." *American Economic Review*, 67(3): 297–308.

Donaldson, Dave. 2018. "Railroads of the Raj: Estimating the Impact of Transportation Infrastructure." *American Economic Review*, 108(4-5): 899–934.

Dornbusch, Rudiger, Stanley Fischer, and Paul Anthony Samuelson. 1977. "Comparative Advantage, Trade, and Payments in a Ricardian Model with a Continuum of Goods." *American Economic Review*, 67(5): 823–839.

Dornbusch, Rudiger, Stanley Fischer, and Paul Anthony Samuelson. 1980. "Heckscher-Ohlin Trade Theory with a Continuum of Goods." *Quarterly Journal of Economics*, 95(2): 203–224.

Eaton, Jonathan, and Samuel Kortum. 2002. "Technology, Geography, and Trade." *Econometrica*, 70(5): 1741–1779.

Eaton, Jonathan, and Samuel Kortum. 2012. "Putting Ricardo to Work." *Journal of Economic Perspectives*, 26(2): 65–90.

Egger, Peter, Reto Foellmi, Ulrich Schetter, and David Torun. 2025. "Gravity with History: On Incumbency Effects in International Trade." *Journal of the European Economic Association*, 23(4): 1350–1396.

Evenett, Simon J., and Anthony J. Venables. 2002. "Export Growth in Developing Countries: Market Entry and Bilateral Trade Flows." Mimeo.

Fallick, Bruce Chelimsky. 1993. "The Industrial Mobility of Displaced Workers." *Journal of Labor Economics*, 11(2): 302–323.

Feenstra, Robert C. 2010. *Product Variety and the Gains from International Trade*. MIT Press.

Feenstra, Robert C. 2016. *Advanced International Trade: Theory and Evidence*. Princeton University Press.

Feenstra, Robert C, Alan Heston, Marcel P. Timmer, and Haiyan Deng. 2009. "Estimating Real Production and Expenditures across Nations: A Proposal for Improving the Penn World Tables." *The Review of Economics and Statistics*, 91(1): 201–212.

Feenstra, Robert C., and Alan M. Taylor. 2017. *International Trade (Vol. 4)*. Worth Macmillan.

Fernandez, Raquel, and Dani Rodrik. 1991. "Resistance to Reform: Status Quo Bias in the Presence of Individual- Specific Uncertainty." *American Economic Review*, 81(5): 1146–1155.

Fieler, Ana Cecília. 2011. "Nonhomotheticity and Bilateral Trade: Evidence and a Quantitative Explanation." *Econometrica*, 79(4): 1069–1101.

Foellmi, Reto, and Manuel Oechslin. 2020. "Harmful Procompetitive Effects of Trade in Presence of Credit Market Frictions." *Journal of Money, Credit and Banking*, 52(6): 1493–1525.

Foellmi, Reto, Christian Hepenstrick, and David Torun. 2024. "Triangle Inequalities in International Trade: The Neglected Dimension." *Journal of International Economics*, 152: 104018.

Foellmi, Reto, Christian Hepenstrick, and Zweimüller Josef. 2018. "International Arbitrage and the Extensive Margin of Trade Between Rich and Poor Countries." *Review of Economic Studies*, 85(1): 475–510.

Foellmi, Reto, Stefan Legge, and Alexa Tiemann. 2021. "Innovation and Trade in the Presence of Credit Constraints." *Canadian Journal of Economics/Revue canadienne d'économique*, 54(3): 1168–1205.

Fouquin, Michel, and Jules Hugot. 2016. "Two Centuries of Bilateral Trade and Gravity Data: 1827–2014." *Vniversitas Económica*, 1–39.

Frankel, Jeffrey A., and David H. Romer. 1999. "Does Trade Cause Growth?" *American Economic Review*, 89(3): 379–399.

Galor, Oded, and Andrew Mountford. 2008. "Trading Population for Productivity: Theory and Evidence." *Review of Economic Studies*, 75: 1143–1179.

Gaulier, Guillaume, and Soledad Zignago. 2010. "BACI: International Trade Database at the Product-Level. The 1994-2007 Version." CEPII Working Papers 2010-23.

Goldberg, Pinelopi Koujianou, Amit Kumar Khandelwal, Nina Pavcnik, and Petia Topalova. 2010. "Imported Intermediate Inputs and Domestic Product Growth: Evidence from India*." *Quarterly Journal of Economics*, 125(4): 1727–1767.

Grossman, Gene M., and Elhanan Helpman. 1994. "Protection for Sale." *American Economic Review*, 84(4): 833–850.

Grossman, Gene M., and Esteban Rossi-Hansberg. 2008. "Trading Tasks: A Simple Theory of Offshoring." *American Economic Review*, 95(5): 1978–1997.

Gurevich, Tamara, and Peter Herman. 2018. "The Dynamic Gravity Dataset: 1948–2016." *US International Trade Commission, Office of Economics Working Paper* No. 2018-02-A.

Head, Keith, and Thierry Mayer. 2014. *Gravity Equations: Workhorse, Toolkit, and Cookbook*. Vol. 4, Elsevier B.V.

Head, Keith, Thierry Mayer, and John Ries. 2010. "The Erosion of Colonial Trade Linkages After Independence." *Journal of International Economics*, 81(1): 1–14.

Head, Keith, Thierry Mayer, and Mathias Thoenig. 2014. "Welfare and Trade Without Pareto." *American Economic Review*, 104(5): 310–16.

Helpman, Elhanan. 2018. *Globalization and Inequality*. Harvard University Press.

Helpman, Elhanan, Marc J. Melitz, and Stephen R. Yeaple. 2004. "Export Versus FDI with Heterogeneous Firms." *American Economic Review*, 94(1): 300–316.

Helpman, Elhanan, Marc J. Melitz, and Yona Rubinstein. 2008. "Estimating Trade Flows: Trading Partners and Trading Volumes." *Quarterly Journal of Economics*, 123(2): 441–487.

Hepenstrick, Christian, and Alexander Tarasov. 2015. "Per Capita Income and the Extensive Margin of Bilateral Trade." *Canadian Journal of Economics / Revue canadienne d'économique*, 48(4): 1561–1599.

Hirschman, Albert O. 1945. *National Power and the Structure of Foreign Trade*. University of California Press.

Hopenhayn, Hugo A. 1992*a*. "Entry, Exit, and Firm Dynamics in Long Run Equilibrium." *Econometrica*, 1127–1150.

Hopenhayn, Hugo A. 1992*b*. "Exit, Selection, and the Value of Firms." *Journal of Economic Dynamics and Control*, 16(3–4): 621–653.

Hsieh, Chang-Tai, Nicholas Li, Ralph Ossa, and Mu-Jeung Yang. 2020. "Accounting for the New Gains from Trade Liberalization." *Journal of International Economics*, 127: 103370.

Hummels, David, and Peter J. Klenow. 2005. "The Variety and Quality of a Nation's Exports." *American Economic Review*, 95(3): 704–723.

Jones, Ronald W. 1965. "The Structure of Simple General Equilibrium Models." *Journal of Political Economy*, 73(6): 557–572.

Kambourov, Gueorgui, and Iourii Manovskii. 2009. "Occupational Specificity of Human Capital." *International Economic Review*, 50(1): 63–115.

Kehoe, Timothy J., and Kim J. Ruhl. 2013. "How Important Is the New Goods Margin in International Trade?" *Journal of Political Economy*, 121(2): 358–392.

Kortum, Samuel S. 1997. "Research, Patenting, and Technological Change." *Econometrica*, 65(6): 1389–1419.

Krugman, Paul. 1979. "Increasing Returns, Monopolistic Competition, and International Trade." *Journal of International Economics*, 9(4): 469–479.

Krugman, Paul. 1980. "Scale Economies, Product Differentiation, and the Pattern of Trade." *American Economic Review*, 70(5): 950–959.

Krugman, Paul. 1991. *Geography and Trade*. MIT Press.

Krugman, Paul, Marc Melitz, and Maurice Obstfeld. 2024. *International Economics: Theory and Policy*. Pearson.

Lancaster, Kelvin. 1957. "The Heckscher-Ohlin Trade Model: A Geometric Treatment." *Economica*, 24(93): 19–39.

Leontief, Wassily. 1953. "Domestic Production and Foreign Trade; The American Capital Position Re-Examined." *Proceedings of the American Philosophical Society*, 97(4): 332–349.

Lerner, Abba P. 1952. "Factor Prices and International Trade." *Economica*, 19(73): 1–15.

Linder, Staffan Burenstam. 1961. *An Essay on Trade and Transformation*. Almqvist & Wiksell.

Matsuyama, Kiminori. 1996. "Why Are There Rich and Poor Countries? Symmetry-Breaking in the World Economy." *Journal of the Japanese and International Economies*, 10(4): 419–439.

Matsuyama, Kiminori. 2016. "Ricardian Trade Theory." *The New Palgrave Dictionary of Economics*, 1–12. London: Palgrave Macmillan UK.

Mayda, Anna Maria, and Dani Rodrik. 2005. "Why Are Some People (and Countries) More Protectionist Than Others?" *European Economic Review*, 49(6): 1393–1430.

McCallum, John. 1995. "National Borders Matter: Canada–U.S. Regional Trade Patterns." *American Economic Review*, 85(3): 615–623.

Melitz, Jacques. 2008. "Language and Foreign Trade." *European Economic Review*, 52(4): 667–699.

Melitz, Marc J. 2003. "The Impact of Trade on Intra-Industry Reallocations and Aggregate Industry Productivity." *Econometrica*, 71(6): 1695–1725.

Melitz, Marc J., and Gianmarco I. P. Ottaviano. 2008. "Market Size, Trade, and Productivity." *Review of Economic Studies*, 75(1): 295–316.

Melitz, Marc J., and Stephen J. Redding. 2014. "Heterogeneous Firms and Trade." *Handbook of International Economics, 4th ed.* Vol. 4, 1–54. Elsevier.

Morales, Eduardo, Gloria Sheu, and Andrés Zahler. 2019. "Extended Gravity." *Review of Economic Studies*, 86(6): 2668–2712.

Nunn, Nathan. 2007. "Relationship-Specificity, Incomplete Contracts, and the Pattern of Trade." *Quarterly Journal of Economics*, 122(2): 569–600.

Olson, Mancur. 1965. *The Logic of Collective Action: Public Goods and the Theory of Groups*, Harvard University Press.

Ossa, Ralph. 2015. "Why Trade Matters After All." *Journal of International Economics*, 97(2): 266–277.

Pavcnik, Nina. 2002. "Trade Liberalization, Exit, and Productivity Improvements: Evidence from Chilean Plants." *Review of Economic Studies*, 69(1): 245–276.

Prebisch, Raul. 1959. "Commercial Policy in the Underdeveloped Countries." *American Economic Review*, 49(2): 251–273.

Rauch, James E. 1999. "Networks Versus Markets in International Trade." *Journal of International Economics*, 48(1): 7–35.

Ravenstein, Ernst Georg. 1885. "The Laws of Migration." *Journal of the Statistical Society of London*, 48(2): 167–235.

Ricardo, David. 1817. "On the Principles of Political Economy and Taxation." In *The Works and Correspondence of David Ricardo*, edited by Piero Sraffa. Cambridge University Press, 1951.

Rogowski, Ronald. 1989. *Commerce and Coalitions: How Trade Affects Domestic Political Alignments*. Princeton University Press.

Romer, Paul M. 1990. "Endogenous Technological Change." *Journal of Political Economy*, 98(5, Part 2): S71–S102.

Rose, Andrew K., and Eric Van Wincoop. 2001. "National Money as a Barrier to International Trade: The Real Case for Currency Union." *American Economic Review*, 91(2): 386–390.

Roy, Andrew Donald. 1951. "Some Thoughts on the Distribution of Earnings." *Oxford Economic Papers*, 3(2): 135–146.

Rybczynski, Tadeusz M. 1955. "Factor Endowment and Relative Commodity Prices." *Economica*, 22(88): 336–341.

Sampson, Thomas. 2014. "Selection into Trade and Wage Inequality." *American Economic Journal: Microeconomics*, 6(3): 157–202.

Samuelson, Paul A. 1954. "The Transfer Problem and Transport Costs, II: Analysis of Effects of Trade Impediments." *Economic Journal*, 64(254): 264–289.

Sawada, Yasuyuki. 2009. "The Immiserizing Growth: An Empirical Evaluation." *Applied Economics*, 41(13): 1613–1620.

Silva, J. M. C. Santos, and Silvana Tenreyro. 2006. "The Log of Gravity." *Review of Economics and Statistics*, 88(4): 641–658.

Smith, Adam. 1776. *An Inquiry into the Nature and Causes of the Wealth of Nations.* https://en.wikipedia.org/wiki/The_Wealth_of_Nations

Stolper, Wolfgang F., and Paul A. Samuelson. 1941. "Protection and Real Wages." *Review of Economic Studies*, 9(1): 58–73.

Taussig, Frank William. 1914. "Abraham Lincoln on the Tariff: A Myth." *Quarterly Journal of Economics*, 28(4): 814–820.

Teti, Feodora A. 2024. "Missing Tariffs." *CESifo Working Papers No. 11590.*

Tinbergen, Jan. 1962. "Shaping the World Economy: Suggestions for an International Economic Policy." The Twentieth Century Fund, New York.

Torun, David. 2025. "Quantifying the Extensive Margins of Trade and Production." Mimeo.

Trefler, Daniel. 1995. "The Case of the Missing Trade and Other Mysteries." *American Economic Review*, 1029–1046.

Trefler, Daniel. 2004. "The Long and Short of the Canada–U.S. Free Trade Agreement." *American Economic Review*, 94(4): 870–895.

Vanek, Jaroslav. 1968. "The Factor Proportions Theory: The n-Factor Case." *Kyklos*, 21(4): 749–756.

Wilson, Charles A. 1980. "On the General Structure of Ricardian Models with a Continuum of Goods: Applications to Growth, Tariff Theory, and Technical Change." *Econometrica*, 1675–1702.

Wolf, Holger C. 2000. "Intranational Home Bias in Trade." *Review of Economics and Statistics*, 82(4): 555–563.

Yanagawa, Noriyuki. 1996. "Economic Development in a World with Many Countries." *Journal of Development Economics*, 49(2): 271–288.

Yotov, Yoto V. 2012. "A Simple Solution to the Distance Puzzle in International Trade." *Economics Letters*, 117(3): 794–798.

Yotov, Yoto V., Mario Larch, José-Antonio Monteiro, and Roberta Piermartini. 2016. "An Advanced Guide to Trade Policy Analysis: The Structural Gravity Model." World Trade Organization, Geneva.

Name Index

Subject Index

An italic *f.* following a page number indicates the following page; *ff.* indicates the following pages.